Catching Up to Crypto

Catching Up to Crypto

Your Guide to Bitcoin and the New Digital Economy

BEN ARMSTRONG

WILEY

Library of Congress Cataloging-in-Publication Data is Available:

ISBN 9781394158744 (Hardback)
ISBN 9781394158751 (ePDF)
ISBN 9781394158768 (ePUB)

Cover Design: Wiley
Cover Image: © binik/Shutterstock; GoodStudio/Shutterstock

SKY10038457_111622

This book is dedicated to the love of my life, my wife, Bethany Armstrong.

Contents

Foreword

Catching Up to Crypto is a book that needed to be written, and there is no better person than Ben to write it! The crypto world is new for most people, and it's moving incredibly fast too. I think I speak for all of us in saying it's a daunting task to stay on top of it. Everything sounds like a foreign language, and getting up to speed with what it's all about means that you always have to ask the "dumb" questions. That never feels good.

However, we're all learning together. Crypto is new for all of us, and there are no "dumb" questions. We're all still beginners, and we all need a good guide and mentor to answer all the questions in our heads. This is what Ben does with this book.

Ben is a deep expert in the space, but he also possesses that magic quality of being a very effective communicator and a champion of helping people understand everything – from the basics to the complexities. This book showcases Ben's ability to help everyone in their crypto journey with the understanding they really need to invest as well as thrive.

The world of crypto really matters. It's not some flash in the pan or a tulip bubble as many in the media will tell you. It's one of the biggest changes to global business models, let alone the entire financial system . . . ever. And it's happening at the fastest pace of adoption of any technology in human history. When something this important is underway, it can create tremendous opportunities for those who take the time to learn, to either invest in the space or to use the technology to grow their own business.

The media paints an image of crypto being about lawless gambling and scam artists speculating around something of no value, but the reality is very far from that. Hundreds of billions of dollars of investment from the smartest VC investors is creating a magnet for the most talented entrepreneurs, developers, marketers, hedge fund managers, asset managers, etc. The smartest, most talented people in the world are now dedicating their lives to crypto, and more than a trillion dollars of value has already been created. However, this is still just the start of this revolution. Even the largest brands, companies, and financial institutions in the world are now developing their own Web 3/ crypto strategy, fueling yet more opportunity and funneling yet more talent and capital into the space.

No one can afford to be left behind. So many people have been let down by the system – sidelined and not given the opportunity to create their own success. Web 3.0 and the crypto world is leveling the playing field, and we all need the knowledge to get started.

I really hope *Catching Up to Crypto* gives you the leg up that you need on the path to your success.

—Raoul Pal
CEO/Cofounder, Real Vision Group
www.realvision.com
@RaoulGMI on Twitter

Preface

People ask me a lot what is the secret to my success. It's simple. It's Bethany. When we got married 13 years ago, we barely knew each other. We'd only dated for seven months before we were married. Looking back, it was quite a risky endeavor. Marriage is a rite of passage for most and I believe most treat it that way. You're constantly looking for the person who will eventually become your spouse. But you can't really understand marriage until you're married. Marriages are notorious for ups and downs. And I can tell you we have certainly seen those. Three kids, five dogs, and a bazillion failed businesses will do that.

I started my first business in 2011 and it was wildly successful. I went from making $25k per year as an assistant manager at a car wash to making $350k within two years. Life was good and we were comfortable. But things dramatically changed over the next few years and we were back to living paycheck to paycheck. When I tell you I tried everything to get our finances back on track, I tried *everything*. Web design, graphic design, animation, SEO, YouTube channel, social media manager, memorabilia, blogs, consulting, creating online courses, flipping things—and those are just some of the many failed businesses I started over the course of a five-year stretch.

And yet, no matter how much I failed, I got back up and went at it again with as much zeal and fervor for the next thing as I had for the previous endeavor. It would have been easy for me to give up and go back to the rat race. But I was determined. And I wasn't in it alone. No matter how many times I failed, no matter how many hard financial conversations we had to have, no matter how poor we were, Bethany never gave up on me. She pushed me and encouraged me and consoled me and motivated me. And when I failed, she was the reason I got back up. She never wavered in her belief that I was going to make something out of myself.

In 2018, we sold our house so we could survive while I started the Bit-Boy Crypto YouTube channel and went full-time in crypto. That's crazy! We moved across the state and only survived on side hustles and the profits from the sale of our first home. The home all our kids were born in. I still don't know how she was able to believe in me *yet again*. But she did.

In early 2020, I sat her down and explained that, though we could barely afford groceries, our life was about to drastically change. I did this because in January of 2020, as clear as day, the Lord spoke to me in a dream and told me that we needed to get our house in order because our lives would dramatically change by the end of the year. I told Bethany that by the end of the year we would be millionaires, we'd own a home, and life would look completely different. She looked at me and said she didn't understand how, but she believed me.

In September of 2020, we bought our second home after two years of renting. With cash. And on New Year's Eve 2020, just like I received in that message, my crypto accounts hit $1 million for the first time. And yes, life looks completely different for us now. I can't stress how grateful and appreciative I am for having such a supportive wife. I could not have done any of this without her.

I would also like to dedicate this book to my three kids: Madden, Zoe, and Blake. I don't know how I was blessed with virtually perfect children because, after the way I behaved as a kid . . . I certainly didn't deserve it. This is an example of radical grace! Sorry, Mom!

In addition, this book is dedicated to everyone who has been with me along the way . . . my parents, my siblings, my grandparents, my Uncle Tim, and of course my best friend, Jim aka *Brooootheeeeerrrrr!*

And of course, this book is dedicated to the largest and greatest crypto community in all the interwebs . . . *the BitSquad!* I would be nowhere without the support of my community. I'm forever indebted to the viewers of my channel. When I meet people at meetups, often they thank me for what I've done for the crypto space. And then I tell them thank you right back. If it weren't for all the loyal BitSquad members that gave me a chance, my channel would be nothing. The community is what makes it great.

This book is for all of you.

Acknowledgments

This book wouldn't have happened without the infrastructure we built at BitBoy Crypto and Hit Network. The amount of streamlining we did to make this book possible in only six months' time was quite the undertaking. Every person on my team has played some role because we are all in this together.

But some specific people need to be particularly thanked for their role in creating this book.

The biggest thank you goes out to Nick Dimondi, the Head of Content at BitBoy Crypto. Nick has helped us to radically transform the direction of BitBoy Crypto ever since he joined the team. Balancing all of the content we produce is difficult, but Nick always delivers on cue. And Nick played the biggest role in helping us get ideas and narratives from the whiteboard into the structure of this book. He organized meetings and managed the project to keep us well ahead of aggressive timelines. Nick is the glue that held this project together. There's no topic that can't be broken down by me, Nick, and a whiteboard. We are dangerous!

Next, *huge* thank you to John Vibes. John has been a writer with BitBoy Crypto for a significant amount of time and was really the workhorse that made this project go. John and I have been in crypto for about the same time and have experienced many of the same things, whether it is libertarian meetups, crashing and hacked exchanges, philosophical battles on decentralization, etc. This resulted in an extremely easy writing process where we debated what should and should not go in this book. It's great to be able to work with people with completely different opinions and experiences. However, working with John Vibes shows that it's way easier when you agree on almost every topic.

Cannot forget to send a huge thank you to my assistant, Allison Fiveash. Without Allison, not only does this book not get written . . . but also I don't eat or go to the doctor, I forget to pick up my kids, I botch up my calendar, and I generally make a mess out of the basic things in life. Allison keeps me on schedule and on target at all times. I don't want to flex, but Allison really is the greatest assistant in the history of assistants.

Thank you to the graphic design team here at BitBoy Crypto for helping us with art mockups for the cover and graphics, specifically Ashley Cooper and Graphic Design Lead Steven Polizzi. I appreciate you.

And of course thank you to my business partner, TJ Shedd, for your overall support. We are the Shaq and Kobe of crypto . . . if they never decided to break up. (Obviously I'm Shaq because I'm taller.) We've already won a ton of championships and there's even more down the road.

Introduction

I have bad news for you and good news.

Bad News: Crypto is hard. Let's get that out of the way right off the rip. Just like building a website was in 1995. Over time it will get easier as adoption grows and simpler processes are introduced. The space is big and it's complicated. Crypto is cutting edge technology, the next step of human evolution in terms of making our lives easier. So it seems to be a bit of a paradox: something extremely difficult to understand that ultimately will make our lives simpler.

Good News: You can learn it. I know this because I learned it. I'm a regular guy. I'm not a technology guru. I'm not a gamer. To be honest, I don't even read books often. I read a lot of tweets, watch a lot of YouTube videos, and break down news articles. I'm not your prototypical technology nerd. So even if you have no understanding of crypto, investing, or technology, I'm here to tell you: I did it and you can too. As I break down my journey in crypto, I think you will understand why I believe you can make it.

The first time I ever heard of Bitcoin was in November of 2012. I was running an online ticket company where I basically sold tickets for events all over the United States on Craigslist. I used an automated ad poster for Craigslist to crank out over 800,000 ticket ads per day across the entire country. The name of the software was called CLAD Genius and it was a killer work of art that made my life 100 times better. To do this, though, I had to post in every local Craigslist. But here was the problem: using automated software was against the Craigslist terms of service.

The creator of the software was Yuri from Ukraine. Craigslist decided to sue Yuri for creating the software. To answer the lawsuit, Yuri would have had to come to America, which is obviously something he wasn't going to do. And since he didn't show up in the States, through ICANN the US government was able to seize Yuri's website and cancel all his payment processors.

To use Yuri's service, we had to pay Craigslist a monthly fee for every license we had. I had 12 licenses and the money added up quickly. And Yuri couldn't just keep his service going for free. So he paused our payments until he could figure something out. For about six months there was no progress until November of 2012, when Yuri sent me an email saying he would begin accepting this new type of digital currency called Bitcoin. I didn't care to learn more about it – all I wanted was to catch up on my payments to keep the software. So I immediately went through all the steps, including creating a wallet with the site Mt. Gox as well as sending and receiving crypto through a company called BitInstant. After a couple days of a learning curve, I was off to the races and running with Bitcoin.

Throughout 2013 I bought more and more Bitcoin. People often think that's how I became wealthy. WRONG! The truth was I didn't understand Bitcoin. If, instead of paying Yuri (who MUST be a billionaire now) every month in Bitcoin, I had simply invested that money and hodled, I would have been worth eight figures in 2017. This haunted me for years. But that's what eventually led me to create my YouTube channel, where I actually have a higher earning potential than I ever would've had if I'd just gotten rich early without doing the work.

In November of 2013, the price of Bitcoin broke $1,000. Suddenly the double digits' worth of Bitcoin I had in my wallet for payments were worth four figures. I decided to sell it. I sold 6 Bitcoin for $1,700. At the time I thought I was a super genius. I took my wife and kids to Florida for a little vacation and spent the rest on some bills. At the peak of the bull run in October of 2021, that dust would have been worth $420,000. This is the mistake that drove me deep into crypto.

Selling Bitcoin was a lot harder than buying, though, because it involved using a third party to do the transaction, including an escrow account on **LocalBitcoins.com**. I posted my price and the available amount, and it matched me with several different investors. I looked at all the choices and one guy stood out, as I could tell he wasn't scamming. We scheduled a meet-up at a local McDonald's.

This is a very important part of the story. We were supposed to meet, but the guy was late. So while I waited I researched Bitcoin – for almost an hour. I guess there was a little voice in my head telling me I should sell *some* Bitcoin, but I wasn't sure I wanted to sell all I had. The idea of Bitcoin sounded so insane, and I could barely understand how to use it. The education available on Bitcoin in 2012 was *awful*. Most of the information out there was poorly written, insanely bad news articles. There was only one YouTube channel, called Bitcoin Unnecessary. So for an hour I tried to grasp who this Satoshi Nakamoto was – the still-unidentified person or persons who invented Bitcoin – and what gave Bitcoin its value. But I just couldn't get all this talk of blockchains, coins, trading, investments, and whatever else. So when the guy finally showed up – he'd gone to the wrong McDonald's – I ended up selling him just 6 Bitcoin rather than cashing it all out. I transferred the Bitcoin to him over Wi-Fi, and he handed me $1,700 and left.

Again, that was in November of 2013. In February of 2014, Mt. Gox – a Bitcoin exchange based in Tokyo, Japan, which handled about 90% of all Bitcoin trading activity – announced that the site had been hacked, and everyone's money was gone. And as I write this in 2022 the Mt. Gox saga is still not over; there are many lawsuit claims still pending.

It is important to note that, even though I didn't sell all my remaining Bitcoin at McDonald's, it's not like I would have actually kept it long term. In fact, I wouldn't have had it at all. Exchanges are vulnerable not just to hacks but also to insolvency and bankruptcy. But because all my Bitcoin was on Mt.

Gox, it would have disappeared anyway. So in reality, while it may seem pretty dumb to have sold 6 Bitcoin for $1,700, given the timing it turned out to be the best decision.

But that didn't help me avoid the pit of regret in my stomach when Bitcoin hurled to the moon in 2017. I didn't think Bitcoin would ever get as popular and maintain the insane prices it did in 2017. In fact, in 2014 when Mt. Gox crashed, because of my lack of education and understanding of Bitcoin, I thought it was a failed experiment that wouldn't come back. But over 2015 and 2016 I watched Bitcoin periodically, and I couldn't believe when prices started rising again. I bought and sold a few here and there with my buddy Jim, but never a significant amount.

Over Thanksgiving of 2017, I watched the price of Bitcoin and altcoins completely rip. Though at that point I did have some exposure to the market, the pain of regret was almost too much to handle. I was living paycheck to paycheck and felt I'd missed my golden opportunity. It had been handed to me on a platter and I had fumbled it. Badly.

But I should have given myself a break. For one thing, as I mentioned, when I tried to learn about Bitcoin in 2012 there were no good resources. Whereas, in 2017 resources abounded. And 2017 saw the ushering in of the Crypto YouTuber/Influencers. I watched *Crypto Daily*, Doug Polk, *Data Dash*, *Crypto Crow*, *Crypto Love*, *Crypto Beadles*, Ian Balina, *Ivan on Tech*, and many more, and learned from all of them. I was inspired by their dedication. Seeing how much fun they were having and how much money they were making, I decided I'd like to join in.

The original idea for my channel *BitBoy Crypto* was to follow the antics of a crypto superhero named BitBoy and his loyal sidekick turtle, Hodl; it was actually called *BitBoy and Hodl*. I worked on characters, memes, animation, and more. However, starting a fun channel in January 2018 at the literal top of the market wasn't an idea that would last and give me the ROI on my time and money that I needed. Nobody was looking for fun in the bear market, so my initial attempts at the channel failed.

In March of 2018, my friend Justin Williams – who is now my VP of NFT Development (and who actually came up with the name BitBoy) – suggested that instead of animation I should start covering crypto news. He told me I had an entertaining personality and a knack for breaking down topics simply. After a couple weeks of his prodding, I made my first crypto news video in March of 2018, and have made on average two to three videos per day ever since. Somewhere along the line, by putting in hard work, I became an expert in both crypto and content creation.

But it wasn't always easy. For a long time people didn't seem to be interested in my content – I wasn't getting views or subscribers – but I kept plugging away and working toward something bigger. Fast-forward to today and I have over 6 million total social media followers, over 300 million views on YouTube, and 1.5 million subscribers. For two years no one watched and

I kept going. Then in 2020 to 2021, I went from 10,000 subscribers to 1.45 million subscribers.

So as you can see, I started out with zero knowledge. The cliché "Rome wasn't built in a day" has proven true in my career as a crypto YouTuber. To truly understand crypto you have to spend a lot of time researching it, watching videos, checking the temperature of crypto culture on Crypto Twitter, and more. You need to immerse yourself in it. You can't possibly know everything in crypto, but you can start with basic concepts and niched areas. That will help you build a foundation.

But here is my promise to you if you read this book: you truly are going to "catch up" to crypto. This book was designed to walk you through the history of crypto so you have perspective on major events. The first section is going to answer a lot of the questions about the early days. Then we're going to stop and enjoy the present for a while as we cover some of the popular narratives and niches relevant to crypto right now. Then we're going to gaze off into the future and project where this all goes. This book will also teach you some basic principles of investing, but this is not an investing book at heart. It's a book of understanding. You will gain incredibly valuable insight and perspective that will propel you further, faster, in any area of crypto you want to dig into.

So enjoy this book and make sure to share it with others interested in catching up to crypto themselves!

CHAPTER 1

The Great Devaluation

Old Money, Central Banks, and the Fed

There is a long trail of victims around the world affected by the crimes that led up to the economic crash of September 2008, when over $10 trillion was wiped out of the American economy and millions of people lost their homes. Homelessness has always been a problem in the United States, but it became much worse after the 2008 crash. In the decade following the crash, large tent villages began to pop up in every major city, and this heartbreaking trend has continued to grow, even after the stock market recovered and soared to new highs.[1]

For nearly a decade beforehand, the government and large financial institutions had promised that everything was okay, even though it should have been obvious that the real estate market was in a bubble. Many economists, like Peter Schiff and Nouriel Roubini, were actually warning that this was the case, but the Federal Reserve (the Fed) and the bankers assured the public that the fundamentals in the market were strong. Ben Bernanke, who was chairman of the Federal Reserve at the time, said that the "troubles" in the "subprime sector" would be "limited," and that they did "not expect significant spillovers from the subprime market to the rest of the economy or to the financial system."[2]

The media was complicit as well. "Mad Money" Jim Cramer was on television night after night telling his viewers to keep their money in failing institutions like Bear Stearns: "Bear Stearns is fine. Do not take your money out. If there's one takeaway, Bear Stearns is not in trouble. I mean, if anything, they're more likely to be taken over. Don't move your money from Bear. That's just being silly. Don't be silly," Cramer shouted at the camera.[3]

Unfortunately, these assurances couldn't have been further from the truth. The market was a house of cards, and it was only a matter of time before it came crashing down.

This crisis began in the real estate markets. In the late 1990s, the Federal National Mortgage Association (FNMA), a government-sponsored financial institution commonly known as Fannie Mae, began experimenting with something called "subprime mortgages." These were basically high-value mortgages that were given to working-class people with low credit scores – essentially, people who weren't actually qualified to receive the loan. As a result they were "highly leveraged": meaning that, ultimately, the debt to the financiers was greater than the combined value of the owners' income and their home.

That's because the banks covered their assets by implementing very strict terms on these types of loans. These loans didn't just have high interest rates; the rates were also adjustable, which meant that they would fluctuate based on market conditions, such as changes to the Fed's balance sheet. In the mid-2000s, the Fed began raising its rates after years of offering cheap money, and interest rates for homeowners began rising to unaffordable levels. People quickly found themselves unable to pay their mortgages, and had to forfeit both their homes and the money they'd invested in them. And because the banks had signed off on way too many of these unconscionably predatory loans, foreclosures began to spiral out of control. Numerous financial institutions were facing ruin as a result of the crash, including many with federal backing, but the government stepped in with a massive $700 billion bailout package to save them and prevent further damage to the economy.[4] In other words, "too big to fail" criminals were given the chance to recover (and rebound) from the consequences of their mistakes – a benefit that taxpayers and small business owners have never received. Wall Street was rescued, but Main Street was left holding the bag, which made it very obvious that our financial system is not designed to protect the average person. Most Americans were furious, regardless of where they fell on the political spectrum. It was one of the few times that the left and the right actually agreed about something. That political cease-fire didn't last very long, however, since the tribes quickly took their grievances in separate directions – through movements like the conservative Tea Party (which began in 2009) and Occupy Wall Street (which began in September 2011). But the crash of 2008 revealed the cracks in the system, and forced people from all walks of life to get more educated about economics.

Central Banks

Those of us who dove into the research eventually learned that most of the financial problems that we see across the world with corruption, instability, and inequality, all seem to trace back to the global system of central banking.

A central bank is essentially a government-focused bank that is tasked with issuing and managing a country's currency. These banks are the most powerful financial institutions in the world, and in many ways they are even more powerful than the governments they're supposed to be working for. In the United States we have the Federal Reserve, which manipulates the global economy through its control of the US dollar, the global reserve currency. While the Federal Reserve and other central banks are primarily single-customer operations that deal with specific governments, they are actually independent institutions. Central banks are not government entities; they are businesses, and governments are their customers.

This means that central banks have no real obligations to the citizens of the countries that they claim to serve, and they often run into situations where their interests clash with those of the general population. The same can be said about many politicians as well, but the organizations that are in control of our money and our economy have much more secrecy – and since they're unelected officials, they don't need to worry about keeping voters happy for the next election. The president and the members of Congress might get all of the attention, but there's an extensive web of unelected, much less visible officials who arguably have more power and influence in the US government. This element of government is often called the "deep state."[5] And since the media usually doesn't pay much attention to them, they're able to both effectively push through their policies and maintain those policies over a long time horizon. High-ranking officials in intelligence agencies often know more about our spying operations than the president or Congress do; and, in many cases, they don't have to answer to elected officials – even when their programs are extremely unpopular with the general public. (We saw this in action in 2013 after computer intelligence consultant Edward Snowden leaked highly classified information from the National Security Agency.) Supreme Court justices also hold more power than elected legislators, and we see this trend in nearly every corner of government. Even in seemingly innocuous sectors like health there are figures like Dr. Anthony Fauci who, having "advised every president since Ronald Reagan,"[6] has a large influence on national policy.

The Federal Reserve is a whole agency of unelected officials, and it isn't even technically a part of the government – it's a private bank that plays by its own rules. This situation is not unique to the United States; there is a network of central banks all across the world that play similar roles in their local economies. These banks often have drastically different policies based on the politics of the region they're located in, but their structures are nearly identical, with small centralized groups of bureaucrats having total control over the money supply. In my view, this experiment has been a total failure everywhere it was attempted, with some estimates suggesting that the average lifespan of a fiat currency is only 35 years.[7] ("Fiat currencies" are legal tender; there's more on them in Chapter 2.) Currencies are typically short-lived, lasting only a few decades before a crash or total debasement of the asset. When governments are able to survive these crashes, they will rarely actually change the name of their currency, but in order to bring their nation's economy back to life they are often forced to drastically change monetary policies in ways that change the fundamentals of the currency, effectively making it an entirely different asset. That's what we've seen in the United States over the past century that the dollar has been in circulation. The dollar has taken many different forms over the years: slowly, and then quickly, descending into a worthless piece of paper due to policies enacted by the Federal Reserve and politicians from both parties. By constantly changing interest rates and tweaking other policies to control the monetary supply, they maintain the stability of the economy temporarily, but it comes at the cost of the long-term stability of the money.

This same scenario has played out many times before throughout history, with empires growing out of control and eventually imploding because their currency was diluted and lost its value. This was one of the primary contributing factors to the collapse of both the Greek and Roman empires, and this cycle has continued to repeat over the centuries. Even now, around the world there are numerous countries like Venezuela, Zimbabwe, and Argentina facing economic collapse for this very same reason.[8] You would think that the people who end up with control of large economies would learn from the mistakes of those that came before them, but it seems the power that comes along with printing money is just too tempting for most bureaucrats to turn down.

The Fed

Central banks and fiat currencies were not always a part of the American story; these were actually among the evils that this country's founders were seeking to escape in the New World. This was one of the many ideals that fell by the wayside in American politics as future generations of politicians and bankers sought new ways to fund their expanding budgets.

The Federal Reserve took control of the US economy in 1914, after many years of debate about whether or not a central bank belonged in America. The bank was established with the support of a powerful coalition of politicians and bankers, led by the infamous J. P. Morgan, but it was still highly controversial at the time. A large economic crash in the early twentieth century known as the "panic of 1907" was used as justification for the new monetary regime. The Federal Reserve was sold to the American public as a solution to market volatility that would prevent future crashes,[9] but in the first years after its creation, the bank would preside over one of the most volatile times that this country's economy has ever seen, followed by a crash that brought the whole world down with it.

The Great Depression brought more extreme changes to the country's monetary policy. In 1933, less than 20 years after the Fed was formed, the

United States in effect took its first step off of the gold standard (which I'll define later on) with the Emergency Banking Act of 1933. (The actual step off the gold standard occurred on August 15, 1971, when President Nixon announced on television that the United States would no longer exchange currency for gold.) In the first years after the policy was implemented in the 1930s, US citizens were legally required to sell their gold to the government far below market prices. Given that these citizens were reimbursed for their gold, historians often debate whether this was technically a confiscation[10] – but it effectively was, considering that they were forced to hand over their gold and they weren't paid a fair price for it.

With the gold standard, all paper money represented gold in a vault somewhere, and was redeemable for gold. The properties of this paper currency were heavily influenced by the gold that backed it. Most importantly, since gold is in limited supply, there is an equal limit to the money that can be printed under the gold standard. But without the gold standard, there is no limit to how much money can be printed. Most banks around the world, including central banks, aren't even required to hold all the paper money they have on their ledgers; they're only required to have a fraction of these reserves on hand, in an arrangement that's aptly named "fractional reserve banking." The logic behind this scheme is that an expanded money supply will free up money for lending, which will create businesses that add measurable value to the economy.

On its face, increasing the money supply sounds great, and it does have some short-term positive effects on the economy. But more money in circulation doesn't mean that everybody is richer; it means that our currency is devalued. Basically (without going too much into the details), with every dollar that the Fed prints, the dollars already in circulation become diluted, and lose a little bit of their value. This causes prices to rise for everything in the market, including the basic necessities needed to survive, in a process known as inflation. Since we were taken off the gold standard – in my view – inflation has spiraled out of control and the purchasing power of the dollar has declined by over 90% when compared to gold.

When compared to the longevity and stability of precious metals like silver and gold, fiat currencies with no backing rarely stand the test of time. Governments haven't seemed to learn their lesson, though, because they continue to roll out these worthless currencies after hundreds of similar experiments have now failed. This is not because they're stupid; it's because keeping the money entirely fiat is the only way to maintain total control, so they see this as the only viable option, even if they know that it will eventually fall apart and hurt a lot of innocent people.

Despite these risks, the US dollar is still the primary global reserve currency today, which means that this is the most commonly used asset for international trade, and is held by central banks all over the world. Most central banks hold a variety of different reserve currencies, and the US dollar has been the most popular for a long time. Having control of the global reserve currency gives the US government an incredible amount of financial power over other countries because it allows them to borrow at a much lower cost, giving them advantages worth over $100 billion per year.[11] This upper hand may soon be coming to an end, as the US dollar slowly loses its dominance on central bank balance sheets.

The share of US dollars held by central banks shrank from around 70% in 2000, to under 60% today.[12] I believe that, at some point, the US dollar will fail and fall from its status as the global reserve currency, and the everyday people of this world will be left to pick up the pieces yet again. The bankers and politicians will insist that the system can be reformed, that everything will be back to normal after a few small tweaks – but since the system is broken by design, it will be impossible to fix. We need an entirely new way of doing business, where power is decentralized in the hands of the many, instead of centralized in the hands of the few.

Some of the smartest people of our time can clearly see the crossroads we're approaching, and they have already begun creating bridges to a better future. As the old and dysfunctional financial system slowly crumbles and fades into obsolescence, we have an opportunity to participate in the creation of an entirely new type of financial network that is open, transparent, and permissionless. If you picked up this book, you probably already know that I'm talking about blockchain technology, crypto assets, and Web3 applications. These innovations will change the world in the coming decades, just as the internet created a world that is unrecognizable from the one I was born into. We are in the very early stages of this transition, and it isn't always going to be easy. But the good news is that the tools that can help us through these times of economic uncertainty are already available. To stay ahead in the new economy, you'll want to learn as much as you can about this technology and figure out how to use it to your advantage. The most important investments you can make in this industry are your time, your brain, and your energy. But note that this space can be a bit overwhelming for newcomers, and things move so fast that it can be hard to keep up, especially if you don't know the basics. In the following pages, we'll track the progress that this technology has made in the short time that it's been around and will dig deep into the most important fundamentals in the crypto industry. It's time to catch up on everything you've been missing in crypto. Let's get it.

CHAPTER 2

Digital Money Tree

eCash, E-Gold, and eBay

Money is such a permanent fixture in our world and in our personal lives, but very few people actually understand how it works, and most people would struggle to even come up with a definition for "money."

Broken down into its simplest terms, money is a representation of value, time, effort, and scarcity. Economists usually point to three principles that separate money from other commodities. In order to be classified as money, a commodity must operate as (1) a medium of exchange, (2) a store of value, and (3) a unit of account. An asset such as money is considered a medium of exchange when it is commonly used and accepted as payment in the economy. Money also serves as a store of value, which means that it can retain its value over time, allowing savers to store their purchasing power for a later date. As for the third principle, units of account are used to measure the prices of goods and to calculate wealth. These assets are divisible into smaller units and they are always fungible, which means that they can be evenly exchanged for other identical assets of the same type and size. For example, one pound of gold will always be considered of equal value as another pound of gold, one dollar will always equal one dollar, and one Bitcoin will always equal one Bitcoin.

That's the technical rundown of how the experts define money, which gives a good overhead view of how it operates on a mechanical level, but it goes much deeper than that. All of the physical and tangible properties that define money are driven by faith. Money is essentially a meme that won't work unless a lot of people believe in it. This is the radical and often overlooked property of money that has allowed it to take so many different forms throughout history.

Crypto pioneer and Gemini cofounder Tyler Winklevoss pointed this out in a statement after Gemini announced that it would begin supporting dogecoin, saying, "Yes, it's a meme coin, but all money is a meme. And all money is both an idea and a matter of faith or belief in it. Over the multi-millennia history of money, the majority of money (be it shells, beads, precious metals, etc.) has been what we the people say it is and believe it is."[1]

The earliest human economies developed around bartering and direct trading, which is a low-velocity form of commerce. This means that value moves very slowly through the economy, usually resulting in stagnant economic growth. Bartering economies depend on the "coincidence of wants" phenomenon, which occurs when two parties each have something that the other wants, allowing them to happily trade the items without a medium of exchange. Unfortunately, the planets don't often align so well, so these coincidences are too rare to support a thriving economy. This problem inspired many ancient civilizations to develop the first money systems, which allowed for economic growth like the world had never seen. Items like shells and beads were the first commodities to emerge from the barter system as mediums of exchange. Much later, with the growth of empires, governments imposed official coins for their kingdoms.

Historians believe that the first regulated coins were used in the ancient kingdom of Lydia, which was located in what is now present-day Turkey. These coins were issued under the rule of King Alyattes (circa 610/619 to 560 BCE). The coins were made of electrum, a natural mixture of gold and silver,[2] which possibly inspired the name for one of the first Bitcoin wallets "electrum." (I'll cover Bitcoin wallets later.) In the years that followed, both silver coins and gold coins were adopted by neighboring kingdoms and spread throughout the continent. Silver and gold remained the most popular mediums of exchange globally until quite recently, but there were a variety of other experiments with different ideas throughout history. Leather was used as a currency centuries ago in places like India and China, which makes sense considering that leather was an extremely important commodity in early human history. Historic currencies weren't always based on commodities, though; sometimes they were purely fiat without anything backing them up. By definition, "fiat currencies" are those that are deemed to be legal tender by government order or decree. The earliest fiat currencies were usually tied to some type of commodity, but rulers quickly learned that these commodities placed limitations on their ability to control or inflate the currency. In Medieval London, traders used small wooden boards called "tally sticks" to keep track of transactions and debts. This early ledger-based system was imposed as a currency by King Henry I around 1100. Even back then this idea was nothing new. Archeologists have found evidence that our ancient ancestors were keeping ledgers with tally marks on animal bones back in the late Stone Age.[3] Centuries ago, most of these currencies were backed by an underlying commodity, but eventually unbacked paper money became the most popular form of fiat currency and still maintains dominance today.

New Money

As we transition into the technological age, the nature of money is starting to change again, but it's not entirely clear what form it will take. There's a chance we'll see a new system of digital money that carries most of the same economic properties as the fiat currencies we see today: with unlimited inflation, tight central bank control, and widespread surveillance.

This is a shift that began in the mid-twentieth century, when banks started using computers to keep track of their accounts and ledgers. Computers and machines also paved the way for the very first credit and debit cards, which allowed people to access all of their wealth and credit with a single plastic card. This innovation made life much more convenient, but it also changed the nature of our economy by diminishing the importance of cash. Although cash is still accepted today, its use has been on a steady decline since debit and credit cards came on the scene.[4]

Banks were not the only ones experimenting with financial technology; computer nerds developed different approaches to digital money as well, and their ideas were far more revolutionary. The earliest users of the internet could see the potential in this new technology, and many of them understood how important it could be for the global economy. They saw that if the internet was going to be a driving economic force, then it would need to have its own financial rails, and perhaps even its own currency.

One of the earliest attempts to financialize the internet was eCash, an anonymous digital currency that was created by a cryptographer named David Chaum and developed by his company DigiCash. Chaum first published the idea for eCash in a 1983 paper that described an anonymous electronic currency that could be sent between personal computers using special software. Unlike the decentralized cryptocurrencies that we know and love today, eCash needed cooperation from banks in order to work, which was a major barrier to mainstream adoption. In the United States, only one bank signed up for a test run of the technology. There was better luck in Europe, with about a half dozen banks adopting eCash, but this still wasn't enough; the idea was just too early. Although the mainstream market wasn't ready, Microsoft saw promise in eCash, and offered to buy DigiCash for $75 million, which was an impressive offer for an internet start-up at the time. Microsoft founder Bill Gates apparently had plans to include eCash in Windows 95. If this deal had gone through, the development of the internet could have looked much different than it does today. Digital currency would have been a native function in personal computers from the very start of the internet age. But Chaum asked for more money, and Gates eventually grew frustrated with the negotiations and rescinded the deal entirely – at a time when DigiCash was struggling to find their place in the market. Negotiations fell through with Netscape for similar reasons. (Chaum had a reputation of messing up deals by asking for too much.) Things got so bad that his employees threatened to quit if he didn't step down and find a CEO who was better at handling business. A new CEO was named, but it was too late. In 1998 DigiCash declared bankruptcy and sold all of its products and patents to a company called "eCash Technologies," leaving DigiCash employees sorely disappointed. In all honesty, it's possible that Chaum's stubbornness saved the world from some serious trouble. Imagine how dystopian the internet would be if Bill Gates and Microsoft were at the center of every single online transaction.[5]

Even though eCash was a short-lived experiment that never fully got off the ground, very important innovations came out of this project, and it inspired a whole generation of programmers and cryptographers to create the ultimate digital money. David Chaum went on to continue his work in cryptography and took a special interest in designing machines that would help make elections more transparent while protecting the privacy of voters.[6]

Around the time that DigiCash was going under, a new currency called E-gold was quickly gaining traction. E-gold was founded in 1996 by oncologist Douglas Jackson and attorney Barry Downey, and took a slightly different approach than eCash. Jackson was not motivated by just money alone; he was an enthusiastic libertarian who truly believed that creating a system of gold-backed money would fix many of the problems in our economy.

E-gold was an online business that allowed users to transfer gold and other precious metals between other accounts on the website. The system was basically a ledger of gold that was held in the bank accounts of Gold & Silver Reserve Inc., the company behind E-gold. However, as E-gold grew, its founders decided to decentralize the governance and ownership of the physical bullion. In a primitive version of the decentralized organizations that we see today in Web 3.0, the bullion was held in a trust called the "e-gold Special Purpose Trust." They also provided regular reports to their users with full transparency of their total holdings and the number and sizes of transactions on the site.[7]

Within three years of its launch, E-gold was recognized by the *Financial Times* (July 13, 1999) as "the only electronic currency that has achieved critical mass on the web."[8] As the site grew in popularity, it started to become a target for hackers and scammers, who used phishing techniques and vulnerabilities in browser software to access passwords and other account information. The site also became a target for regulators, who worried that it was being used for illicit activity, like money laundering, drug smuggling, and fraud. It is true that some criminals used the site, but they represented a very small percentage of E-gold's user base. The staff of E-gold also worked with law enforcement to identify and track down users who were involved with illegal activity. In the end this was not enough, because the government came down hard on E-gold, filing a massive indictment against its founders in 2007, when the site was at its peak. The founders were charged with money laundering, conspiracy, and operating an unlicensed money-transmitting business.[9] The charges were brought because the website did not collect information on its users or implement any KYC (Know Your Customer) policies, a process that became mandatory after the 2001 passing of the USA PATRIOT Act. The founders of E-gold were luckily able to avoid serious jail time, but the legal battle destroyed the E-gold business and it went offline forever.

Though Jackson faced a maximum sentence of 20 years in prison and a $500,000 fine, Judge Rosemary Collyer showed leniency because it was clear that Jackson had not intended to break any laws. All of the founders received sentences of house arrest, probation, and community service. When the site finally shut down in 2009, it had over five million accounts.

The E-gold case had a chilling effect on the digital currency scene, forcing many developers to go underground, develop pseudonymous online identities, and continue their work in the shadows. This was not that much of a change for some, considering how strong the culture of privacy and anonymity was among the earliest contributors to this industry. But this culture was not necessarily shared by the millions of people who were coming online for the first time. In an interview with *Forbes* after the downfall of DigiCash, David Chaum pointed out, "As the Web grew, the average level of sophistication of users dropped. It was hard to explain the importance of privacy to them."[10]

New Ways to Spend

The users who were coming online for the first time wanted something easy, and PayPal filled that gap. As many readers likely know, PayPal is a simple payment processing tool that allowed users to send instant transactions to other accounts after providing their bank account information. Unlike E-gold or eCash, PayPal doesn't have its own native currency; it was just a digital wallet that allows users to send and receive fiat currency.

PayPal rose to prominence by targeting the growing eBay market, where users were still buying items online by mailing personal checks and money orders. PayPal solved a major problem for eBay users by allowing them to send money instantly, which resulted in a more seamless shipping experience. PayPal still faced many of the same problems that E-gold did – with hackers luring users into various scams, and with criminals using the platform – but the company was careful to stay compliant with government regulations in the United States, especially when it came to KYC enforcement. By 2006, PayPal had already amassed over 100 million users, making it the most successful online payment platform in the world. PayPal became so popular that it began changing social norms about buying online, especially regarding giving websites one's personal financial information. After becoming familiar with PayPal, people were more likely to give their credit card information to other trusted online platforms like Amazon or Netflix – which paved the way for the massive economic boom that followed. Unfortunately, this growth has come at a cost. All of our most sensitive financial and personal data is stored on centralized servers that have become a gold mine for hackers. According to a study by the online consumer research group Comparitech, over 12,000 data breaches were reported in the United States between 2005 and June 2020. These breaches have led to millions of people having their identities stolen every single year, with no sign that the trend will slow down any time soon. According to the Federal Trade Commission, identity theft cases have almost doubled between 2019 and 2020, rising from $1.8 billion in 2019 to $3.3 billion in 2020 and then $5.8 billion in 2021.[11]

We trust the most popular apps and websites to protect our data because the businesses behind them are so powerful, but it's important to remember that our security and privacy isn't always a priority for these companies. In fact, their business model is to sell our data to the highest bidder, in an arrangement that many critics have called "surveillance capitalism." (This term was coined by Shoshana Zuboff, author of *The Age of Surveillance Capitalism*.) This is essentially a system where the products are free but profits are generated through the capture and sale of data. Surveillance capitalism was pioneered by Google, who was the first tech giant to introduce targeted advertising, but it is now the most common means of monetization on the internet. And it's not just advertisers that have access to this data either; access is available to anyone willing to pay – including politicians, government agencies, terrorists, and hackers. Data collected by social media platforms have also been used by third parties to influence elections and provoke violence between increasingly hostile political tribes on both sides of the aisle. Ultimately, these companies can't be trusted with either our money or our data. Even if they were trustworthy, their platforms are still vulnerable to hackers ready to compromise our accounts.[12]

There is a better way of doing business but the solution lies in decentralization and privacy, which are not compatible with the dominant business model in Silicon Valley. Luckily, the next era of the internet will not be built and owned by the incumbent tech giants that dominate our world today.

CHAPTER 3

First-Gen Giants

Cypherpunks and Disruptive Tech

The internet that we know and love today wouldn't be possible without cryptography, which keeps information secure as it travels around the web. Without cryptography, hackers would have easy access to all of our email and social media messages, making financial applications like online banking entirely impossible. Even credit card payments require advanced cryptography to ensure that the information is seen by only the intended recipient. Back in the early days of the internet, however, this was one of the most controversial aspects of the new technology. Government agencies, especially in the United States, had grown accustomed to easily searching through mail and phone calls to gather intelligence on criminals and innocent citizens alike. The idea of people being able to encrypt their communications online terrified governments and threatened one of their most important sources of control – information. The US government actually classified cryptography as a "munition of war" because having the edge in developing or cracking cryptographic messages can tip the scales during times of war. The US government and its allies had the strongest encryption in the world at the time, and they wanted things to stay that way.[1]

Experts in computing knew that encryption was going to be an essential safeguard for internet users as the technology became more mainstream. Though the US government agreed with this in theory, it also wanted the power to crack the codes. Regulators have harassed cryptographic developers since World War II, forcing them to release weaker versions of their products to the public so they could be easily cracked by government agencies. This was especially true for products that were sold overseas; because the US government essentially viewed encryption as a top-secret weapon, developers were sometimes accused of threatening national security when they sold encryption software internationally.[2]

This is what happened to Phil Zimmermann, the creator of PGP (Pretty Good Privacy) Encryption, which was used to encrypt email conversations. PGP's encryption was too strong for the government to crack, and the software was distributed worldwide, which made Zimmermann public enemy #1 with the US government and the National Security Agency (NSA). Zimmermann was a true believer in cryptography, and released the PGP software for free because he feared that the government would try to ban it. In 1993, Zimmermann became the target of a criminal investigation for violating the Arms Export Control Act. He was accused of threatening national security by exporting weapons, even though the alleged "weapon" was simply computer code. He and other privacy advocates of the time saw this as a free speech issue, and they fought the case on constitutional grounds.[3] After all, computer code is a form of expression and speech; it consists of numbers and letters that people type into a computer, so it operates in a similar way to the printing press.

To illustrate that releasing PGP was an act of free speech, Zimmermann published a book that contained the source code and began shipping it internationally. This was an epic 4D chess move because, if the government wanted to come down on him, they would have to ban a book, which put them in clear violation of the First Amendment. It was also popular for privacy advocates to wear T-shirts with the source code printed on them in a trendy act of civil disobedience.[4] The government ultimately closed their investigation into Zimmermann in 1996 without pressing charges. As it happens, their persecution actually made PGP more popular, and strengthened a community of online privacy advocates who were already beginning to organize. Zimmerman was just one of many software developers who would go head-to-head with the government in the early 1990s. Even Netscape, one of the first internet browsers, was forced to create an entirely separate version of their software for international users that had weaker encryption than the US versions.[5] A culture of resistance began to form among software developers at the time who saw encryption and privacy as a basic human right.

Cypherpunk

The most radical programmers in those days subscribed to something called the cypherpunk email list. (The name "cypherpunk" merges the techno-futurist theme of "cyberpunk" with the cyphers of cryptography.) This was long before social media, back when most online communities used email lists to communicate. This list community formed in 1992 just when the war on crypto was starting to heat up. It was started by a group of programmers and privacy advocates who regularly met in San Francisco to discuss the battle for privacy online. Eric Hughes, John Gilmore, Jude Milhon, and Timothy C. May were among the founding members of the group.[6]

Eric Hughes handled much of the administration of the mailing list. He was also the author of the group's mission statement "A Cypherpunk's Manifesto," which advocates privacy, freedom of speech, and even digital money. John Gilmore is one of the founders of the Electronic Frontier Foundations, an organization that has been on the frontlines of the battle for online freedom since the very early days. The very first cypherpunk meetings were also held at the headquarters for Cygnus Solutions, a company that Gilmore cofounded. Jude Milhon was a lifelong activist who was heavily involved in the civil rights struggles of the 1960s; she was arrested on numerous occasions after the protests she helped organize. She brought her activism to her job in programming, where she advocated for women in tech and other causes like the war on encryption. Though some deem that Eric Hughes coined the term "cypherpunk" in publishing his manifesto, Timothy C. May specifies in his "Cyphernomicon" that the coining credit goes to Jude Milhon.[7]

Timothy C. May was arguably the most radical founder of the cypherpunk movement. He was a crypto-anarchist to the core, and thought the internet combined with strong cryptography could put the average citizen on a level playing field with the government. In 1994, he published "The Cyphernomicon," which laid out the cypherpunk philosophy in detail. The work made predictions about how the internet and cryptography could change the world, and how these tools could be used for both good and evil. May argued that the good far outweighed the bad; he believed that restricting important rights like privacy and free speech would be worse than any negative outcome that this technology could create. Some of the most interesting predictions he made were in the realm of digital currency. Fifteen years before Bitcoin, May predicted that "sophisticated financial alternatives to the dollar, various instruments, futures, and forward contracts," would be made possible by cryptography. Cryptocurrency was actually an extremely popular topic on the mailing list, which grew to over 2,000 members by 1997. Cryptocurrency was seen as the holy grail of cryptography because it would allow people to transfer value, not just information, across the internet safely and anonymously.[8]

There was a deep mistrust of government and fear of government surveillance in the cypherpunk culture. These were the people who were building the future of the internet, so they understood how dangerous and powerful this technology could be if it was abused by authority. With these concerns in mind, they did everything they could to build their systems in ways that empowered the average person. Cryptocurrency was a priority because it was obvious to those working in the industry that the financial system would eventually go digital, which could take society in an entirely dystopian direction if it wasn't handled carefully. If the financial systems that developed online were too easy to control or too centralized, oppressive regimes could easily seize funds from their citizens or prevent them from interacting in the economy. To avoid this dystopian future, the cypherpunks dreamed of a decentralized, borderless, and private digital currency that operated with the same properties as cash or gold.

Many of the early cypherpunk members started developing their own cryptocurrencies and shared their progress on the mailing list. The first to market with a viable product was Adam Back, whose open-source project

Hashcash introduced "proof-of-work" (PoW) mining as a mechanism for verifying digital coins. Although Hashcash used digital coins in its system and had *cash* in its name, it looked nothing like the cryptocurrencies that we know today. Put simply, Hashcash was a system that required email users to spend a small amount of computational power in order to send their messages – although under the hood it was far more complex than that. In theory, the Hashcash algorithm would cause a wait time and power expense that would be unnoticeable to the average user but would make it infeasible for spammers to send out thousands of emails. This mechanism of using computing power to verify online activity is why it's called "proof of work." And though Back is sometimes credited for this invention, it was actually an idea that had been circulating in technology publications for years; it's often traced back to Cynthia Dwork and Moni Naor's 1992 paper "Pricing via Processing or Combatting Junk Mail."[9] However, Back was the first to execute on this idea, and he was the first to incorporate digital coins into a proof-of-work system – even though the coins were just used for internal operations, and were not tradeable or transferable. And though Back's Hashcash was short-lived and proved difficult to scale for the mass market, other cypherpunks took notice of how he incorporated proof-of-work into his system, and realized that this function could be used to secure cryptocurrency.

In 1998 another member of the cypherpunk mailing list, Nick Szabo, proposed a cryptocurrency called Bit Gold, which called for a tweaked version of the Hashcash proof-of-work algorithm to verify the money. (Nick Szabo is also the initial creator of smart contracts, the technology that makes decentralized platforms like Ethereum possible.) Bit Gold was never actually built, but the revolutionary concept solved some major problems that had been challenging crypto programmers for years. Szabo proposed using proof-of-work in a decentralized way to solve the digital currency "double spend problem." This essentially means that it would prevent the creation of counterfeit cryptocurrency. With printed money, counterfeiting happens when someone is able to print bills that appear identical to legal tender. But in cyberspace, someone could just tamper with the records of balances and transactions in order to produce as much money as they want. Previous digital currencies like Digi-Cash avoided the double-spend problem with a centralized registry to keep track of the transactions, but this is a major weakness that could be vulnerable to attack. For a cryptocurrency to be truly viable, it could not have a central point of failure – it would need to be decentralized, and there could be no single authority in control. Bit Gold's proof-of-work system required computers to solve a series of cryptographic puzzles in order to mint new coins. These puzzles also served to independently time-stamp the creation of new money. Records of these results were to be stored across all of the computers that run the software, and they would each be verifying the activity on the network, keeping the other participants honest.

Ultimately, Bit Gold's fate was similar to many other early cryptocurrencies – it never came to fruition. But the concept laid the foundation for further innovation in the field. In 1998, Wei Dai released an informal whitepaper describing his B-money: "a scheme for a group of untraceable digital pseudonyms to pay each other with money and to enforce contracts amongst themselves without outside help." Dai is best known for developing an open-source library of cryptographic algorithms and code. He was also honored in the language of Ethereum, becoming the namesake for the smallest subunit of Ether, the "Wei"; in addition, the Maker coin is called a "Dai."[10]

Hal Finney, a developer for the PGP corporation, took the ideas about cryptography that cypherpunks were experimenting with at the time and built a model for a new digital cash proof-of-work system called Reusable Proof-of-Work (RPOW). Finney launched the software for RPOW in 2004. Though it didn't gain any traction, it added yet another piece to the puzzle, and laid the foundation for more development in the crypto space.

Disruptive Tech

Cryptocurrency may have been the holy grail, but it wasn't the only thing that the cypherpunks were excited about. Another disruptive innovation to come out of the group was decentralized file sharing. Early file-sharing platforms like Napster (started in 1999) were peer-to-peer, allowing users to trade music directly with one another. But because, in the case of Napster, the service relied on a centralized indexing service hosted by its owners, it was vulnerable to legal shutdown orders. That didn't take very long; after being relentlessly pursued by the music industry, Napster was forced to shut down in 2001 after just two years in operation.

The record companies probably thought they had dodged a bullet with Napster. But in the same month that Napster was shuttered, July 2001, a cypherpunk named Bram Cohen launched a decentralized file sharing platform called BitTorrent.[11] Unlike Napster, BitTorrent did not require a central server to operate. Instead, it pulled bits of data – which were spread across a whole network of computers that agreed to share the files – and compiled them into a complete file. This made it pretty much impossible to shut down the network entirely, and also allowed for the sharing of larger file sizes like videos – threatening to eat Hollywood's lunch too. Since BitTorrent could not be shut down, Hollywood and the music industry were forced to adapt to the shifting culture and changing demands of their customers. Today there may be fewer millionaire rockstars than there were in the 1990s, and Web2 (which is the internet without blockchain; I'll cover Web 1, 2, and 3 more in Chapter 17) streaming services are far from perfect, but the number of people who are able to earn a living with their music is magnitudes higher than it was before BitTorrent. The impact that BitTorrent has had on our culture and some of the most powerful industries of our time exemplifies the cypherpunk philosophy and strategy: writing code can allow the average person to change the world.

The infamous hacktivist and prisoner Julian Assange was also an early subscriber and contributor to the cypherpunk mailing list. Assange had a reputation for being one of the most provocative members of the movement. In his early years he found himself on both sides of the law, first getting arrested for hacking in 1991, and then later using his computer skills to help Australian police track down child predators in 1993. Nowadays, Assange is best known as the founder of WikiLeaks, an online organization that publishes news leaks and classified documents contributed by anonymous sources. Although WikiLeaks did not formally launch until 2006, Assange began working on the idea as far back as 1999, when he registered the domain **leaks.org**.[12]

The WikiLeaks project was inspired by one of the most important values of the cypherpunks: "privacy for the weak, transparency for the powerful."[13] Throughout most of history it has been the other way around, with those in power having total secrecy, and those under them having no privacy. This is one of the imbalances that many cypherpunks were hoping to correct with the software they developed. Without transparency, governments can never be accountable to their people; without privacy, the people can never be free. Giving people tools to maintain privacy online was controversial, but exposing government crimes and secrets was even more of a threat.

It's important to remember that the cypherpunks were not a monolithic force. These were thousands of people with various ideas about life and how this technology should develop. There were plenty of disagreements and a multitude of approaches to doing business, just as there are today in the crypto industry. Not all of the cypherpunks were anarchists, either; some of them were suits who played by the rules. For example, Marc Andreessen, the billionaire entrepreneur and investor behind Mosaic, Netscape, and now A16z, was on the cypherpunk mailing list.[14]

Encryption was a necessary component of the products Andreessen was building at the time. And though he was careful to comply with regulators, his more rebellious counterparts in the movement were happy to risk their fortunes and freedom to disrupt the system. However, Andreessen's compromises were likely necessary to get the internet to where it is today. Netscape was also able to make important contributions to cryptography at the time, especially in the development of SSL, an encryption-based internet protocol. Effecting change from working within the system and working against it from the outside are both strategies with merit. This movement would have never been possible if there weren't people on both those paths, approaching the realm in their own way.

Although Netscape was quickly displaced by other browsers, Andreessen has grown into a major power player in the tech world, funding a ton of start-ups that would become foundational applications for the internet, including Facebook, Foursquare, GitHub, Pinterest, and Twitter. His investments are made under his venture capital firm Andreessen Horowitz or A16z. After building the first generation of the internet and placing big bets on the winners of the second generation, Andreessen now sees a bright future in Bitcoin, crypto, and Web3. In 2021 and 2022, A16z announced the launch of numerous multibillion-dollar funds specifically focused on the blockchain space.

CHAPTER 4

Genesis Block

Satoshi Nakamoto and Bitcoin

O n October 31, 2008, a member of the cypherpunk mailing list (which by then had changed its name to the Cryptography Mailing List) by the name of Satoshi Nakamoto posted the following message: "I've been working on a new electronic cash system that's fully peer-to-peer, with no trusted third party. The paper is available at: **http://www.bitcoin.org/bitcoin.pdf**."[1] This paper, "Bitcoin: A Peer-to-Peer Electronic Cash System," is also referred to as Satoshi Nakamoto's white paper. But though the initial posting specified *"I've* been working," the paper itself includes such wording as "The solution we propose begins with a timestamp server." To this day it is not known who exactly the paper's author is, or even if Satoshi Nakamoto is more than one person.[2] Since this persona is usually referred to as just "Satoshi," I'll do the same, with no reference to gender. The paper's Bitcoin would be decentralized and anonymous, just as the cypherpunks had always imagined; it also had many similarities to the software that had come before it, and Satoshi referenced the early cryptocurrency projects that provided any inspiration or research for the development of Bitcoin, including Nick Szabo and the proof-of-work concept.

At first, Satoshi's post was met with a bit of skepticism, because many people had started to believe that it was impossible to create a truly decentralized digital currency, especially since there had been so many other projects that never got off the ground. But though others had generated novel concepts, Satoshi also changed the game entirely by combining the best ideas from the industry and taking them to the next level. In fact, there's a very good chance that Satoshi could be one of those early giants. Given how much regulatory uncertainty there was around this technology, the mysterious pseudonym was a necessary safety measure at the time.

The persecution of E-gold founder Douglas Jackson (see Chapter 2) had the cypherpunk community on edge, and for good reason: the feds didn't want people to exchange value across the internet without there being an accessible record of the transactions. Two of the most important cypherpunk values – anonymity and no permission requirement – are the basis for creating a truly free currency, but these values are incompatible with the US "Bank Secrecy Act," a policy enacted in 1970 that requires financial institutions to report high-value transactions and keep records of account balances for government inspections.

Bitcoin's economic model was also in total opposition to the one adopted by the United States and most governments around the world, wherein strong central banks control an infinite money supply. Instead, Bitcoin would be limited to only 21 million coins, and they would be mined slowly over the course of many years. This approach ensures that Bitcoin would be a relatively scarce asset depending on demand. The mining would be done by a decentralized network of computers spread out all over the world, who would use their computing power to secure the network in exchange for an occasional Bitcoin reward.

A few months after publishing their white paper, on January 9, 2009, Satoshi released the first version of Bitcoin software. Satoshi also mined the first block, called the "genesis block," and it had a reward of 50 Bitcoin. Satoshi included a message in the transaction that cited a British newspaper headline from *The Times* that said, "The Times 03/Jan/2009 Chancellor on brink of second bailout for banks."[3]

The genesis block was mined in the wake of the financial crisis of 2008, when the massive bailouts given to irresponsible banks were at the forefront of the conversation. Bitcoin was not a direct response to this single event, but the crisis was a perfect example of the systemic problems that Bitcoin was hoping to solve. The traditional banking system is plagued by corruption, and so many important moves take place in the shadows. Bitcoin, on the other hand, is transparent, with an open ledger showing all the transactions that take place, with accounts represented by a long alphanumeric code. Nowadays these transactions are no longer anonymous because there are sophisticated tools that can link transactions to real identities, but back in the early days of Bitcoin all of the transactions were mostly anonymous, as Satoshi intended. Anonymity was not a threat to the system's integrity because the platform was open source and could not be unilaterally changed by its founders. Users did not need to trust in an organization, government, or founder; they could trust and rely on the code.

The first person to run the Bitcoin software aside from Satoshi was cypherpunk Hal Finney. On January 10, 2008, the day after the software was released, Hal Finney posted "Running Bitcoin" on Twitter. Though the post now has thousands of likes and retweets, it went mostly unnoticed at the time.[4] Two days later, on January 12, Satoshi sent Hal Finney 10 Bitcoin in the first Bitcoin transaction. It seemed that the software worked, but it wasn't entirely perfect. Finney dug into the code over the next few days and kept in constant contact with Satoshi through email, reporting bugs and suggesting improvements. Bitcoin had no price back then and it was only being used by a small handful of cryptographers, who began pitching in to develop the system. Finney was definitely one of the most enthusiastic developers on the project. He was also among the first to make over-the-top predictions about where the price of Bitcoin would go.[5]

About a week after the genesis block was mined, Finney predicted that Bitcoin could reach USD $10 million per coin one day if it were to become the world's dominant payment system. Finney was so closely connected with the project early on that many people in the industry think that he is Satoshi.[6] Sadly, the genius of Hal was cut short when he was diagnosed with Amyotrophic Lateral Sclerosis (ALS) in late 2009; he had to cash out most of his personally held Bitcoin to pay for medical bills. He continued to work on the Bitcoin project as he battled the illness, but he tragically passed away on August 28, 2014. Before his death, he made arrangements with Alcor Life Extension Foundation to be cryopreserved.[7]

Finney had retired from his job at the PGP Corporation in early 2011, and Satoshi stopped publicly posting around the same time – which many people believe is evidence that Finney and Satoshi were the same person. Some investigators have argued that the two had a similar writing style, with both of them using a double space after each sentence and writing in British English. All comparisons of writing samples from Satoshi and Finney also show that they had a similar writing style. It is unclear how scientific this actually is, but there is a website called "I Write Like" that takes writing samples and compares them to famous authors. Samples from Satoshi and Finney always turn up as the same author, H. P. Lovecraft, for whatever that's worth.[8] However, there are also some holes in this theory as well. For example, Satoshi is said to have never owned a Macintosh computer, and reportedly didn't know how to code for Macs. Finney did own a Mac, which leads some to believe that Satoshi must be someone else.[9]

A few months before Finney passed away, a *Newsweek* journalist identified one of Finney's neighbors as being a likely Satoshi Nakamoto candidate – a man named . . . Dorian Nakamoto, whom the journalist seemed to think had been hiding in plain sight that entire time. Those who believe that Hal Finney was Satoshi believed that he could have used his neighbor's name to throw investigators off his trail. The 64-year-old Dorian Nakamoto was a retired physicist and engineer who, according to the *Newsweek* article, had previously worked on classified projects for the government and corporations. But, aside from his name, this was really the only similarity between him and Bitcoin's inventor. Dorian Nakamoto denied the allegations and insisted that he had no knowledge of cryptography or peer-to-peer networks. He added that the situation brought "much confusion" to his family, at a time when he was dealing with serious health problems. In response the Bitcoin community rallied behind him, donating over $20,000 to cover his medical bills and the legal expenses for clearing his name.[10]

There are different theories about other early cypherpunks being behind the Satoshi moniker, such as Nick Szabo or Adam Back, but most of them have strongly refuted these accusations. Adam Back has said that he hopes Satoshi's true identity is never revealed, because that would ruin a part of what makes Bitcoin special. In a 2020 Bloomberg Interview, Back said, "If you read about a technology, you try to figure out who is the CEO of a company, and people want to ask questions. Because Bitcoin is more like digital gold, you wouldn't want gold to have a founder. For Bitcoin to keep a commodity-like perception, I think it's a very good thing that Satoshi stays out of the public eye."[11]

All of the early contributors feel pretty much the same way, except for a controversial figure by the name of Craig Wright, who has maintained for several years that he was a part of a team that was behind the Satoshi Nakamoto name. He is the only person who has been bold enough to attempt to claim the title, and he has made a lot of enemies as a result.

Craig Wright had his house raided by Australian Police hours after *Wired* and Gizmodo both identified him as a likely Satoshi candidate. Shortly after, however, *Forbes* published an article – "Time to Call a Hoax? Inconsistencies on 'Probable' Bitcoin Creator's PhD and Supercomputers Revealed" – suggesting that previous reports had been based on false evidence that was intentionally planted by Craig Wright himself. Very few people believed Wright's story, and he made himself a target for authorities in Australia who became very interested in his businesses and their potential tax obligations. But he had a few supporters too. Two early Bitcoin contributors, Gavin Andresen and Jon Matonis, defended Wright and publicly stated they believed his claims about inventing Bitcoin.[12] This was certainly an unpopular opinion among the Bitcoin community, most of whom had started to call Wright a fraud. Not many people would believe his claims unless he was able to sign a transaction from one of Satoshi's addresses. He promised to do this on numerous occasions but never followed through. While he was making these claims, he was also filing patent applications for pretty much anything related to Bitcoin and other cryptocurrencies, which goes against Satoshi's open source values. By this point he started to lose prominent supporters like Gavin Andresen, leaving him with only a small cult following. His claims would lead to years of legal battles with governments and former associates that will likely continue for most of his life. Wright is regularly on both sides of the court, as a defendant in some cases and a plaintiff in others. In one early lawsuit filed against him, some disturbing details were revealed that shed some light on his character. Dave Kleiman, one of Wright's associates from the early days of Bitcoin, had passed away in 2013 after a battle with the pernicious staph infection MRSA. The two had shared assets, and Kleiman's family was legally entitled to his share. Wright was accused of forging signatures that transferred all of Kleiman's assets into his control, essentially stealing from a dead colleague.[13]

It turned out that Satoshi was right to remain anonymous, because whenever a theory about their true identity reached the news, it became clear that law enforcement agencies all over the world were determined to track down this mysterious figure. To this day, nobody has been able to confirm they know Satoshi's true identity, although everyone has their favorite theory. Hal Finney seems to be the most popular theory among early Bitcoiners, but with any luck we will never find out.

A Culture Is Born

In the very first years of its development, Bitcoin was just a passion project among a small group of people who volunteered their time to its development. There was no price for Bitcoin, and although the early users made transactions to test things out, nobody was actually buying anything with Bitcoin. That all changed on May 22, 2010, now known as Pizza Day in the crypto community, when the first retail purchase was made with Bitcoin. A programmer and early Bitcoin adopter named Laszlo Hanyecz posted a thread on the Bitcointalk forum where he offered to pay 10,000 Bitcoin to have a few pizzas delivered to him. At the time Bitcoin had no formal price and was worth basically nothing, but someone took him up on his offer and paid to have a nearby Papa Johns deliver the pizzas in exchange for the 10,000 BTC. Happy with the exchange, a few days later Hanyecz posted, "I will trade 10,000 BTC for 2 of these pizzas any time as long as I have the funds. I usually have plenty."

Hanyecz maintained this offer for several months, and gave multiple other early adopters the same deal. And though many have put a dollar amount on what those Bitcoins were eventually worth, Hanyecz says he has no regrets – he was a part of Bitcoin history, and his transaction helped to prove the Bitcoin use case and to hype up the community. Also, as an early contributor to the Bitcoin community, chances are that he continued to accumulate the asset while it was only worth pennies. But he keeps his current net worth unknown. Aside from a few annual podcast appearances, Hanyecz has maintained a relatively private life, and has not sought to capitalize on his Bitcoin fame.[14]

Hanyecz was the first, but he was not alone. In the earliest years of the Bitcoin experiment, the true believers were doing everything they could to spend their Bitcoin. The initial idea for the network was for it to be a decentralized and private payment system with a built-in scarce currency. So, naturally, the only way to gain adoption would be to actually spend the currency and convince merchants to adopt it. There was an expectation that the price could become astronomical someday, but everyone understood that this would not happen until a large number of people were holding and spending Bitcoin.

Two months after Pizza Day, Jed McCaleb, (soon to become a tech entrepreneur), read a July 11 article about Bitcoin in Slashdot and decided to build a key piece of infrastructure for the network: a Bitcoin exchange. Instead of starting from scratch, McCaleb used the domain and infrastructure from an old project that he'd abandoned years before when it failed to gain traction: a platform for trading cards for the Magic: The Gathering card game ("Mt. Gox" is short for Magic: The Gathering Online eXchange). With these quick and somewhat sloppy moves, McCaleb was able to launch his Bitcoin exchange seven days after first reading about the technology; he announced it in a post on Bitcointalk on July 18, 2010. The site didn't get much traffic at first, but the users slowly began to trickle in over time.[15]

Bitcoin for President

At first, only the cypherpunks and hardcore hackers were interested in Bitcoin, but it quickly became an intellectual curiosity for Libertarians and Anarcho-Capitalists who had an interest in alternative currencies. In fact, in the early emails between Satoshi and Hal Finney, Satoshi described Bitcoin as being "very attractive to the libertarian viewpoint." Indeed, many Libertarians were attracted to Bitcoin, not only because of its privacy ethos but also because of its sound-money policy, which seemed to be inspired by the Austrian School of economics,[16] one of the core components of western Libertarian philosophy. The Austrian perspective is based on the work of Ludwig von Mises and other free market economists such as Murray Rothbard, Friedrich Hayek, and Carl Menger. One of the core tenets of this philosophy is that the private sector *companies* can do pretty much anything the public sector *governments* can do, and much better. Whether it's roads, schools, police, courts, or money, Austrian School economists see a potential reality where all of these public services are better delivered by a collection of businesses, charities, collectives, and private foundations. Something like Bitcoin fits in with this model perfectly because it is private money that is totally outside the control of the state.

The Austrian perspective is somewhat contrarian in modern economics because it is very different from the Keynesian philosophy, which is the dominant economic model throughout the world today. The Keynesian school of economics takes its name from John Maynard Keynes, an economist from the mid-twentieth century who advocated against free markets and called for government intervention in the economy. Keynes was also a strong advocate of governments spending money that they don't have, and printing money to pay for expenses. Keynes believed that the benefits of these policies outweighed the costs because control of the monetary system typically allows governments to keep the system stable – but it doesn't always work out that way. As discussed, these policies can lead to problems like inflation, but Keynes didn't think that inflation was a problem. As far as he was concerned, it was just an example of the system working as it should, and it caused problems in only a few rare, extreme cases.

Bitcoin was hotly debated in Libertarian circles from the very beginning, and not everyone was on board. Much of the older guard were lifelong gold bugs who refused to believe that any digital currency could ever have value. Peter Schiff is among this crowd of Libertarian gold bugs who failed to see the magic in this new technology.[17] There was also some initial resistance in corners of the Libertarian movement that were heavily influenced by conspiracy theories. For decades there was a major talking point in conspiracy culture that warned about the central banks of the world joining together to implement an all-powerful global digital currency that would totally enslave humankind with debt and surveillance. But this wasn't just a conspiracy theory; a global digital currency has been on the agenda of the global central banks for decades. There was even a cover story in the January 1988 edition of *The Economist* where the headline told readers that a global currency would launch in the next 30 years.[18] These are all legitimate concerns about how central banks would handle a global digital currency. To my mind, Central Bank Digital Currency (CBDC) is worth worrying about – the currencies controlled by the central banks that offer no transparency and no privacy. This is the complete opposite of Bitcoin, which is decentralized, open source, and private. Most Bitcoiners will admit that privacy on the network has eroded as the ecosystem has grown, but there are now other cryptocurrencies and applications that focus specifically on privacy. There is also hope that privacy can someday return to Bitcoin through some type of update or layer 2 integration.[19] But these nuances can be difficult to grasp, especially for those encountering this strange technology for the first time.

Still, despite these internal controversies, Bitcoin continued to find vocal advocates in the Libertarian movement during the first years of its development. Some of them were public figures, like Max Kieser, Charlie Shrem, and Roger Ver. But ultimately it was yet another anonymous and mysterious figure that would take Bitcoin to the next level and catapult it into the mainstream.

CHAPTER 5

A Short Course in Blockchain

Hashing, Mining, and Forking

In this chapter I'm going to give you a primer on the core technology that powers crypto: the blockchain. It's important to say up front that crypto is based on code and math; that's what makes it special. And the nitty-gritty of crypto, the blockchain, is university-level math that's difficult to grasp. In fact, this chapter is hardly going to scratch the surface of the nuts and bolts of blockchain. So if you're feeling overwhelmed, that's okay – just hang on. If at the end of this chapter you want to learn more you should pursue that curiosity; good blockchain developers are few and far between.

Blockchain 101

"Blockchain" is a confusing term that conjures up mental images that make it harder to conceptualize. You can thank David Chaum for the name. Suffice to say that a blockchain is a database in the same way money is. It's a way to organize information that's easy to sort through. But the beauty of blockchain isn't that it's a new method of storing information (which it is); the beauty is in *how* the information is put on to this chain of spreadsheets *and* is shared and distributed across thousands of computers. So let's break down the core elements of blockchain.

Blocks and Chains

The "block" in the blockchain is a spreadsheet with some special instructions and a bunch of transactions. Every blockchain starts with one block – the "genesis" block. After a certain amount of time, the programming of the blockchain closes the genesis block (which has a height of zero) and adds another block on top of it – building "height." As time goes on more and more blocks are stacked on top. For instance, the genesis block of Bitcoin started on January 3, 2009. Fast-forward to when President Obama was elected to a second term on November 6, 2012, the block height was 206,860; and when the Braves won the World Series on November 2, 2021, the height was 707,957. Each block ranges in size depending on how heavily the network is being used, but all together the entire Bitcoin blockchain is over 425 gigabytes at the time of this writing.[1]

Now, let's say you opened up a block "explorer" (which is the blockchain equivalent of a search engine) and took a look at what was going on under the hood. It's all metadata, a bunch of text that makes sense only to the Blockchain. The structure of a block is set up like this:

1. Block Size: the size of the block (in bytes);
2. Block Header: the information needed to link this block to the chain;
3. Transaction Counter: the count of how many transactions have taken place in this block; and
4. Transactions: the actual transactions recorded in the block (for example, "5BTC from X address to Y address").

Those are the four elements that make up a block on the Bitcoin blockchain. And since every block is unique and cannot be changed – which is the whole point of blockchain – they each need their own ID. That's where the *hash* comes in.

Hash

Using the word "hash" when talking about numbers and math can sound a bit odd. But hashing a number is the same idea as chopping up potatoes to make hashbrowns: taking something uniform and scrambling it up. A simple definition of "hashing" is that it's a mathematics term for running some data through a formula. A hash is the result that comes out of the formula – like a plate of hashbrowns you order at Waffle House. Hashing is the process of working out that formula – when the line cook pulls out the knife and starts chopping away. In the end you get a mess compared to what you started with, but it's a delicious mess. Each block in a blockchain has its own unique identifier along with its block height. This unique hash ID locates that block in relation to the parent block (the block that came before it).

So hash is math. Cool. But how does that relate to crypto assets? Well, the computer doing all this math is called a miner (more on that later), and its job on the network is to complete the necessary cryptographic work on the blockchain to gain the "block reward"– some amount of crypto currency. In the early days of Bitcoin you could mine on a laptop because the amount of hashing needed to figure out the block wasn't that hard to do. That amount of hashing work is called "hashrate," and it's a unit of power. In the early days, Satoshi Nakamoto mined thousands of Bitcoin on their home computer,[2] but a part of the Bitcoin code makes adjustments that requires more computing power in order to verify the network. The code adjusts the *difficulty* of the hash to scale with how many blocks are being created. Not too many, and not too slow. Bitcoin likes blocks to be mined about every 10 minutes, so the Bitcoin code adjusts the hash difficulty dynamically to hit that sweet spot. It's complicated and takes a lot of work. That's why we call it *mining*. (More on that ahead.)

Mining

The concept of "mining Bitcoin" conjures images of gnomes using pickaxes to pull golden coins from a mountain of 1s and 0s. While I wish that were the case, the day-to-day process of mining crypto is a little more grounded in reality and a lot better for society. The process of mining is essentially computers validating transactions on a blockchain and checking their work against others on the network in order to achieve consensus. The validation work is done through a cryptographic algorithm that forces the mining machine to match the previous block's hash or digital fingerprint by guessing its hash. Once a block is confirmed, the work of validating a new block (a group of transactions on a spreadsheet) is rewarded with tokens specific to the blockchain the computer was working on – BTC for mining on the Bitcoin network and LTC for mining on the Litecoin network.

Similar to how 1 dollar is made up of 100 pennies, a single Bitcoin is divisible by 1 million. The smallest unit of a Bitcoin is called a "Satoshi" – or "sat" for short. This what it means when you hear crypto people talking about "stacking sats": just like putting change in a jar, they're building their stack of bitcoin one Satoshi at a time. Other coins have denominations that get really small too; Litecoin has "litoshis," Ethereum has "wei" and Dogecoin has "koinu."

But the process of mining a crypto asset isn't just about consensus and making new blocks to get the blockchain up and running. It's about security. The more computers that are on the network doing the mining work, the harder it is for a bad actor to try to manipulate the assets. That manipulation can happen several ways, but the most common is the 51% attack. When the hashrate is commandeered by a hacker up to no good, the network can be manipulated to spend coins twice, change payment addresses, or do lots of other nefarious things.[3] Needless to say, this is very bad for the asset and erodes trust in its integrity.

I said earlier that the code adjusts the difficulty of the hash. It does that because security is so important: the higher the difficulty, the more work it takes to solve a block, and thus the more secure the network. It wasn't long after the Bitcoin went live that Nakamoto was no longer able to mine just on their laptop. But the Bitcoin code was online, free to everyone. So more people jumped on the network and started mining. This created a positive feedback loop: (1) Additional miners (2) increase the hash difficulty, which (3) improves security, which (4) increases trust in the network, which (5) increases the value of Bitcoin, which (6) inspires more miners to join the network, which continues the process.

That's a beautiful thing. So the hashrate of Bitcoin started at basically one hash per second. Two years later, the hashrate was 5 Gigahash, or 5 million hashes per second. At the time of this writing, the Bitcoin hashrate is 239 Exahash, or 239 quintillion hashes per second.[4]

That's a lot of potatoes.

With all that math happening at the speed of light, the likelihood of a hacker taking over that much *power* in the network decreases as long as more people participate. In fact, the Bitcoin network wields so much power – and is so spread out across thousands of businesses, governments, and individual miners – that, today, it's basically impossible to hack the Bitcoin network.

This isn't true of most networks, though, and it wasn't always true for Bitcoin, which had to go through a lot of turmoil in its early years to become what it is today. I cover that turmoil later on in this book, but it involves something called a blockchain "fork," which I'll cover lower down.

Blockchain 201

So we've covered the basics. Now let's look at the ways blockchains have evolved over the years.

Consensus Mechanisms

Let's review a bit. Up until now the consensus mechanism described was what's called "proof-of-work" (PoW) in action. In PoW, computers compete to solve a math problem; the first to finish is rewarded with tokens for doing so.

But there's another means of getting consensus on a blockchain that's done without all this guesswork and hashing. This is called "proof-of-stake"

(PoS). First mentioned as an alternative to "proof-of-work" (PoW) in the Bitcoin talk forums on July 11, 2011, proof-of-stake was seen as a means to scale up Bitcoin faster, reduce transaction costs, and allow for more transparency when voting on proposals to the code.[5]

In proof-of-stake there are no miners verifying transactions; instead there are "validators"—token holders that have committed or "staked" a certain amount of their tokens to a node on the network. A node is simply a piece of software running on a desktop computer that is tied directly to the full blockchain and is managing the tokens being staked in addition to "minting" new blocks. Note the difference in terminology: blocks are *mined* on PoW and *minted* on PoS blockchains.

Whereas with PoW consensus is reached via competitive computing, with PoS consensus is reached via validators that have been chosen by the algorithm. Once a validator checks its work against the results of the other validators chosen for that block, and everything is good, a reward is released to all the stakers involved. Validator selection is somewhat randomized, but it's also weighted to favor older, more established nodes, bigger nodes, nodes that have had more up time, etc., etc. This evens out the playing field and helps protect the network from a bad actor gaming the system.

There are many strong opinions about cryptographic consensus mechanisms and which one is better, but my take is this: there is room for both. Each adds value in its own way, and allowing crypto to innovate means being open to developing new tech.

Forks

There's a saying in crypto that "Code is law." That means any change to the programming of a blockchain, a crypto wallet, or a smart contract should be regarded as changing a law – in other words, something to be taken seriously and with careful consideration by a democratic body.

A blockchain never breaks; it either stops or forks. A stoppage is pretty self-explanatory; transactions just stop being processed. But a fork is different: it's a split in the river of data – that's been decided upon by vote. For example, Ethereum has had several forks, and you can follow the paths all the way back to the Ethereum genesis block.

Forks are a natural part of a blockchain's growth and progress forward as a technology. When patches or upgrades are voted in on a blockchain, that changes the river of data, and therefore pushes the river on to a slightly different path. The forks that retain a blockchain's compatibility with their previous blocks is called a "soft" fork. This is relatively easy to manage and happens relatively often.

A fork that is more drastic or contentious is called a "hard" fork. Sometimes they're intentional; for instance, both Litecoin (October 2011) and

Ravencoin (January 2018) are hard forks of Bitcoin.[6] They used the Bitcoin code as a launch pad, changed some things, and then proceeded as their own unique blockchain. Other hard forks are more controversial; that will be covered in later chapters. For now, suffice it to say that a hard fork on an existing blockchain requires a lot of effort to pull off.

Blockchain 365

All things of value require effort and time. It takes effort to get gold and oil out of the ground, it takes effort to make a worthwhile piece of art, and it takes a lot of time to make a relationship valuable. The same is true for Bitcoin. All that computing power (or effort) comes at a cost, and that cost is energy. The average Bitcoin-mining facility can consume enough electricity to power a dozen Walmarts. In fact, one Bitcoin-mining computer is really just an array of computer chips called ASICs, or Application Specific Integrated Circuits, and can have over 100 chips inside it. An obsolete ASIC miner can consume 3,000 watts of power per hour, and miners run 24/7, 365. That's like running your microwave oven all day and all night. That's a lot of effort to make some magic internet money. But that's the amazing thing about Bitcoin and proof-of-work: it's a form of money that uses the greenest available energy. As of 2022, over 70% of bitcoin mined used green energy, and mining operations are incentivizing power-grid improvements and green-energy alternatives everywhere they pop up.[7] There is much to be said about the energy consumption of Bitcoin, but suffice to say, a lot of it comes from centralized powers that feel threatened by a form of money they can't control. I don't know about you, but I like my money backed by math and electricity instead of war and oil.

CHAPTER 6

A Necessary Evil

Silk Road's Original Sin

O nline marketplaces for things like drugs, weapons, secrets, and even assassinations were predicted and regularly discussed by the cypherpunks in the early days of the internet. Some of them saw this capability as a necessary evil that was outweighed by the benefits the technology would bring; others saw it as a public good that would bring necessary change to oppressive and outdated laws. This concept was detailed by Timothy May in his 1997 paper "Untraceable Digital Cash, Information Markets, and BlackNet," where he discussed how private digital transactions should be recognized as a natural right protected by the Constitution. He admitted that digital cash would also make it easier to commit crimes, but he felt that was a fair trade-off for the privacy and freedom that it enabled. In the paper, May revealed that in 1993 he had created a proof-of-concept for this idea that he called "BlackNet," which he had run anonymously up until then. BlackNet was an online marketplace for illegal information, including government secrets and recipes for drugs or banned chemicals. BlackNet even had its own native currency, called "CryptoCredits," and used anonymous email services called "remailers" to allow users to communicate privately. The currency was limited because it had no use outside the system and could not be exchanged for real money.

May wrote: "BlackNet is nominally non-ideological, but considers nation-states, export laws, patent laws, national security considerations and the like to be relics of the pre-cyberspace era. Export and patent laws are often used to explicitly project national power and imperialist, colonialist state fascism."[1]

May's views were controversial, even among cypherpunks, some of whom hoped that systems could be designed in ways to prevent negative externalities like crime while still maintaining privacy and freedom of speech. Although BlackNet was a working prototype, it was also just an experiment that only a small handful of people knew about. At the time the internet wasn't as pervasive as it is now – back then it was more of a novelty, only used by nerds, universities, and governments – and only a fraction of users were interested in illicit uses of cryptography. The technology was also very rudimentary back in those days, so the idea was a bit too far ahead of its time. Although this discussion remained on the fringes, it did catch the attention of the libertarian philosopher and activist Samuel Edward Konkin, who had been pondering how technology could disrupt the state since the 1980s. Konkin was somewhat of a misfit among American Libertarians because he was vehemently opposed to the Libertarian Party and political participation altogether. He believed that politics was a lost cause, and that participating in elections and campaigns actually strengthened the power of the state by giving it more credibility. But he didn't advocate for violent revolution either; instead, he called for a strategy of "counter-economics" that sought to weaken the power of the government through illegal financial activity such as tax evasion, smuggling, and running small businesses without licenses and permits. The counter-economic strategy also called for direct market competition with government services in hopes of replacing them with free-market alternatives and rendering them obsolete – an act that is typically seen as illegal, if not treasonous. Examples of this strategy in action could include launching an alternative currency to compete with the Federal Reserve, starting a private security organization to compete with the local police, or developing a mutual-aid society to compete with government welfare. But in order to work, these alternatives would need to serve their communities better than the government agencies they were intended to replace. Konkin expanded on this strategy in his most famous work, "The New Libertarian Manifesto," which introduced a philosophy based on counter-economics called "Agorism." In addition to advocating for things like tax evasion and black-market activity, Agorism also called for a radical self-reliance, which advocated avoiding any dependance on the government and doing everything possible to help others also become less dependent.

Konkin also subscribed to the Austrian School of economics, a late-nineteenth-century school of thought that sees government services as being essentially monopolies that become corrupt because they don't actually need to serve their communities in order to stay in business. Regardless of how many people are dissatisfied with the service they're getting, their tax dollars will keep on funding that service. Some of the most popular Austrian economists of the day, like Murray Rothbard, thought they could use the political system to slowly introduce more free market policies over time. This approach favored working within the system to create change. Konkin, on the other hand, felt that there was no hope in creating change through the political system, so he favored a more radical approach. He believed we should all start carefully and strategically breaking laws and challenging government power with our own unregulated businesses. In a research paper titled "The Second Economy and the Destabilization Effect of Its Growth on the State Economy in the Soviet Union: 1965–1989," economists Vladimir Treml and Michael Alexeev suggested that it was just this sort of counter-economy that led in part to the fall of the Soviet Union, where smuggling, tax avoidance, and daily acts of civil disobedience had become a way of life in response to all-encompassing regulations.[2]

Konkin passed away in 2004, so he only got to see the very beginning of the internet revolution, but toward the end of his life the technology he'd been imagining for years was starting to hit the market. In a 2002 interview, Konkin was asked about the cypherpunks and their overlap with the Agorist philosophy and replied: "The Cypherpunks provide a useful tool/weapon for the Counter-Economy." He also praised cryptography, rejoicing that the government "cannot reach the invoices, inventory lists, accounts and so on of the Counter-Economist," when encryption is used.[3]

Because Konkin's ideas were radical, even among libertarians, he had played the role of the underdog, and he had embraced it. When he passed, a half-hearted memorial in the Libertarian magazine *Reason* started out by reporting that Samuel Edward Konkin III had died and "deserves to be remembered." It ended with the lines: "Konkin isn't the sort of figure who's likely to receive an obit in the newspaper, so I feel obliged to offer at least a sketchy memorial here."[4] Konkin may not have been a celebrity activist, but his work was extremely influential, especially among early Bitcoiners who believed they were creating the type of "counter-economy" that he had envisioned. His philosophy of direct action was the driving inspiration behind the first online drug marketplace, Silk Road.

Silk Road

After six months of development, Silk Road launched in February 2011. It couldn't be found through traditional web browsers; you needed a special encrypted browser called Tor to access it. In addition to privacy, Tor also gives users access to a part of the internet known as the "deep web," which is not indexed by search engines and doesn't appear on normal browsers. The deep web includes a large volume of material that is totally legal and necessary for operating many websites, but it also includes encrypted areas known as the "dark web," where illegal activity often takes place and illegal services are offered, involving stolen data, assassinations, and the like. Very few people even knew that this corner of the internet existed until Silk Road started hitting the news. Silk Road got off to a very slow start, only finding users among the most extreme crypto-anarchist Bitcoiners. However, things started to take off in June 2011 when *Gawker* published an article about Silk Road titled "The Underground Website Where You Can Buy Any Drug Imaginable."[5]

The website was founded by a mysterious figure known as Dread Pirate Roberts, a name taken from the novel *The Princess Bride*. In one of his many philosophical posts for Silk Road users, Roberts cited Konkin as an influence and inspiration. In a post explaining his ideological background, Roberts said: "I read everything I could to deepen my understanding of economics and liberty, but it was all intellectual, there was no call to action except to tell the people around me what I had learned and hopefully get them to see the light. That was until I read [J. Neil Schulman's] *Alongside Night* and the works of Samuel Edward Konkin III. At last the missing puzzle piece! All of the sudden it was so clear: every action you take outside the scope of government control strengthens the market and weakens the state."[6]

The mystery and hype about Silk Road, and the increased traffic on Silk Road, proved to be Bitcoin's first truly viral moment, and the *Gawker* article was the first place that many people initially heard about cryptocurrency.[7] There had been coverage of Bitcoin via tech sources like *Wired*, but that wasn't at the forefront of pop culture like *Gawker* was. Plus, decentralized digital cash doesn't capture national attention in the way that online drug marketplaces do. As the article made its rounds across social media, more and more new users began flocking to Silk Road – and they needed Bitcoin if they wanted to buy anything. Once they were able to figure out how Bitcoin worked and how to buy it, Silk Road users had a very similar user experience to what Amazon or eBay offered at the time; this included photos and descriptions of the items along with prices, and a detailed review system that helped to keep the transactions honest – weeding out the dishonest sellers, no pun intended. To ensure that the sellers followed through on their promises to deliver, there was an automated escrow system where the funds would be locked until the buyer confirmed that the package had been received. In the June 2011 *Gawker* article, author Adrian Chen cited "1/8th of pot on Silk Road [selling] for 7.63 Bitcoins," when one Bitcoin was about $8.67. In 2011, a bag of psychedelic mushrooms sold for upwards of 40 Bitcoin, or a bag of weed for 20 Bitcoin. (Given that, on November 10, 2021, one Bitcoin was valued at $68,789 – the highest to date[8] – many early Bitcoiners might see those purchases as their very own "pizza days" to look back on with regret.)

As the Silk Road grew in popularity, Roberts became a sort of cult symbol in the Libertarian movement. His supporters were amazed that someone could break the law so brazenly and get away with it. The fact that he was largely motivated by Libertarian ideals also gained him a ton of support in that community. Libertarians argued that the Silk Road was saving lives because the review system was preventing addicts from buying dirty adulterants like fentanyl. They also argued that keeping drug deals off the streets was reducing robberies and violent crimes.[9]

Of course, not everyone agreed. Many thought that the Silk Road represented a serious threat to civilization. The idea that anyone could get drugs any time they wanted seemed like just too much temptation. There were concerns that overdoses would increase and that cartels would use the site, and not everyone thought that undermining the government was a good thing. There were also a lot of people in the Bitcoin community and development team who did not want to be associated with Silk Road, and weren't happy that something so controversial was Bitcoin's "killer app." That most people who had heard of Bitcoin associated it with drugs distracted attention from the technology's core value proposition: decentralized digital cash with a sound monetary policy.

Law enforcement also became increasingly concerned about this politically motivated kingpin and his dark web marketplace. US Senator Chuck Schumer took a special interest in the case and demanded that the Drug Enforcement Administration (DEA) and Department of Justice (DOJ) find a way to shut the site down. At first it seemed like an impossible task because law enforcement officials were so unfamiliar with the terrain in cyberspace, but after about two years of investigation and undercover operations they were able to close in on Silk Road. Dread Pirate Roberts was arrested in a public library in San Francisco in October 2013, and was shortly thereafter named as Ross William Ulbricht. At that time he was charged with money laundering, computer hacking, and conspiracy to traffic narcotics.[10]

For all his talents in creating and running Silk Road, and keeping himself anonymous for so long, Ulbricht hadn't fully covered all his tracks. On January 27, 2011, using the name "altoid," he had posted on Bitcointalk and shroomery.org mentioning he'd come across an "anonymous market online" and wondered if anyone had heard of it and what they thought about it; he then provided the link to Silk Road. These appear to have been Silk Road's "Grand Opening!" announcements. Eight months later, altoid posted on Bitcointalk putting out feelers seeking to hire an "IT pro in the Bitcoin community" for "a venture backed Bitcoin startup company." As his contact info he gave his email address – his full name **@gmail.com**. Eventually, after exhaustive investigating, IRS Special Agent Gary Alford was able to connect the digital dots and uncover his identity.[11]

Ross Ulbricht was no angel, but I think his case was an injustice, and he never really had a shot at a fair trial. Authorities in New York hated the idea of a decentralized currency, especially if some of its most vocal builders are openly calling for the disruption of the Federal Reserve. After all, NYC is the home of Wall Street. In the documentary *Banking on Bitcoin,* Alex Winter, director of the film *Deep Web,* states that Ulbricht's case was much more about Bitcoin than it was about Silk Road. And that the fact it was tried in the southern district of New York demonstrates that Bitcoin was seen as a threat – and that "the idea that somebody could create a marketplace where you could freely transact without oversight or regulation had to be dealt a massive and public blow."[12]

Ulbricht's hard-core brand of Libertarianism was also something that made the prosecutors extremely uncomfortable. Let's not forget that he made law enforcement look foolish and incompetent too. Everyone in the establishment wanted to make an example out of him. The trial lasted less than a month, and the jury convened for less than four hours. Judged guilty on all seven counts – distributing narcotics, distributing narcotics by means of the internet, conspiring to distribute narcotics, engaging in a continuing criminal enterprise, conspiring to commit computer hacking, conspiring to traffic in false identity documents, and conspiring to commit money laundering – Ulbricht received a double life sentence without the possibility of parole. At his sentencing in May of 2015, US District Judge Katherine Forrest stated: "Your case is without precedent. You are first. For those considering stepping into your shoes, they need to understand, there will be very severe consequences. There must be no doubt that lawlessness will not be tolerated."[13]

Like I said, Ross Ulbricht was no angel. But why did he get a *double* life sentence without the possibility of parole? (As a point of comparison, Sinaloa Cartel leader Joaquin Guzman – El Chapo – was sentenced in 2019 to life in prison for "conducting a continuing criminal enterprise, including large-scale narcotics violations and a murder conspiracy, drug-trafficking conspiracies, unlawful use of a firearm, and a money laundering conspiracy. . . Trial evidence proved the cartel [engaged in] murder, kidnapping, torture, bribery of officials, and other illegal methods."[14])

The DEA press release about Ulbricht's sentencing conveys that six overdose deaths have been linked to drugs purchased from Silk Road; one victim was found at his computer with the Silk Road site on his screen. It also characterizes the site as a "sprawling black-market bazaar" offering "unlawful goods and services," including computer-hacking services, malicious software, and forged documents. But that's not even the whole story.

On October 1, 2013, a separate indictment had been filed in Maryland alleging that, in addition to the aforementioned activities, Ulbricht had requested and paid for the torture and murder of one of his employees, Curtis Green, who had apparently stolen [$350,000] from him and other users of the site. These murder-for-hire charges never made it to court. Reasons for this include the pertinent fact that the charges were false and the supposed evidence faked – and that the perpetrators of that sham were in fact under investigation during the same period. At the end of a six-year vow of silence he agreed to in relation to a movie deal, Green admitted in a December 2018 interview with KSL TV 5 that two FBI agents, Carl Force of the DEA and Shaun Bridges of the Secret Service and NSA, had forced him to fake his death in exchange for a reduced sentence for his involvement with Silk Road. But you don't need to take his word for it, because those same officers were both convicted of "breathtaking" abuse of power in relation to the case, involving skimming many Bitcoins for themselves, plus laundering. Ex-DEA Agent Carl Force was sentenced to six years' imprisonment for "extorting Silk Road" of $50,000, and former Secret Service Special Agent Shaun Bridges pled guilty to "diverting . . . into his own account" $350,000 worth of bitcoins during the Silk Road investigation – the same $350,000 that Curtis Green had supposedly stolen, for which reason Ross Ulbricht had supposedly arranged for his murder. According to reporter Lee Munson: "Bridges's plea agreement brought to light how he obstructed the investigation of Ulbricht and Silk Road through his takeover of Green's administrator account. He also impeded investigations into his own wrongdoing by making several false or misleading statements."[15]

Let's back up a bit and repeat some pertinent dates. Ulbricht was indicted, charged, and arrested in October of 2013. He was sentenced in May of 2015. Carl Force pled guilty a month later, in June 2015. Shaun Bridges pled guilty two months after that, in August 2015. Was the murder-for-hire indictment allowed to float so as to sway the court of public opinion? Those murder charges weren't dropped until July of 2018 – on account of the Supreme Court having declined to consider reducing his sentence. Many of Ross's supporters don't believe these accusations are true, and even Curtis Greene, who was the alleged target of the hit, has spoken out on numerous occasions about how he did not believe that Ulbricht ordered to have him killed.[16]

The Streisand Effect

The downfall of Silk Road created a gap in the online drug trade that an army of newly minted Agorists was happy to fill. Instead of making an example out of Ulbricht to discourage similar activities – as US District Judge Katherine Forrest demonstrated in her comments quoted earlier – the case ended up bringing more attention to the dark web and inspired a flurry of copycat websites.[17] This is similar to the wave of file-sharing websites that launched after the downfall of Napster. It is very hard to hide information like this on the internet, and things tend to spread faster when it's information that people would like to cover up. This online phenomenon is so common that it resulted in the coining of the phrase "The Streisand Effect," named after the actress Barbra Streisand, who fought to keep photos of her mansion off the internet – only to bring more attention to the photos through her legal actions against those who sought to publish them.

And so the authorities are now caught up in a never-ending game of Whac-A-Mole in cyberspace, just like they are on the streets. Through the years, drug marketplaces have continued to pop up on the dark web, and law enforcement continues to shut them down.[18]

After sentencing, Ross Ulbricht expressed remorse in a letter to the judge, saying that, "Silk Road turned out to be a very naive and costly idea that I deeply regret." In the years since his conviction, he has relentlessly fought for a reduction in his sentence. He keeps in contact with his supporters through a Twitter account that is managed by his mother, Lyn, and a team of friends. Lyn has now dedicated her life to her son's case, regularly traveling to speak at crypto conferences and taking interviews with Libertarian podcasts to advocate for his release. Ross has continued his activism from behind bars, writing, creating art, and getting involved in prison reform. In late 2021, he auctioned off some of the artwork that he made in prison, raising millions of dollars for prisoner-related charities and his own fight for freedom. Ulbricht said that a large portion of the funds will be used to help support the children of parents who are in jail on drug-related offenses. A petition for Ulbricht's release on Change.org has received nearly a half million signatures at time of writing, making it one of the top petitions on the site.[19] Various updates, including all his trial documents, can be found at FreeRoss.org.

Outlaws are often polarizing and seen as either total heroes or total villains, but the truth usually lies more in the middle. They are often just average people responding to the struggles and incentives of their time. Silk Road put Bitcoin on the map, and there is a very good chance that this technology may have never caught on without that original sin, but Bitcoin was already starting to grow up by the time the original dark web marketplace closed for business in October 2013. And though the price of Bitcoin crashed for a short time after the seizure of Silk Road, it quickly rebounded, in large part because it was already starting to find greater use cases outside of the dark web. As it happens, there was a serious macro situation taking form that would finally give Bitcoin's unique monetary policy its time to shine.

CHAPTER 7

"Mo' Money, Mo' Problems"

BitInstant and BitLicense

Whenever it faces adversity, Bitcoin has a way of bouncing back and becoming stronger than ever. And though we see this only every so often now, back in the early days it was a regular occurrence. Bitcoin was challenged constantly, and every time it seemed to learn and grow from its mistakes as if it had some type of super-intelligence. There have been so many pivotal moments in the history of Bitcoin where monumental successes would not have been possible without previous misfortunes. Silk Road had tarnished the crypto industry's mainstream reputation in ways that we are still dealing with today, but it also acted as a proof-of-concept that established Bitcoin as a decentralized and censorship-resistant form of money. This is a use case that is important to everyone, not just criminals – though many enemies of privacy would have you believe that only criminals use this tech. In 2013, as the international news was filled with stories about Silk Road, the Mediterranean island of Cyprus was sliding into a major financial crisis. The country's government and banks were in debt to other countries and financial institutions like the European Central Bank. Many of these problems were brought on by a global recession, but later exacerbated by corruption in the country's government and banking sector. To cover these debts and prevent the economy from collapsing, the government of Cyprus decided to literally steal money from its citizens' bank accounts with a policy called the "Economic Adjustment Programme." Larger percentages were taken out of private savings accounts, and there was nothing anyone could do. People were lined up around the block at ATMs, attempting to get as much money as they could out of the failing banking system.[1]

In those initial weeks where bank accounts in Cyprus were at risk, the price of Bitcoin jumped from around $20 at the end of February to nearly $100 in the middle of March. The price continued to rally throughout April, reaching over $200 before cooling off for a short period of time.[2] The people of Cyprus were in a desperate situation, and some of them heard stories about how Bitcoin could be used to move and store money that you don't want the government to interfere with. It is not clear how many citizens of Cyprus began using Bitcoin because of this incident, but this crisis was a major turning point for Bitcoin's narrative and its path to greater adoption.[3] Bitcoin continued to rally throughout 2013 and reached a new all-time high of about $600 in November of that year,[4] when Bitcoin was recognized as a legitimate asset in a Senate hearing. Leading up to the event, the Federal Reserve chairman of the time, Ben Bernanke, praised the cutting-edge technology in a letter to the Senate. Bernanke said that crypto assets like Bitcoin "may hold long-term promise." The hearing itself covered many of the concerns that the government had about the technology, from Silk Road to money laundering and the potential threat to the dollar. Much of the dialogue was based on false narratives and misunderstanding, but they were still taking crypto seriously as an emerging asset class, which gave it a new level of credibility.[5] Bitcoin began 2014 strong, extending its parabolic run into the new year and reaching a new all-time high of over $850 at the beginning of February.[6]

But then things really started to fall apart. Mt. Gox, the world's largest Bitcoin exchange, which was processing over 70% of the world's Bitcoin trades, went offline. Mt. Gox filed for bankruptcy and revealed that in a giant hack they had lost 744,408 Bitcoin, which represented hundreds of millions of dollars' worth of user funds.[7] Later investigations showed that this actually had been a slow hack over the course of several years that had gone undetected until it was far too late. The problem seems to have started way back in March of 2011, when Mt. Gox founder Jed McCaleb sold the site to French developer Mark Karpelès – whom he'd never even met – and left the project. Within three months there was a massive security breach on the exchange, with 25,000 BTC stolen from 478 accounts. The hacker gained control of the account of a Mt. Gox auditor, and then tampered with the exchange's software to temporarily manipulate the price of Bitcoin. The exchange managed to recover from the attack, but this vulnerability and others remained, allowing the hacker to continue to steal money in very small increments – for years. The fact that Jed McCaleb had sold the company so soon before the first hack has provoked suspicion that he knew about the vulnerabilities before handing the company over. Some have even suggested that he was involved in the hack because he had intricate knowledge of the site's flaws. This is all speculation. But former Mt. Gox traders filed a lawsuit against McCaleb in 2019, accusing him of "'fraudulent' and 'negligent' misrepresentation" of the website by not revealing its vulnerabilities when he sold it. McCaleb shot back at the plaintiffs, calling their suit "frivolous" and insisting that his predecessor was "totally incompetent" and "ran the site into the ground." The Tokyo District Court agreed with McCaleb, deeming that Karpelès's management was "a total mess" and that he was guilty of "data manipulation" – tampering with the books to hide the missing Bitcoin – but found him not guilty of embezzlement.

We may never know what actually happened, but the collapse of Mt. Gox was a major blow to the crypto industry.[8]

The market was bound to cool off at some point – it couldn't go straight up forever with no breaks. But the huge losses that happened on Mt. Gox caused further damage to the industry's reputation and scared away many new investors, who rightfully didn't trust the centralized exchanges available at the time. But Mt. Gox taught the industry an important lesson very early on: Security is essential. After the Mt. Gox hack, "Not your keys – not your coins" became a battle cry for early Bitcoin adopters, who urged investors to use hardware wallets and other methods of self-custody and cold storage.[9] Mt. Gox became an object lesson to teach other crypto exchanges just how badly things can blow up if security isn't taken seriously. It would be a long time before Bitcoiners started to trust exchanges again, and many early adopters continue to avoid exchanges at all costs. But people still needed a place to buy Bitcoin. Many different players saw a massive opportunity in the fall of Mt. Gox – some of whom were already in play.

BitInstant

The competitor with the biggest head start was BitInstant, which launched in 2011, not long after Mt. Gox imploded. The founders of the exchange – Charlie Shrem and Gareth Nelson, who were both in their early twenties – looked to their more experienced angel investors for guidance. Unfortunately, these investors had competing values and, thus, very different visions for the crypto industry, which was a constant source of struggle within the company.

One of the earliest investors was a Libertarian entrepreneur named Roger Ver, an extremely vocal advocate for Bitcoin in the first years of its development. Ver became known as a prolific investor who focused specifically on Bitcoin and crypto projects. In addition to his contribution to BitInstant, he was also among some of the first investors in Ripple, Blockchain.com, BitPay, Kraken, Bitcoin.com and many others. Somewhere along the way, mainstream media sources like CNBC started calling him "Bitcoin Jesus," and it really seemed like he was stepping into the role of an important messenger for this new technology. The fact that Ver was getting so much media coverage early on is surprising, considering that his vision for Bitcoin was similar to that of the original cypherpunks and Silk Road founder Ross Ulbricht. He was also an Agorist and a proponent of the Austrian School; he felt that Bitcoin could be used to diminish the power of the government and bankers – which would in turn create more freedom for the average person. This also meant that Ver had no problem with laws being broken if he felt that those laws were unjust. He detested any type of government regulations – from taxes to drug prohibition – and he saw Bitcoin as a powerful tool that could help people undermine these regulations. From his perspective, the fact that this technology could be used to help people do things like launder money was one of Bitcoin's most important features. These were among the talking points he used when describing this new technology to fellow Libertarians. Sure, he liked to make money, he'd say, but these philosophical beliefs were the driving factor behind most of his decisions.[10]

These beliefs would later clash with BitInstant's most high-profile investors, the Winklevoss twins, who famously had their concept for "The Facebook" stolen by Mark Zuckerberg. They were pariahs in Silicon Valley because of their feud with Zuckerberg, the new nerd king of Palo Alto, and none of the important establishment players wanted to deal with them out of fear that they would miss out on an opportunity with Facebook. But though the twins may have been outcasts among the elite, as far as Roger Ver was concerned, they were the epitome of the establishment. They wanted Bitcoin to be regulated and they wanted every project that they were involved in to follow strict regulatory guidelines, including KYC requirements, which was an extremely controversial take back in those days, because it required users to give up their privacy. The "Winklevii," as some call them, believed that Bitcoin was an important invention with huge potential, but they wanted to work with the government and bankers to bring them into the industry, not to use this technology against them. Obviously, as soon as the twins got into BitInstant with a $1.5 million investment in 2013, they began to run into conflict with Roger Ver.[11]

Of course, passionate parties having different or even opposing visions is a common occurrence in business, and often there is merit to both sides of the argument – as was the case with BitInstant. Ver was correct in trying to preserve the original values and ethos of the crypto culture; but at the same time, the Winklevii were right too: this technology was not going to go mainstream without being regulated to some degree. This clash of personalities would become largely irrelevant within a year after the twins made their large investment, because BitInstant was charged with knowingly transacting with Robert M. Faiella, the "BTCKing," who exchanged Bitcoin for Silk Road users. Cofounder Charlie Shrem was arrested for "conspiring to commit money laundering, operating an unlicensed money transmitting business, . . . [and] willfully failing to file any suspicious activity report regarding Faiella's illegal transactions." Shrem pleaded guilty to a reduced charge of aiding and abetting unlicensed money transmission, and was sentenced to two years in prison; he was released after one year. In later interviews, Shrem said that he was young at the time, and just didn't see a problem with what he was doing. BitInstant was shut down in late January 2014, within weeks of Mt. Gox shuttering – with the major difference that BitInstant users got their money back so the market had less reason to panic.[12]

Regulators Take Notice

After these events, regulators in the United States stepped up enforcement – and once again, the state of New York took a special interest. This would be a good time to introduce a concept known as "regulatory capture," which describes situations where regulatory agencies are totally controlled by the most powerful people in the industries they're supposed to be regulating. Instead of protecting consumers, these agencies end up protecting their corporate friends from legal liabilities – while also preventing competition from smaller companies that don't have the money to bribe government employees. This type of arrangement has developed in many sectors of our economy, but it is ever present in our banking system and financial institutions. Many times this comes in the form of campaign contributions – which are basically bribes. But also high-ranking CEOs from heavily regulated industries are given seats on regulatory agencies, where they are in control of the markets in which they hold significant stock. This is so common that it's known as the "revolving door" strategy in politics. For an example of this type of arrangement we don't need to look any further than Gary Gensler, the current SEC regulator (since April 2021) who was previously an employee of Goldman Sachs (1979–1997).[13] Once they're in positions of political power, regulators often do the bidding of the banks they're loyal to. And when they claim that this is necessary to maintain "financial stability," often what they really mean is the stability of the traditional system. This is why so many regulators seem intent on stopping crypto – or at least slowing it down. Anyone with a financial interest in the dominance of the traditional system would want to prevent competitors from entering the market, right? As a result of this conflict of interest, many regulators haven't been making good faith efforts to understand the crypto industry and truly protect investors.

This fact became obvious after the first major piece of crypto regulation, New York's BitLicense. The framework for the license was designed and introduced by New York's first Superintendent of Financial Services, Benjamin Lawsky, who was previously the chief counsel to Senator Chuck Schumer. The BitLicence, which came into effect on August 8, 2015, required crypto businesses to go through a rigorous registration process in order to legally operate in the state of New York. This sounds simple enough but the process was extremely expensive and time consuming, making it impossible for most crypto start-ups to actually get a license. Even if the business wasn't based in New York, they would still need to obtain the license in order to serve customers from the state. The move sparked outrage among builders in the crypto community and many companies that were based in the state decided to move out. The most notable crypto business to leave town was the centralized exchange Kraken, which also blocked New York residents from using their service. Other companies in the industry began taking the same approach, opting to entirely cut off customers from New York rather than submitting to the BitLicense.[14]

The industry showed that its legs were longer than the arms of the law. If regulations were too heavy in one jurisdiction, they would simply move to another and continue operations as usual. This works across state lines and even better across national borders. This is a phenomenon known as "jurisdictional arbitrage" and it happens in many industries; entrepreneurs flee areas with harsh regulations and move on to regions that have friendlier policies. But the permissionless and global nature of crypto makes it much easier to move around because global service can be provided from pretty much anywhere. Another workaround is the fact that users in more repressive jurisdictions can use VPNs (Virtual Private Networks) to access the blocked sites.

Despite the widespread defiance to this new law throughout the industry, there were some companies that decided to play nice with regulators. After their blunder with BitInstant, the Winklevoss twins decided to open up their own heavily regulated exchange in the state of New York, the belly of the beast. Their exchange, Gemini, was the second crypto businesses to obtain the BitLicense and become fully regulatory compliant for residents of New York.[15] The prominent exchange Coinbase opted in as well, getting their BitLicense in 2017, two years after Gemini. Although it took them some time to get in the good graces of regulators, Coinbase had an early advantage over Gemini in that it was heavily supported by big VCs in Silicon Valley, including Andreessen Horowitz and the Digital Currency Group.

The regulatory crackdown may have slowed the industry down a bit, but it didn't stop us. It even made us stronger in many ways. We also proved that we can just open up shop anywhere in the world.

CHAPTER 8

What the Fork?

The Block-Size War

The early days of Bitcoin were fun and exciting for almost everyone involved. The stakes weren't extremely high in those first few years, and early adopters were experimenting with an interesting new technology that had the potential to change the world. The Bitcoin community was filled with rebels, nerds, and dreamers – with most Bitcoiners fitting into all three categories. Many of the early builders and advocates of Bitcoin had deep philosophical motivations for their participation in the space – as can be seen with some of the figures we've covered so far. However, there was no general consensus on what the philosophy of Bitcoin actually was. Although many early developers were vocal Libertarians, the technology was neutral – so any individual could envision it working exactly as they thought it should be designed, serving whatever they thought its global role should be. There were often lively debates on popular forums like Bitcointalk and Reddit, and given how it was such a small and close-knit community, the atmosphere was usually friendly and collaborative.

Many early adopters felt that the Bitcoin network was a democratic system because there was no leader or CEO. However, as soon as Bitcoin started making people serious money, it ran into troubles with scaling, and disagreement emerged over how the protocol should be developed and governed. One of the original pitches for Bitcoin was that it is a cheap, fast, and easy way to send money, for which reason it gained a fair amount of early adoption. But as more people began using the network – again, the difficulty with scaling – many found the fees and slow transaction times unreasonable. This became extremely frustrating for Bitcoiners who were trying to onboard merchants and spread the gospel about crypto. Many of the active members in Bitcoin's Reddit discussions believed that the scaling dilemma should be the community's #1 priority, but not everyone in the industry was concerned. Most of the Bitcoin developers at the time were not in a rush to reach mainstream adoption and felt that the technology was still in a somewhat experimental phase – although there were a few key developers, such as Mike Hearn and

Gavin Andresen, who were heavily focused on the scaling issue.[1] Hearn was a Google engineer before leaving that behind to work on Bitcoin. Andreson was one of the most prolific Bitcoin developers when it was first getting off the ground; he worked directly with Satoshi in the beginning when very few people were interested. When Satoshi decided to retire, their final communication under that name was sent to Andreson, sharing some parting thoughts about the future of the project: "I wish you wouldn't keep talking about me as a mysterious shadowy figure, the press just turns that into a pirate currency angle. Maybe instead make it about the open source project and give more credit to your dev contributors; it helps motivate them." Days before, Satoshi had written to Mike Hearn, saying, "I've moved on to other things. It's in good hands with Gavin and everyone."[2]

Before leaving, Satoshi also handed over to Andreson control of the Bitcoin website and repository.[3] Needless to say, Andreson's opinions carried a lot of weight in the community. But Bitcoin's development was still an open-source endeavor, and the network was intentionally designed to prevent one person from gaining too much power. So Andreson had to debate with the other developers to get them to agree to any change he wanted to implement. Throughout 2014, debate had begun to heat up about a proposed solution to the scaling issue: increasing Bitcoin's maximum block size, which was 1 MB. Andreson and Hearn were in favor of raising the block size, which would drastically reduce the fees and transaction times on the Bitcoin blockchain. They wanted to see this change implemented as quickly as possible, but a majority of the other developers had concerns – they felt it needed to be done very slowly and carefully. For Andreson, Hearn, and the other advocates of bigger blocks, it started to seem like the other developers were stalling. "Big blockers," as they came to be called, felt that time was running out. Bitcoin had captured the world's attention, but that attention span is only so long, and many Bitcoiners were worried that this small window of time would be their only opportunity to reach mainstream adoption. This was a legitimate concern at the time, as many merchants were canceling their Bitcoin payment options, and it was becoming increasingly difficult to onboard new users. In early 2015, Andreson and Hearn started to campaign for bigger blocks among the broader Bitcoin community, and asked for support in pushing through this new rule change. Then, Mike Hearn made a Bitcoin Improvement Proposal (BIP), which called for a hard fork that would introduce new software called "Bitcoin XT," bringing with it new upgrades, including a block-size increase to 8 MB.[4]

A "fork" in blockchain programming is essentially a split in the chain. This can happen one of two ways: in the form of a "soft fork" or a "hard fork." As the names seem to imply, hard forks are much more serious and dangerous than soft forks. Hard forks are updates to the protocol that are not compatible with previous versions, which either nullifies the old chain or creates a situation where there are two different networks and assets that grew from the same root. Soft forks, on the other hand, are backwards-compatible with previous versions, so they allow for upgrades to take place more seamlessly and with less risk.

Initially, Hearn's idea for a hard fork didn't get much attention, because working with a new software client would be a drastic departure from how Bitcoin had been developed up to that point. But Hearn's proposal started gaining traction after Andreson publicly supported it. Even though Andreson was also a big blocker, his decision to support the proposal was still shocking to many in the Bitcoin community because the move was so aggressive. This is when things really got heated and when factions began to form. It was becoming obvious that there were many different people who had different visions for Bitcoin, and it was becoming very difficult for them to work together. On one side there was the vision of the big blockers: private digital cash that can be sent instantly for just a few cents – and on the other side there were the small blockers, who saw Bitcoin's high fees as a good thing that helped secure the Bitcoin network and were simply a by-product of the network's success. They wanted to ensure that Bitcoin's blocks were always filled, and that prices were always relatively high, because there were concerns that a surplus in block space could cause something called a "fee death spiral." In the case of this catastrophic event, the supply of blockspace would be too large for the demand, causing a collapse in fees, possibly to zero, which would leave the miners with no payment and the network with no security.[5]

In addition to these different strategies and concerns, each side had its own different way of looking at Bitcoin. The big blockers were most interested in the economics of the system – many of them actually had a background in economics; whereas the small blockers were usually more technically minded and better with coding. There were certainly some great programmers on the big-block side, but they were outmatched by their small-block opponents, who seemed to have a deeper knowledge of cryptography. And though the big blockers often recognized this fact, they still insisted that the design of Bitcoin should be just as much informed by economics and game theory as it is by cryptography and programming. Many of them also believed that public opinion among the community should have some role in shaping the governance. The small blockers saw things differently. They saw Bitcoin as an extremely complex system that most people are unable to understand, so they didn't really value the opinions of people who they felt were less educated on the subject than they were. When it came to the debate over block size, the small blockers did raise some very legitimate concerns. They pointed out that if big blocks were rushed before other key upgrades were completed, it would become more difficult for smaller miners to earn Bitcoin rewards, further centralizing control of the mining hashrate into the hands of industrial-scale miners. Most agreed that a moderate block-size limit would be needed at some point, but the size of the increases that were being proposed, and the speed at which they would be rolled out, was way too aggressive for many

Bitcoin developers. The fact that this change was being proposed through a hard fork was also a major point of controversy. The prospect of forcing through rule changes in this manner threatened to split the community – and possibly even split the blockchain into two competing networks. As far as the big blockers were concerned, desperate times called for desperate measures. From their perspective, Bitcoin was in imminent danger of failure due to its scaling problems.[6]

Shots Fired

In the summer of 2016, the situation had escalated so much that big blockers were effectively banned from making their case for the rule change on the most popular Bitcoin forum on Reddit, /r/Bitcoin. The forum was filled with posts advocating for bigger blocks because the everyday users and traders in the community wanted lower fees and improved user experience. This annoyed the small-blocker developers, who felt that the big blockers were ignorant and reckless – so moderators blocked all conversations about block size from the forum. They said that this was to avoid "confusion" about Bitcoin's roadmap and to allow the developers to have their technical discussions in peace.[7]

Gregory Maxwell, a prominent Bitcoin developer who cofounded Blockstream with Adam Back in 2014, deepened the divide between the two camps when he began making posts saying that big blockers were not technically sophisticated enough to understand what they were advocating for. In a Reddit post, Maxwell suggested that the big blockers were just armchair quarterbacks, portraying them as NASCAR fans in "beer cup hats" who shout out bad advice to the pit crew mechanics. Maxwell compared himself and the other developers to the mechanics in the pit crew, saying, "While they're busily debating compression ratios and high octane fuel and the seeming impossibility of getting the car to safely go much faster with the current state of technology you have a guy standing on the sidelines with a beer cup hat, saying, 'No problem guys: let's remove the brakes!' and the crowd goes wild: Finally someone who cares about speed."[8]

Maxwell became extremely unpopular because of his somewhat elitist attitude toward the nontechnical Bitcoin community, and Blockstream – one of Bitcoin's top development companies (which, again, he'd cofounded) – started taking heat on social media, especially from the big blocker camp. It didn't help that the vast majority of the developers in favor of small blocks were employed by Blockstream at the time. The community was upset that the developers seemed to be excluding them from a decision-making process that they thought was democratic. After weeks of openly suppressing content about the debate over block size on the r/bitcoin reddit forum, one of the moderators, Theymos, made a lengthy post on the subject, making his case against both the block-size increase and against democracy in "private and independent forums on the free market": "Just because many people want something doesn't make it right," Theymos wrote, adding: "If 90% of r/Bitcoin users find these policies to be intolerable, then I want these 90% of r/Bitcoin users to leave. Both r/Bitcoin and these people will be happier for it." He closed with: "The purpose of moderation is to make the community a good one, which sometimes includes causing people to leave." The "policies" referenced in the post was the forum's temporary ban on all block-size-related conversation on the r/Bitcoin subreddit; Theymos recommended that those who disagreed could "move to a different subreddit" so that "r/Bitcoin can get back to the business of discussing Bitcoin news in peace."[9]

This was a massive turning point. Many retail investors felt that they were no longer welcome to be a part of the Bitcoin community unless they went along with what the Blockstream developers wanted. The censorship was condemned by leaders in the space from both camps, including Andreas Antonopoulos and Vitalik Buterin.[10] The censorship issue also forced many of the libertarians in the industry to join the war and pick sides, most notably "Bitcoin Jesus" Roger Ver. Ver was already siding with the big blockers because he was frequently running into problems trying to onboard merchants due to the high fees and long waiting times. Ver became increasingly vocal as the censorship picked up on Reddit, and was quickly recognized as a leader in the big block camp. This also made him public enemy #1 for the small blockers, who did everything they could to discredit him on a personal level.[11]

At this point some important terminology started to take shape that distinguished the key players in the war from one another. The small blockers who continued working on Bitcoin's original client began referring to themselves as "Bitcoin Core" – and separated themselves from developers who began working on other clients. The Bitcoin Core team maintained control of r/Bitcoin – the most popular Reddit forum – and assumed the role of Bitcoin's main developers. Other devs who publicly argued for bigger blocks or began working on different clients had their admin privileges revoked on the forum, and were considered to no longer be Bitcoin developers. According to Bitcoin Core, the developers building on other clients were now working on altcoins. In addition, links for exchanges like Coinbase and miners like Bitmain were removed from the official Bitcoin.org website for this reason as well; thereafter, big blockers used Bitcoin.com to get their message out.[12] Another distinction that small blockers were making at this time was what actually constitutes a Bitcoin "user." According to them, only Bitcoiners who run a full node can technically be considered "users," but this framing of the Bitcoin community entirely left out the average traders and retail Bitcoin holders. The semantics of this are important because if the network is governed by its "users," the definition of the word "user" will impact who is allowed to participate in governance. Among the factions that were fighting for influence were the miners, the developers, and the community.

The miners wanted hashrate to determine the governance because they were in charge of the hashrate. They also wanted bigger blocks because that would give the miners that were already established a huge advantage over hobbyists and newer miners. The developers believed that users who are running full nodes should be responsible for governance – and of course, the vast majority of them were running full nodes. Meanwhile, the nontechnical Bitcoin community of traders, holders, and libertarians were hoping that there would be a public discourse on important topics that would allow community sentiment to impact the future of the network. This was just as much a battle over Bitcoin's governance as it was a battle over its block size.

During the conflict, there were numerous conferences hosted around the world where parties on both sides of the argument gathered to discuss the future of Bitcoin scaling and make the case for their desired outcome. The first conference was hosted by Blockstream in Montreal, Canada, in September 2015, and it was called "Scaling Bitcoin." Very little progress was made at the conference, and the two opposing sides didn't come any closer to an agreement. The big blockers were disappointed that the conference was more of a presentation than a negotiation, so they considered the event a failure. Many of them began calling the conference "Stalling Bitcoin" and called for more urgency in the debate. Note that the big blockers were having trouble finding support for their alternative client Bitcoin XT; it was eventually abandoned by its supporters within a few months. In January 2016, Mike Hearn, one of the main developers behind XT, declared Bitcoin a failed experiment in a controversial blog post where he announced that he was leaving the industry and selling all of his coins. He did go on to take a CEO role at a blockchain enterprise company called R3, but whether or not he ever reinvested in crypto is not public knowledge. After the failure of XT, two more alternative Bitcoin clients were spun up by the big blockers, Bitcoin Classic and Bitcoin Unlimited, both of which accomplished very little aside from infuriating and galvanizing the small blockers.[13]

Things got even worse for the big blockers after Gavin Andresen put his support behind Craig Wright, the man who still to this day claims that he is Satoshi. We covered Craig Wright in Chapter 4, but now he enters our story again, unfortunately. In a 2016 blog post, Andreson claimed that Satoshi had returned, and suggested that he had seen "cryptographic proof" that Craig Wright was in fact Satoshi. This "proof" was later published on Wright's blog, but the post didn't actually offer any evidence that Wright was Satoshi. The Bitcoin community was unconvinced, but Wright supported big blocks, so Andreson continued to see him as a key ally. Some critics have speculated that Andreson was desperate to get his way in the conflict so he was resorting to extreme measures, while others think that he was deceived by Wright. Either way, Wright was welcomed by the big blockers with open arms, which majorly hurt their credibility. After making his blog post declaring that Satoshi was back, Andreson had his access removed from the Bitcoin website and repository. First, Bitcoin Core claimed that they suspected he was hacked because the blog was so ridiculous, but then after finding that it was real they decided it would be best to not add him back regardless. Gavin Andresen's reputation would never recover from his attempt to cast Craig Wright in the role of Satoshi.[14]

Meanwhile, the small blockers came up with a technical solution that was somewhat of a compromise. It was an upgrade called "Segregated Witness," or "SegWit," which freed up block space without increasing the block size, and fixed an assortment of bugs to improve the security of the network. Most importantly, this upgrade would be achieved through a soft fork instead of a hard fork, which would not require a new client or risk a chain split. Unfortunately, SegWit ended up increasing the tensions among the warring factions. They had become so distrustful of each other that it was too late for compromise; the conflict had become about a lot more than just block size.

ASICBoost

According to the small blockers, there were also some nefarious reasons for the opposition to SegWit, particularly among miners. On April 5, 2017, Mr. "beer cup hat" Gregory Maxwell sent a letter to the Bitcoin mailing list accusing one of the world's largest mining firms of opposing SegWit for financial reasons. According to Maxwell, many miners were opposed to SegWit because it prevented something called Covert ASICBoost, a function that would give them massive power over the system.[15] Although he did not mention them by name, Maxwell was referencing the large Chinese mining firm Bitmain, and many journalists were quick to pick up on this and publish the accusations. Bitmain responded with an evasive press release; though they denied running Covert ASICBoost on the main Bitcoin blockchain ("mainnet"), they admitted to both running it on testnet and filing patents for it[16] – which was a sketchy denial at best, if not a downright admission of guilt. They may have not run ASICBoost on mainnet, but they were testing it out on something called a "testnet," which is a practice blockchain where developers can run experiments without risking real money. In other words, Maxwell's concerns were well founded. ASICBoost has radically changed the mining industry – although today we have a slightly different version than the one he feared in 2017. Now, over 60% of the miners in the industry use Overt ASICBoost, which has still added a degree of centralization to the network, but is not nearly as bad as Covert ASICBoost, which was less transparent and allowed miners to tamper with the transactions. To be fair, the big blockers leveled similar accusations against Bitcoin Core and Blockstream, saying that their business model was dependent upon small blocks and that they held patents related to SegWit.[17]

In 2017, many miners, including Bitmain, were refusing to upgrade to SegWit, insisting that their hashing power should determine which upgrades go through. This was a potential disaster considering how many bugs SegWit fixed – as well as the potential for a Chinese mining firm with a patent to supercharge mining hardware. At this point, an unlikely mediator stepped in: crypto-market entrepreneur Barry Silbert.[18]

Silbert began his career shortly after college with the 2004 launch of a company called SecondMarket, a website for trading alternative financial investments. While many across the country were losing their homes and savings during the 2008 financial crisis, SecondMarket made Silbert a fortune. The company's impressive returns amid the downturn caught the attention of international investors; SecondMarket even started to build a relationship with the World Economic Forum (WEF). As Bitcoin started catching media attention, Silbert shifted his focus; in 2015 he sold SecondMarket to Nasdaq and started Digital Currency Group.[19] Ever since, he has played a major role in the crypto industry, and Digital Currency Group now has its hands in nearly everything.

At the height of the hostility in the block-size war, the Digital Currency Group hosted a conference in New York called Consensus, where some of the most powerful participants in the space gathered to finally come to an agreement for the good of the industry. However, Blockstream representatives refused to show up, leaving at the table 50 other representatives from a variety of different development companies, exchanges, and mining firms. They came to an agreement that seemed to give both sides what they wanted: SegWit would be implemented for the small blockers, and the big blockers would get a small increase of 1 MB blocks. However, Bitcoin Core rejected the deal; they would support only SegWit, not the block increase, and they would not compromise. As a result, many of the miners planning to support the block increase lost confidence and backed out. This was a major turning point for the small blockers; now they were in control. The big blockers would not get their way, at least not on the "official" Bitcoin chain – they would need to fork off to their own chain.

In mid-2017, the big blockers decided they would proceed with a hard fork because the developers would not raise the block size. The hard fork created its own currency that would compete directly with Bitcoin: Bitcoin Cash, with the ticker BCH. When the fork took place on August 1, 2017, Bitcoin holders were rewarded with an amount of Bitcoin Cash that was equal to the figure in their BTC wallet. Now the race was on to see which side could gain the most market share and the highest price, claiming the title of the "real" Bitcoin. The community again had a seat at the table, and could place bets on which vision they believed in the most. Some users decided to sell their BCH to buy BTC or vice versa, depending on which side of the war they were on; other investors hedged their bets and held onto both, wanting to have a piece of the winning pie regardless of which direction things went.

The Bitcoin Cash community was extremely enthusiastic at first, and the movement's leaders – like Bitmain and Roger Ver – poured millions of dollars into marketing and merchant onboarding, especially in developing countries. However, that enthusiasm soon diminished due to infighting and a bear market that caused most of retail to flee the space. The Bitcoin Cash community was ultimately split after Craig Wright decided to launch his own fork, which he called Bitcoin SV, or Bitcoin Satoshi's Vision. A small cult following that believed Wright was Satoshi went along with him into that project, but the asset hasn't really done anything in terms of price or development since its launch. After this second fork, many of the big blockers became fed up with Bitcoin altogether, and decided to venture out into the realm of Ethereum and the altcoins, which we'll cover in the next chapter.[20]

At first, this flight to other projects was welcomed by the most hard-core Bitcoiners; because they felt there were too many people trying to change Bitcoin and influence the network, they were excited to have less interference at a pivotal time. But after a while, some members of the Bitcoin community started to become extremely hostile to other projects and other communities. This is where "toxic Bitcoin maximalism" really started to take hold. In crypto culture, maximalism is the view that only one particular crypto asset is worth investing in. So Bitcoin maximalists invest only in Bitcoin, and there's really nothing wrong with that. However, there are some Bitcoin maximalists who are very toxic, calling everything else a scam and attacking other communities because they are working on or investing in something other than Bitcoin. This group got larger and more vocal than ever after the scaling debates and Bitcoin forks.[21]

So, what became of Bitcoin Cash? Suffice to say, it's on life support. Developers are still working on it, and it's still used as a currency sometimes, especially in the developing markets where it was heavily promoted. Roger Ver continues to promote Bitcoin Cash and has taken significant losses for his big bet on the hard fork. He has also been vilified by the Bitcoin community, who cast him as an enemy and never looked back. A lot of Bitcoin maximalists like to say that he was greedy and just wanted to run his own chain, but most of the people who spent any time working with him insist that he was motivated by his deep philosophical belief that digital cash was a better way of subverting the government than digital gold was. BCH was never able to return to its all-time highs in the following cycle, and the future is certainly looking rough from an investment standpoint. The industry has grown to the point that there are now faster and more convenient forms of digital cash, with many options to choose from, and Bitcoin Cash has fallen into the background – just like Litecoin and many other crypto assets that were once at the top of the charts but are now mostly unknown to new entrants.[22]

Throughout the block-size war, the number of competing cryptocurrencies and crypto assets began to accelerate rapidly; when many Bitcoin users and developers realized their vision for this technology was different than Bitcoin Core, they saw it was best to go elsewhere. In fact, they were told to leave the community if they didn't agree with the plans that Blockstream had for Bitcoin Core.[23] But maybe this was for the best; Bitcoin is probably better off with a very slow and meticulous development process that prioritizes security over scalability. Also, as much as the Bitcoin maximalists like to deny this fact, the thriving market of competing crypto assets that we have today actually makes the industry a more innovative space that can generate even more wealth than Bitcoin could on its own.

At the end of the day, the block-size war was both a power struggle and a conflict over the future of Bitcoin. Both sides had some very intelligent people with some great ideas, and both sides used dirty tricks to advance their cause. The small blockers were wrong to censor the Bitcoin community and talk down to them, but many of their technical concerns like miner centralization were dead-on. Their vision of Bitcoin as a reliable store of value is also why many of us have been able to make a lot of money in these markets. The big blockers weren't innocent either; they were wrong to force rule changes and rush consensus. But their fight for private digital cash was an admirable one, and they had many valid criticisms about Bitcoin's development.

If all these players had been able to set aside their differences and their egos and come to a reasonable compromise, we might have been better off as an industry today. These incredibly talented and skilled people were fighting against each other instead of working together, which seems like a lot of wasted creativity. Sure, competition is great, and it's a good thing that protocols can fork when there is disagreement. It's also great that we have a wide variety of crypto assets outside of Bitcoin. But we could have done without the polarization and tribalism that grew from this conflict.

CHAPTER 9

The Future Is Born

Ethereum and Smart Contracts

A Russian Canadian named Vitalik Buterin was among the early Bitcoiners who had a different vision for what the crypto industry could be. Buterin first learned about Bitcoin in 2011 when he was just 17 years old. That year he founded *Bitcoin Magazine,* one of the first "Bitcoin only" media publications. He quickly made a name for himself with his writing and, despite his young age, became one of the first thought leaders in the industry. Even from those very earliest days, Buterin imagined blockchain technology being capable of much more than just cryptocurrency. He saw a future where a wide range of digital assets would power a vast network of decentralized applications.[1]

As the name implies, a decentralized application is internet software that is not controlled by a single entity. This is in stark contrast to the huge popular services that we see on the internet today, like Facebook, Gmail, Twitter, Uber, or Spotify. All of these services and their parent companies have a top-down organizational structure, where the owners and board members make all the rules and collect all the revenue. Decentralized applications work much differently, with a more horizontal system of organization and rule making. The most successful decentralized applications also tend to give their users a share of their revenue, whether in the form of airdrops, staking rewards, or dividends. Airdrops are essentially deposits of free crypto into your account in reward for being an early user of a platform.[2]

Decentralized applications take out the intermediary, which often doesn't need to be involved in every single transaction. For example, Spotify is an application that connects musicians with their fans, and they do provide a good service for both, but they are often criticized for not paying creators enough and for sometimes engaging in censorship. If it were a decentralized, peer-to-peer application with no intermediary, artists would be free to express themselves as they wished and would receive a majority of the revenue they earned. Their fans might even be able to get free money, in the form of a token airdrop, just for being an early or frequent user of the platform. Side note:

Some might wonder what incentive entrepreneurs would have to take risks when building projects like these, but recall that founders of crypto projects are generally not short on cash these days, and there is still a ton of money to be made for founders of decentralized applications.

With most of these platforms, the governance and ownership of the platform is decentralized thanks to a token, often called a governance token. Founders are entitled to a fair share of these tokens when the project launches, which rewards them for their efforts, but then the promise of further financial gain incentivizes them to continue working on the project, since they'll naturally want those rewards to be worth as much as possible. The owners of most decentralized applications are Decentralized Autonomous Organizations, or DAOs. It sounds complicated, but these are basically cooperatives or "co-ops" powered by blockchain technology. Basically, a DAO is an organization that is owned and governed by large groups of people, and the technology involved allows certain parts of the operations and governance to be automated.

Buterin and many others in the industry thought it would be possible to build this future on top of Bitcoin, and throughout 2013 a few projects were working on this exact idea. It was a movement called "Bitcoin 2.0," which involved protocols built on top of the Bitcoin blockchain to allow it to do more than just send and receive value.[3] One of the ideas that developers were working with to make decentralized applications and metacoins possible was "smart contracts," a concept first introduced by the cypherpunk Nick Szabo in the early 1990s. You may remember Szabo as the creator of BitGold and one of the only developers referenced by name in Satoshi's famous Bitcoin white paper. Szabo defined smart contracts as "a set of promises, specified in digital form, including protocols within which the parties perform on these promises."[4] Think of a smart contract as a system programmed to deliver certain outcomes when it receives a certain input; it essentially automates the deal-making process. One of the most rudimentary examples of this technology is a vending machine in the physical world, which is programmed to dispense the selected item when it receives the required amount of money. Now just think of those same mechanics being applied to online transactions. The possibilities are endless.

Two of the top projects with the Bitcoin 2.0 vision were Colored Coins and Mastercoin, which were trying to make it possible to host decentralized applications and launch additional tokens on the Bitcoin network. These additional tokens were called "metacoins." Buterin began working with these teams and contributing to these projects because he saw a ton of potential in combining smart contracts with Bitcoin. In 2013 he helped the team at eToro write their "Colored Coins" white paper. Around the same time, Buterin offered suggestions to the Mastercoin team to make their protocol more functional. When the team politely declined to go forward with his plan, he decided to develop a separate project. He was still a Bitcoiner at heart, but he knew it would be a very unpopular political decision to build his project on top of Bitcoin, as Mastercoin did, because a large faction of Bitcoin developers had been extremely vocal about how they did not want those kinds of applications to be built on top of Bitcoin. Mastercoin was already being accused of bloating the blockchain with their complex protocol, a major point of contention on Bitcoin forums. So Buterin wrote a white paper for his concept of a smart-contract-powered blockchain, which he called Ethereum. Encouraged by the feedback he got from a few Bitcoiners, he published the paper in late 2013 – and it went viral. Many talented people wanted to get involved, and Buterin was happy to bring on anyone who was interested, so the founding team got very big very fast. Ethereum ended up with eight founders, each of them having unique personalities and visions for the project.[5] For the purpose of this story we're going to focus on only half of them: Vitalik Buterin, Charles Hoskinson, Gavin Wood, and Joseph Lubin.

The Ethereum Team

Charles Hoskinson was another early Bitcoin adopter. In 2013 he'd cofounded a blockchain project called Bitshares, a blockchain focused on hosting decentralized applications and "stablecoins" – one of the first platforms of its kind. Hoskinson had stepped down as CEO shortly before reading Buterin's white paper; it's not entirely clear why he left, but it was apparently not on good terms. He'd apparently claimed the title of CEO for himself – after which Buterin dubbed himself C-3P0 of Ethereum.[6] This example of different cultures and philosophies was just one of many factors that caused tension among these eight very different people – who ranged from squatter anarchists and hackers to traditional finance and tech investors. (All of these different personalities were working together in the same house in Miami in the early stages of Ethereum's development.) Hoskinson envisioned Ethereum as the leading blockchain corporation, so he was actively seeking VC funding and running Ethereum as a boss would run a company. This approach clashed with the view of Buterin and many of the other early founders, who were against hierarchy and saw Ethereum as a nonprofit foundation. They didn't want it to be a corporation – which also meant they didn't even want Ethereum to have a CEO. There was also a split between the programmers and the nontechnical members of the team who handled the day-to-day business operations. Each side saw the other as expendable – and not truly deserving of a founding-member role. Gavin Wood, the project's CTO and lead developer, was especially critical of what he perceived as a lack of work or lack of usefulness on the part of some of the other team members. He also had a hard time recognizing the value of nontechnical work. To his credit, Wood did do most of the original coding for the project, and he wrote the Ethereum yellow paper, which explored its technical nuts and bolts.[7]

The most well-connected of the eight cofounders was Joseph Lubin, who'd been college roommates with the famous Wall Street investor Mike Novogratz and had previously worked for Goldman Sachs. And while very few on the Ethereum team trusted Lubin because of his Wall Street connections, they also knew that those connections would help them succeed. The project was formally announced to an excited crowd at the Bitcoin conference in Miami in January 2014.[8]

The team decided to launch Ethereum by raising funds for the development and sustainability of the project via a new process called an ICO. ICO stands for Initial Coin Offering, a play on the term Initial Public Offering or IPO, which is used to describe equities. In fact, there was some serious concern at the time that the SEC might end up labeling these offerings as securities, which made the ICO concept very controversial, even in the Bitcoin community. The Ethereum team delayed the launch of their ICO for a few months while Joseph Lubin pulled some strings in Wall Street and Washington, DC, to get them some legal clearance. The wait was worth it. In June 2014, William Hinman, the director of corporate finance for the SEC, issued a public statement declaring that the agency would likely not consider Ethereum or Bitcoin to be securities. Hinman explained that Ether, Ethereum's own cryptocurrency, could be compared to fuel because of how it functions as a utility on the network.[9] This statement would later be a point of controversy, because Hinman's law firm, Simpson Thatcher & Bartlett, had received substantial payments for reviewing and advising Ethereum's ICO plan. According to information obtained by the nonprofit Empower Oversight Whistleblowers & Research (EMPOWR), Hinman personally received a significant amount of that money. The payments were reportedly filed under "retirement benefits." The Ethereum team often gets accused of dirty dealing in this situation; many believe that they directly greased the palms of bureaucrats to get the green light for their ICO.[10] Others would say they sought advice from a powerful and connected legal firm, and that such advice is not cheap. They were doing what most businesses need to do in this regulatory environment: seeking out guidance from well-connected professionals. I happen to agree with this latter view, and consider that Hinman was taking advantage of the political "revolving door" that was covered in Chapter 7. In 2017 he left the Simpson Thatcher & Bartlett law firm to go work at the SEC for a few years. While at the SEC, Hinman was in a position to shape the regulatory framework for sectors that he had a personal interest in. He returned to the law firm in 2020.

Blast Off

In the lead-up to the ICO, tensions continued to mount among the team members. The disagreement about whether Ethereum should be a nonprofit or corporate entity was a very touchy philosophical issue that neither side was willing to concede, and a mutiny against Charles Hoskinson formed among a contingent of employees who didn't want him as a boss.[11] This is another one of those situations, much like the block size war covered in the previous chapter, where well-meaning and intelligent people became enemies because they had different visions for the same blockchain. At the end of the day, Buterin had the final say on which direction Ethereum would take, and he decided to go the nonprofit route. In fact, by 2016, Buterin was the only founding member left. Some of the other cofounders went on to start companies to build Ethereum infrastructure, wallets, and applications – while others went on to build their own Ethereum competitors,[12] which we'll cover in a later chapter. And even though they'd all left before the project got off the ground, everyone listed as an Ethereum cofounder received a large chunk of Ether when the network finally launched.[13] The rollout was extremely slow; the ICO took place between July and August 2014, but the network launched a full year later, in July 2015. This means that anyone who invested in the ICO had to wait a whole year before they could cash out or begin speculating on the price. The crowdsale raised an estimated $18.3 million,[14] which was astonishing at the time, but meager compared to the crowdsales that the Ethereum network would later make possible.

The DAO

As soon as Ethereum launched, developers began experimenting with it and building the first decentralized applications. The biggest early project was simply called "the DAO," which was only intended to be a placeholder name, since the founders – Simon Jentzsch, Christoph Jentzsch, and Stephan Tual – hoped that the community would later come up with their own name. Launched in April 2016, the DAO raised roughly $150 million,[15] vastly more than Ethereum itself had gathered during its ICO. The DAO was intended to be a decentralized venture capital firm that would fund a variety of blockchain projects, and it was one of the most popular things in crypto at the time.

To ensure its safety, the developers had the code audited by the same team that audited the code for Ethereum, but the audit missed a few bugs – not just in the DAO, but in the Ethereum code itself.[16] Because of these bugs, any smart contract built with certain parameters was at risk, and the DAO was one of these contracts. One month after the DAO launch, a developer published a paper pointing out the vulnerabilities in the DAO code; other developers continued to raise concerns over the next month. Before the DAO could decide how to proceed, an attacker (or team of attackers) began siphoning funds from the DAO on June 17, 2016. Though the team quickly noticed, there was nothing they could do to stop it. They did have one advantage: the smart contract was designed such that funds were locked in an account for 28 days before they could be withdrawn. But the developers' options were limited, and their attempts to outhack the hackers proved fruitless.[17]

Ultimately, Ethereum developers were left with just two options: conduct a hard fork to create an entirely new blockchain where the hack hadn't occurred, so the DAO investors didn't lose their money; or do nothing and let the chips fall where they may.[18] It may seem like an obvious solution to just do the hard fork and cancel out the hack, but remember that hard forks were extremely controversial. Though part of this controversy was due to the difficulty involved and the risk of creating two competing chains, there was also the historic, cypherpunk philosophical opposition to the idea of a hard fork. And though the philosophical influence of the cypherpunks had waned a bit as more mainstream users flooded the space, many of the builders and adopters still respected that history. There was a belief among the cypherpunks that "code is law": that code, not courts and government agencies, was the regulatory framework for the internet. From this perspective, making fast and unilateral changes to the code for any reason was similar to a dictator changing the laws on a whim. Also, there was a belief among the most extreme cypherpunks that hackers didn't actually do anything wrong when they exploited code. To them, the original coder was to blame for enabling the vulnerability in the first place; the hackers simply outsmarted the sloppy developers.[19]

However, if developers want to keep their products safe, they're going to need to be able to make updates, because software is rarely ever perfect when it launches. Not even Satoshi Nakamoto was capable of launching a perfect project; Bitcoin has had plenty of transitions and upgrades along the way, such as SegWit and the more recent Taproot upgrade. Ultimately, the DAO decided to go ahead with the hard fork – which was popular among everyone who had lost their money, but extremely unpopular among Bitcoiners, who saw the move as a betrayal of crypto values. When the hard fork took place, the old chain was expected to die because it would have been unprofitable to mine – the miners would just receive expired ETH that was essentially worthless. And while we don't know who mined the zombie chain, it is a bit suspicious that certain Bitcoin maximalists quickly came out of the woodwork to support the coin of the hacked chain, which was called "Ethereum Classic." Barry Silbert of the Digital Currency Group tweeted, "Bought my first non-bitcoin digital currency . . . Ethereum Classic (ETC). At $0.50, risk/return felt right. And I'm philosophically on board."[20] Blockstream cofounder Gregory Maxwell, who led an army of small-block maximalists at the time, joined in and began taunting Buterin on Twitter about how he was supporting ETC.

As for who was responsible for the DAO hack itself, they were never formally charged or even named. However, podcaster and author Laura Shin used new tools from the data analytics firm Chainalysis to track key transactions at the time, and determined that former TenX CEO Toby Hoenisch was the most likely suspect. TenX was a crypto wallet that was also accused of insider trading and scamming users, so Hoenisch would fit the profile.[21] This is a very strange case though; technically, the crime that was committed was erased because the hack was nullified by the Ethereum fork as if it had never even happened, so the victims were made whole again. Hoenisch has denied the accusations,[22] and there has been no further news since Shin published her initial report.

Ethereum managed to survive the attack. So did Ethereum Classic – though it's just hanging on by a thread, thanks mostly to Barry Silbert. It's basically just a memecoin for maximalists at this point, as no development has taken place on it in years; it just pumps every now and then during bull markets.[23] (A bull run is when prices steadily rise.) Interestingly, this situation turned out a bit differently from the Bitcoin fork, which resulted in the original chain becoming the dominant version. In the case of Ethereum, the newer chain became dominant, and the original faded into the background. In both cases though, there was a strong social consensus for the winner, so the sentiment of the community matters much more than which one won out.

CHAPTER 10

Digital Gold Transformation

Cryptocurrencies and Crypto Assets

W ith communities forking off into different tribes and new blockchains launching on a regular basis, by the time that crypto winter hit in 2018, the once small and fringe Bitcoin community had grown into a full-fledged cryptocurrency industry. However, the term "cryptocurrency" is a bit of a misnomer that has caused a lot of confusion about these markets over the years. People get the idea that the crypto industry is a big casino where traders are placing bets on one very specific vision: a future medium of exchange that will replace fiat currencies like the dollar. This is a gross over-simplification of the space that leaves out some of the most interesting innovation happening here. To be fair, degenerate gambling and poorly designed Ponzis have consumed some corners of the crypto market,[1] and the original mission of Bitcoin was to become a transactional currency accepted by retailers around the world, so it's understandable that people get confused.

Once Bitcoin got out into the wild and started developing a user base, it took on a life of its own – and it quickly became apparent that although it wasn't great as a transactional currency, it had serious utility as a store of value. Satoshi's original plan was for Bitcoin to be both a store of value and a medium of exchange, but there are a few factors that make Bitcoin inefficient as a transactional currency. Bitcoin's volatility makes it a bad unit of account; and as the price goes up over time, there is a stronger incentive for people to hold Bitcoin than there is for them to use it as a currency. Another problem is that Bitcoin became very slow and expensive as more users came on to the network and demand for block space increased. As of this writing, it typically takes at least a few minutes for a Bitcoin transaction to go through, and the fees can be upwards of $20, even for very small transactions.[2] In some cases for small transactions, the fee may be higher than the amount that was actually sent. This makes retail adoption effectively impossible.

On the other hand, Bitcoin's scarcity, resilience, and strict monetary policy make it an incredible store of value, so after the fork Bitcoin's narrative and development ethos began to shift stronger in that direction. This kind of thing happens often in start-ups and business ventures: a "pivot," where a project finds a product–market fit in a place that is entirely unexpected and a vast departure from where they initially planned to develop a user base. There are plenty of examples of this happening in recent history. Instagram was originally a competitor of the local search-and-discovery mobile app Foursquare before the team realized that their best feature was their photos, so they decided to optimize for that. YouTube was originally a video-dating website (with the slogan "Tune In, Hook Up") before its pivot into social media, and Facebook started out as the short-lived Facemash – a Harvard knock-off of Hot or Not, which was a photo-rating site created by Berkeley grads for the purpose of objectifying one's peers. (This was separate from the Winklevii suing Mark Zuckerberg for copying their ConnectU networking site.)[3] These are just some of the many successful companies that started out with an entirely different use case than the one they have today.

Bitcoin Becomes Digital Gold

In the case of Bitcoin, because there is no single boss or CEO to make these decisions, this pivot happened more naturally as a result of Bitcoin's growing pains with scaling – although Bitcoin Core developers certainly played a major role in this shift, as we saw with the block size war. After the Bitcoin forks took place in 2017, developers of the dominant chain that maintained the BTC ticker had a clear plan to prioritize decentralization and permanence over properties like speed, fees, and extra features. These design choices further accelerated Bitcoin's transformation from magic internet money into digital gold.[4] It might seem like a bit of a technicality, but once Bitcoin became digital gold instead of digital cash it was no longer really accurate to think of it as a cryptocurrency; it had become more of a "crypto asset."

The same can be said for the many other blockchain projects that were launching and being developed at the time: "cryptocurrency" isn't really an accurate description of what projects like Ethereum or the DAO were building either. Projects like Ethereum built smart contract platforms to enable decentralized financial applications and perhaps even a new layer for the internet. There was also a barrage of tokens, such as Maker or Basic Attention Token, whose developers hoped would serve as equity or utility for some of these potential decentralized applications.[5] These are tokens on crypto rails that can be traded, but they are not cryptocurrencies – they are crypto assets.

Of course, volatile assets can be used as a medium of exchange in a pinch, but they're not ideal, especially for everyday use. The people behind projects like Bitcoin Cash, DigiByte, Dash, and Litecoin still hope their digital coins will become currencies and compete with the dollar, but the hype for these offerings dried up with the rising popularity of stablecoins.

Stablecoins are crypto assets that are a single price, usually on par with a dollar. Stablecoins are perfect for transactions; they provide the self-custody and ease of cross-border transfer that crypto makes possible – while maintaining a stagnant price, which is essential for any good currency. To date, stablecoins are the only actual cryptocurrencies in the market; all of the other coins and blockchain projects are various types of crypto assets. This is an important distinction because, as noted earlier, "cryptocurrency" is a limited term that has pigeonholed the industry into a very narrow public image that doesn't fully represent the full scope of what's happening here. Some people in the industry continue to push this narrative, ever hopeful that Bitcoin and other blockchains will entirely replace traditional finance and fiat currencies,[6] just as many of the early cypherpunks like Timothy May and Hal Finney had envisioned it. Perhaps over the long arc of history, in a hundred years or so, this transition may actually happen – but it's not happening any time soon.

We need to be realistic about the world we're living in today, where the legacy establishment is still extremely powerful. And although Bitcoin has proven to be resistant to nation-state-level attacks and bans, it's not entirely immune to influence from governments and institutions. In fact, governments and traditional institutions like Goldman Sachs and Citigroup have become the Bitcoin industry's largest and most important sources of liquidity. These institutions have hundreds of millions of dollars or even billions invested in these assets, so together they make up a significant portion of the market. As of June 2022, institutions hold 6.47% of all the Bitcoin that will ever exist.[7] These more traditional traders and investors are far more interested in the store of value use case for Bitcoin because they don't have the same philosophical aversion to dollars that the early cypherpunks did. The same can be said for most of the retail investors that have entered the space in the past several years. The vast majority of the people in the market now were attracted to the technology because they see an opportunity to make money and they want to achieve financial freedom – and a lot of them have entirely different political views from the crypto-anarchist early adopters who loved Bitcoin because they saw it as a tool for undermining corrupt governments. These militant cypherpunks kept the faith, but as the years have passed their demographic ratio in the Bitcoin community has steadily diminished as the community grew, reaching more of a mainstream audience.

The dollar will likely remain the primary transactional currency in the United States for years to come, even if it moves on to crypto rails as some type of central bank digital currency. The world is in need of a credibly neutral settlement layer that isn't controlled by either a single country or a conglomerate of powerful countries. Maintaining control of the world reserve currency has given the States an advantage in international trade – but this has come at the expense of other countries around the world, which strains diplomatic relations in the long run anyway.

Halving

Since gold was long recognized as the most stable and reliable asset to hold during times of economic uncertainty, it is only natural that many of the first digital money platforms took inspiration from gold. I believe that Satoshi Nakamoto had this in mind from the beginning; they even used the word "mining" for the minting of Bitcoin. The metaphor fits perfectly because Bitcoin and gold share many of the same properties, especially scarcity, resilience, and strict monetary policy. So it makes sense that it was the narrative of "digital gold" that really connected with the masses, helping them to start to embrace Bitcoin. But Bitcoin is actually better than gold in many ways. When it comes to scarcity, Bitcoin is hard-coded to have a fixed supply; only 21 million BTC will ever be mined. This ensures that Bitcoin is a deflationary asset – whereas new gold is mined every day, constantly adding supply to the marketplace.[8] Bitcoin is also far more practical to store or transport; Bitcoin keys can be remembered, held on a hardware wallet, or retained on a small piece of paper. This is especially important for people attempting to flee oppressive regimes without having their wealth confiscated. Intermediaries are also required to transfer gold, especially across international lines, which can be a lengthy process – but with Bitcoin you can send as much as you want, anywhere, in just a few minutes.

So it turned out that the small blockers were right after all: Bitcoin works best as a store of value. After the forks took place, the people who wanted Bitcoin to be a medium of exchange or a platform for decentralized applications found other communities where they could build their dream – which allowed Bitcoin to settle into its natural place as digital gold. Merchant adoption of Bitcoin began to slow, and many retailers who signed up to accept Bitcoin later reversed their decision on account of the fees and wait times. This was no problem for the diehard Bitcoiners, though, as they had little interest in spending their Bitcoin anyway.

The term "hodl" was one of the most famous memes of the Bitcoin world: a misspelling of "hold," taken from a post in the early days of the Bitcoin talk forums, where one early Bitcoiner told other forum members he was going to "hodl" even though the price was crashing.[9] Sometimes this is great advice, especially when you're just buying and holding and considering a longer time horizon. But to make the most of these markets, you need to pay close attention to the Bitcoin cycles, and try to take profits while Bitcoin is going up, and then reaccumulate when it's going down. This is easier said than done, but some aspects of Bitcoin's design make these cycles somewhat predictable. As noted, there will never be more than 21 million Bitcoin in the total circulating supply, and these coins will be slowly mined over time. The release schedule is determined by a mechanism called the "halving": every four years, the production of BTC on the network is cut in half. Technically, this happens every time 210,000 blocks are mined, which works out to roughly four years. The first Bitcoin halving took place in 2012, when the reward for mining a block on the Bitcoin network went from 50 BTC to 25 BTC. In 2016, a second halving event cut the rewards down to 12.5 BTC per block. And then on May 11, 2020, just before a massive bull run kicked off, the reward was reduced down to 6.25 BTC per block. The next halving, expected to happen sometime in early 2024, will further reduce the incoming supply down to 3.125 BTC per block.[10]

The important point is that the Bitcoin bull cycles have traditionally been driven by the halving, because the reduced inflows of new Bitcoin increase the value of the total supply. Of course, demand also plays a role in these market dynamics. The shock to the global financial markets at the next halving is sure to make heads spin, as institutions who were used to buying at the current supply are suddenly going to have to compete much harder to purchase the same amount of Bitcoin for their customers and products. The fact that YOU can buy the very same asset that major hedge funds, banks, and sovereign wealth funds are fighting over should make you feel like a winner.

The CEO Of Bitcoin

You can't talk about Bitcoin these days without referencing one man who has become one of the biggest Bitcoin advocates in the world. Michael Saylor, MIT graduate, cofounder of Microstrategy, and the unofficial "CEO of Bitcoin," has been bullish on Bitcoin ever since March 2020 when he watched the world governments' response to COVID-19 – which he described as "shaking his faith"[11] in the traditional finance system. From there he took a personal journey of discovery around Bitcoin and came to the conclusion that Bitcoin was the only way to save the economy. "After scientifically studying everything on Earth, I've concluded bitcoin is the best inflation hedge."[12] Since then he has undertaken one of the largest and most aggressive Bitcoin purchasing plans in the history of crypto. Say what you will about Saylor, he put his money where his mouth is. And Saylor's company Microstrategy now sits on a Bitcoin horde of over 130,000 BTC at the time of writing.[13] Saylor took it upon himself to teach his peers of CEOs, angel investors, and entrepreneurs about the revolutionary technology that powers Bitcoin and how it's the best asset to those in the face of all of this economic uncertainty. In February 2021 Saylor launched "Bitcoin For Corporations," which taught business leaders how to buy and hold Bitcoin as a means of increasing their companies' value.[14] The two-day conference was a success and catapulted Saylor into the crypto conversation as **the** Bitcoin Guy for talk shows, podcasts, news segments, and conferences. What makes Michael Saylor different from most Bitcoiners or Bitcoin Maxis is that he doesn't seem to care about Ethereum and altcoins. Instead he thinks they should be regulated as securities or treated like any other tech company. Instead of hating on altcoins, Saylor is hyper-focused on the merits of Proof of Work, the fact that Bitcoin is a hard asset, and why the current financial system is a scam.

CHAPTER 11

Crypto Turning Point

The Crypto-Rich

As we've covered in the previous chapters, the crypto industry was in an experimental phase for the first few years of its existence, and was taken seriously by only a core community of nerds, rebels, and true believers. But before long it was clear that some real value was being created with this technology. By 2016, Bitcoin was regularly trading above $500.[1] There were also new competitors, dubbed "altcoins," popping up every day, creating new opportunities for people who felt they were late to Bitcoin. The businesses developing around crypto were getting very rich very fast, and so were their customers. Eventually, the mainstream started to take notice and they wanted a piece of the action too. Many users in the United States started their journey with Coinbase (launched in 2012 in the US), where they purchased their first Bitcoin. Coinbase supported only Bitcoin and Litecoin at the time, so many of its customers transferred their BTC to other exchanges[2] like Bitfinex (launched in 2012 in Hong Kong), Cryptopia (2014, New Zealand), Poloniex (2014, United States), and later Binance (2017, China, then Japan), where they were able to exchange their BTC for a variety of different crypto assets that seemed to have a lot more room to grow.

Binance had a late start compared to its competitors, but it quickly dominated the market; by April 2018, it had become the largest cryptocurrency exchange in the world with a market capitalization of $1.3 billion. Binance became so popular so fast because it usually offered the widest selection of the major altcoins on the market, and many of the smaller ones too. It also had a better interface and user experience than many of its competitors. Binance was founded by Changpeng Zhao, who is more commonly known as CZ. After learning about Bitcoin in 2013 during a game of poker, he decided to dedicate himself to the crypto industry. He also claims that he sold his apartment to buy Bitcoin when it was about $600, and then continued to hold even after the price crashed down to $200. And though a *Forbes* article pegged him as going "From Zero to Crypto Billionaire in Under a Year," he had nearly two decades of applicable experience before he founded Binance, starting with the Tokyo Stock Exchange.[3]

This is an important point, because such overnight success stories create a false idea that people are lagging behind if they don't get rich after a year or two. These things can take time, even in the fast-paced world of crypto. (It took me nine years of learning and perseverance before I became a millionaire from crypto.) When the market was starting to heat up in 2017, the media coverage of crypto was making it seem like anyone who invested a few hundred dollars into an ICO was rich within a month, but there were plenty failed projects too. Remember, ICOs are Initial Coin Offerings, where tokens that represent equity in a project are launched to help bootstrap the venture and raise funds for development. This was a fairly regular occurrence before Ethereum came on the scene, but Ethereum's infrastructure made it much cheaper and easier to launch an ICO, so before long a new one launched every single day. The total crypto market cap was exploding with new wealth.[4]

Meanwhile, Bitcoin experienced a halving event in mid-2016; in the months following, the price of Bitcoin nearly doubled, to over $1,000 by January 2017. These factors would converge to create one of the most insane years that crypto had ever seen. By the beginning of 2017, crypto was already starting to get major airtime on the mainstream media. Some of this coverage reflected celebrity interest: some of it genuine, some of it paid advertisement. Crypto was no longer just a weird internet novelty – especially with Bitcoin reaching an all-time high of $3,000 in June, and countless other projects achieving massive valuations.[5]

Traditional financial institutions began taking notice as well, but they didn't favor this new technology and its rabid band of traders. Warren Buffett, legendary investor and owner of Berkshire Hathaway, made headlines after saying that Bitcoin was "probably rat poison squared" during an interview with CNBC. JPMorgan Chase CEO Jamie Dimon was one of the most vocal critics of crypto in the banking industry. At the Barclays investment conference in September of 2017, Dimon declared onstage that Bitcoin was a "fraud," indicating he'd fire anyone at the bank that he found trading crypto. (He publicly "regretted" that statement just four months later, by which time Bitcoin trading had gone from $4,200 to $14,000.) Maybe his comments were just psyops and misdirection, because just two years later JPMorgan would become the first bank to launch their own cryptocurrency, the JPM Coin. In 2022 they would also be the first bank to open a branch location in the metaverse. Despite JPMorgan's experimentation with blockchain technology, Jamie Dimon continues to be antagonistic to the crypto community, even to this day.[6]

Buy Bitcoin

Of course, crypto enthusiasts and industry insiders saw the rejections from traditional finance as a victory signaling widespread awareness, but this movement managed to maintain a sense of humor. One of the highlights of the 2017 bull run was when a heroic prankster held up a yellow legal pad that read BUY BITCOIN during Fed Chair Janet Yellen's July testimony for the House Financial Services Committee. The "Bitcoin Sign Guy" (as he was named) was quickly removed, having broken the no-sign-holding rule, but the sign had been caught on camera and made national headlines, becoming a bigger story than the Fed meeting itself.[7] The US government was still not taking crypto seriously, so the Fed didn't comment on their photobomber at the time, but governments around the world were starting to recognize that this technology had value.

For example, in 2016 Japan had been the first country to recognize Bitcoin and other cryptocurrencies as money. Other governments such as Singapore or Malta offered tax breaks and loose regulations to lure promising crypto projects into their jurisdiction. The industry exploded with new start-ups, protocols, and white papers ambitiously promising to change the world with blockchain technology. Some hoped that every single application would have a token and every company would have a blockchain within just a few years. From Uber to AI and social media, there were calls to "decentralize everything," and there was more excitement about crypto than ever.[8]

Ever since fintech companies like PayPal started making it easier for people to transfer money, banks had been desperate for a technological solution to cross-border payments and other complex transactions. Enter Ripple, whose native currency, XRP, serves as a bridge currency for international settlements. So, whereas most other projects in the crypto market sought to entirely replace or even destroy banks, Ripple's raison d'être was to help banks run more efficiently. This controversial entity was cofounded (with Arthur Britto and Chris Larsen) in 2011 by the controversial figure Jed McCaleb, who'd recently sold the doomed Mt. Gox exchange he'd launched the previous year. Ripple enjoyed the greatest gains in the 2017 bull run, increasing by 36,000% – it rocketed from a mere fraction of a penny, $0.0063, in January to $2.28 by December.[9] (McCaleb left Ripple in 2013 and went on to found Stellar, another crypto project with the same MO as Ripple.)

Unlike McCaleb's previous effort Mt. Gox, Ripple is still a massive success. (It later faced intense regulatory scrutiny over its ICO, but we'll cover that in detail in another chapter.) McCaleb managed to avoid getting wrapped up in the legal case, despite making billions from the ICO and dumping his tokens on a scheduled basis since receiving them. XRP was dubbed "the banker's coin" by many early Bitcoin adopters, who felt Ripple was consorting with the enemy. XRP was just one of many so-called altcoins that outshone Bitcoin during the bull run of 2017.

"Altcoin" is yet another terrible term that unfortunately managed to cement itself into crypto culture. Initially it made sense, because the first crypto assets that hit the market after Bitcoin were mostly Bitcoin forks with small tweaks that were said to offer better performance, usually at the cost of security. In these cases, the term altcoin made sense because they were alternative versions of Bitcoin. However, by 2017 a variety of different use cases were being developed for blockchain technology, and many of these had entirely different token models and infrastructure. Ethereum, for example, inspired a long list of competitors to build their own smart-contract platforms, which represented an entirely new sector of the blockchain industry. Another top performer for this bull run was a smart-contract platform called Cardano, founded by Charles Hoskinson. (You may recall that Hoskinson was briefly Ethereum's CEO before the project launched its ICO.)

Dan Larimer, another member of the interesting cast of characters, created EOS, which holds the record for the largest ICO ever, raising roughly $4.1 billion. EOS was marketed as an "Ethereum killer" that would offer a faster, cheaper, and more scalable smart-contract blockchain. This was one of the most hyped projects of that era, and a lot of people truly believed it would become the dominant smart-contract platform. However, EOS failed to attract enough developers, and it lost investor confidence after it was reported to be a glorified database with no level of decentralization. A 2018 paper – published by Bitmex Research and written by members of Vulcan Labs and blockchain testing company Whiteblock – concluded that EOS is "fundamentally similar to a centralized cloud computing architecture without the fundamental components of a blockchain or peer-to-peer network." According to the cryptocurrency blog Fully Crypto, Bitmex republished the paper two weeks after first releasing it – and then took it down again. EOS published their own counterclaim as well, retorting: "Yes, EOS is a blockchain."[10] Larimer later stepped down from the project, and then rejoined – but EOS is widely recognized as a dead blockchain.

Larimer has a habit of creating ambitious projects and then abandoning them once they're too much to handle. Backing up a few years, Larimer had cofounded BitShares in 2013 with Charles Hoskinson, but he later left to found Steemit in 2016, a blockchain-based social media site that rewarded users with tokens for the upvotes that they received. The platform worked great at first and fostered an active, friendly, supportive community. But it was quickly gamed by token farmers with bots, which means that there were sophisticated users who built bots to post and vote all day so they earned an outsized share of the reward tokens. Then these users became whales (entities with cryptocurrency-filled pockets) and started taking over – rewarding themselves with free money, or using their tokens to censor posts they didn't like. (When it became apparent that the platform was beyond repair, Larimer hopped off to raise money for EOS.)[11] While Steemit struggled to keep its users onboard, crypto billionaire Justin Sun swooped in to purchase it. Sun is a crypto founder famous for his smart-contract blockchain TRON. Sun had a reputation for being a bit of a grifter and a copycat – it was widely reported that the TRON white paper was just a collection of plagiarized excerpts from other projects' white papers. Steemit users protested the TRON acquisition with a hard fork and became their own community-led blockchain called Hive. Unfortunately, Hive still inherited Steemit's broken tokenomics model that allows whales to game the system, so it suffers from many of the same problems. Justin Sun went on to acquire the pioneer file-sharing application BitTorrent, the classic crypto exchange Poloniex, and several other blockchain companies.[12]

Moonboys and Lambos

The 2017 bull run was also marked by obnoxious displays of wealth, which is why mainstream media came to define crypto as excessive "moonboy" culture. The newly crypto-rich consumed so conspicuously, and social media posts about new Lamborghinis became so common, that the "lambo" meme has been forever cemented into crypto culture. Toward the end of the cycle, some really crazy things started to happen, and there were signs that the party would probably be coming to a close. But many of us were caught up in the excitement and the vision of a decentralized future, and we didn't want to see those signs. And many of us new to these types of markets hadn't yet learned how to look out for "top signals": indications that the market is frothy or overheated. But no matter how promising a new technology or asset class is, it will not go straight up forever.[13]

There will always be somewhat of a cyclical nature to markets. This strikes at the core of human psychology, which exist in all markets, from old to new. At some point the people who got in early are going to sell and take profits, which will start a cascade of selling pressure that the demand side is usually unable to maintain. This is where we see the transition from a bull market to a bear market, where prices fall 20% or more. It's pretty much unavoidable regardless of what you're trading. Assets with a long history tend to be more stable during both good times and bad, but newer assets tend to be more volatile. Many who are new to trading don't realize this, and are seduced into buying when the hype is at its peak – thinking the increased value makes it a sure thing. In reality this is usually the worst time to buy, but when you're in the midst of a bull market it's very difficult to tell where the top is – especially with crypto, where valuations so often exceed our expectations.

Even experienced traders had a problem timing the top of the market in 2017; every week brought even more hype and higher prices, so it felt like we were at the top for most of the year. Traditional brands were tripping over themselves to attach their names to blockchain projects or make callouts to crypto culture in their advertisements. One of the most ridiculous examples was when the New York–based beverage company Long Island Iced Tea changed its name to Long Blockchain Corp. The stunt pumped the small company's stock by 450% and gained it a ton of free publicity. Paid celebrity endorsements started to get out of hand too – especially when the celebrities didn't disclose that their posts were paid sponsorships, leading to serious financial penalties. Rapper and producer DJ Khaled was fined $152,725; for his secret agreements with dubious ICOs, boxer and promoter Floyd Mayweather was fined $614,775.[14]

Of course, as more giddy users got on the networks the most popular blockchains started to suffer major throughput and scaling challenges. As Bitcoin was breaking all-time-high records throughout 2017, the community clashed over how and when to scale to meet user demand. Ethereum was facing similar problems with high fees and slow transactions during times of congestion, and some of the applications building on the network found there was a limit to how many users could be reached. The Bitcoin and Ethereum communities both had extensive roadmaps to improve their scalability, but these were long-term plans that couldn't quickly enable mass adoption. These technical realities likely contributed to the end of the bull run, which was sudden. On December 17, Bitcoin hit an all-time high of $19,783.21; days later, it dropped 30%.[15]

There were a few who managed to come out on top though. Probably the most famous example was Charlie Lee, the founder of Litecoin, who sold his massive holdings in the project in late 2017 at the very top of the crypto cycle. He sold claiming that his stake was a conflict of interest, and promised he'd continue to work on Litecoin.[16] But Litecoin never returned to its former glory; despite consistent development, it's considered by many to be a dead project.

Vitalik Buterin, the eccentric and noble founder of Ethereum, also sold at the top. On Buterin's orders, the Ethereum Foundation sold an estimated 70,000 ETH when the asset was at its all-time high of about $1,400, making nearly $100 million on the trade. At the time, Vitalik was publicly vocal about how he felt the market was overheated. He was also critical of the excessive culture of greed that had come to define the industry, and threatened to leave crypto if things were going to be that way. In a controversial Twitter post, Buterin wrote we "need to differentiate between getting hundreds of billions of dollars of digital paper wealth sloshing around and actually achieving something meaningful for society."[17]

Buterin seemed to sense that the market was out of balance, and he made a smart decision that helped Ethereum weather the crypto winter and continue to build while the market was down. But not everyone was so lucky or so wise. I personally held all the way to the bottom thinking that the market would turn around any minute, as did many people I knew. We were still luckier than some investors, though; some lost everything in scam projects, hacks, or insolvent exchanges. The media sentiment on crypto quickly turned sour, with sources calling the whole industry a scam months after telling their audience to buy at the top.[18] Many retail investors left the market with a very negative view of the industry, but a few true believers remained.

CHAPTER 12

New Layer to the Internet

Decentralized Finance

E thereum proved that blockchains could be more than just currency networks – they could build a new layer to the internet. But what does that mean exactly? As you undoubtedly know, the internet started out with very basic functions of text and image display. Over the years and as technology has improved, additional "layers" have been added to include more functionality. But despite all the growth of the past few decades, we still don't have a financial layer. A few companies like PayPal and Stripe have developed some solutions for transferring value online, but these are centralized third-party services that have to be integrated with applications – they are not natively a part of the application's infrastructure. Smart-contract platforms allow for the financial layer to be built into the applications themselves as a core part of their infrastructure. There are a few major benefits to this approach. Not only is it more decentralized and secure, but it also opens up new possibilities for features and functionality. With applications building on top of the same financial layer, they can now connect and collaborate in ways that were never possible before. This idea is known as "composability," and sometimes industry insiders use the phrase "Money Legos" to describe how some financial applications are able to plug into one another and build on top of each other.

The concept of a "new layer to the internet" has been thrown around since the early days of Ethereum; it was even discussed on the Bitcointalk forum in relation to the potential of blockchain technology. However, the term "layer 1" wasn't in the discourse until both Bitcoin and Ethereum began running into scaling challenges. One of the most popular solutions proposed in both communities was the idea of adding additional blockchains on top of the base layer. The additional layers would allow for more activity while still benefiting from the security of the base layer. Ethereum and Bitcoin are the main blockchains focused on scaling through "layer 2" networks. Bitcoin developers are working on something called the Lightning Network, a second layer that will increase speed and lower transaction fees, but it seems to be a long way off from becoming a reality. On Ethereum, these layer-2 networks are still in the process of being developed as well, but a few, like Optimism and Arbitrum, have already launched as of mid-2022 and are steadily onboarding users as of this writing.[1]

Many of Ethereum's competitors disagree with this layered approach, and are instead trying to create platforms with scalable base layers. This is a massive challenge. Many of Ethereum's early competitors from the 2017 cycle fell apart during the bear market, or failed to reach their previous all-time highs when the momentum finally returned years later. EOS was probably the most spectacular failure, fading into obscurity within a year of raising over $4 billion in the largest ICO ever. The team behind TRON, another top contender from the 2017 cycle, continues to develop their network and market the blockchain heavily – but it doesn't get a whole lot of use and the price was never able to recover after the bear market. However, TRON is not entirely dead, thanks to Tether, one of the most popular stablecoins on the market. Tether is on multiple different blockchains including Ethereum and TRON. Since it's much cheaper to send Tether on TRON, the TRON blockchain sees a decent amount of volume – despite not having many other popular applications or utilities.

Cardano was one of the only smart-contract blockchain projects aside from Ethereum that managed to maintain a strong community during the crypto winter following the 2017 bull run. This is in part because Cardano founder Charles Hoskinson was very approachable and started doing regular AMAs – "Ask Me Anything" sessions, often held randomly on YouTube – with his community members, fielding even the difficult questions. In 2018, Cardano was mostly still in development, and smart-contract functionality hadn't yet launched. This was one of the things that Cardano did differently from the competition. Cardano took a slow-and-steady approach to blockchain development, conducting scientific research and then developing their platform accordingly. This was a controversial strategy because many investors feared that Cardano was lagging behind its competitors, who were rushing to market. But Cardano came back stronger than ever in the next cycle, so the plan obviously worked.[2]

Ethereum also received plenty of criticism during the bear market. Many Bitcoin maximalists blamed the price crash on the ICO mania that Ethereum's infrastructure had enabled (as noted in Chapter 11). In addition to their financial loss, many investors also resented that their dreams to decentralize the world had come up short. But there was still a strong Ethereum community of users and developers that continued to believe in that vision even after prices crashed below $100. Over time, developers started launching some very interesting projects on Ethereum in the midst of the bear market.[3]

DeFi

One of the first pieces of this next puzzle was a protocol called Maker. Maker is a platform that creates the decentralized stablecoin DAI. It isn't very flashy and it didn't fatten many wallets, but it was one of the first building blocks of the DeFi ecosystem on Ethereum. DeFi stands for "Decentralized Finance," a term used to classify the decentralized blockchain applications that provide financial services. DeFi was coined by Ethereum builders who were kicking around ideas in a shared Telegram chat in August of 2018. The chat included Inje Yeo of Set Protocol, Blake Henderson of 0x, and Brendan Forster of Dharma.[4]

The next piece of the puzzle came into place when a few decentralized exchanges began popping up to allow peer-to-peer trading of ERC-20 tokens, which are tokens that are deployed on the Ethereum blockchain. The earliest exchanges to get significant use were EtherDelta and Bancor. EtherDelta was the first to launch, on July 12, 2016, and was much more popular than its competitors thanks to its head start. But the project was short-lived: in December 2017, a hacker compromised the site and scammed users out of roughly $800,000. Then in November 2018 the SEC also came after the platform, accusing them of running an unregulated security exchange.[5]

Bancor launched on July 12, 2017, raising a significant ICO of $153 million – the highest ICO at the time – but it's remained one of the lesser-known decentralized exchanges on Ethereum. It's surprising that Bancor never really took over, because they launched with such a revolutionary design. Bancor was the first Automated Market Maker (AMM), which means that instead of using an order book that matches individual trades with one another, Bancor's trades were facilitated by liquidity pools and smart contracts. Liquidity pools are accounts filled with large amounts of crypto that have been collectively locked up by different users on the platform in exchange for a reward. These liquidity pools are secured by smart contracts, which means that even though this big pile of money is in one account, the platform is coded to allow the depositors to withdraw only their own money – and no one else's. With this AMM, users trade with the smart contracts instead of directly with one another. The AMM model was initially proposed by Vitalik Buterin in 2017.[6]

Bancor wasn't the only exchange to answer the Market Maker call; another AMM called Uniswap launched in November 2018. And quickly dominated the market because it allowed anyone to create a liquidity pool for their own token, making it easier than ever for developers to create listings for the crypto projects. Bancor was a bit more selective about the tokens allowed on their platform, which is why I think Uniswap was able to corner the market so quickly.[7]

Uniswap became so popular that it spawned a host of competitors with the same model, as we often see in the open-source world of crypto. One of

Uniswap's most formidable competitors was a small project called SushiSwap that was launched by an anonymous team in August 2020. At face value, there was nothing particularly special about SushiSwap. The ace up their sleeve was a brilliant strategy later dubbed a "vampire attack," where a hostile exchange attempts to lure their rival's customers away with financial incentives. SushiSwap began giving large token incentives specifically to Uniswap's liquidity providers in the form of their own token, SUSHI. The trick worked, and was able to draw away an estimated $1 billion in liquidity as soon as the platform went live because investors were already waiting to transfer. The SushiSwap team presented themselves as heroes fighting for the common trader because of the rewards they offered, which started to shift the momentum in the race.[8]

This was somewhat of an existential crisis for Uniswap, who appeared to be losing the moat they were establishing in the decentralized exchange sector. They had to do something to recapture that liquidity and win back the momentum, and it had to be big. In response to the vampire attack, in September 2020 Uniswap launched the biggest airdrop that the industry had ever seen. As a part of the distribution for their UNI token, Uniswap sent out thousands of dollars' worth of tokens to every single Ethereum address that had ever used the platform. They also began offering token incentives for liquidity providers, which brought back many of their original customers. The airdrop made international headlines, even outside of crypto in the mainstream media. Now even more eyes were drawn to DeFi, where the financial applications seemed to be giving away free money to people just for being customers. Uniswap was the talk of the industry for a while after that – which regained the momentum that was lost during the vampire attack and made Uniswap more popular than ever before. The rivalry between Uniswap and SushiSwap continued, but Uniswap became the clear victor as time passed on. SushiSwap faced a series of challenges, including accusations of scams, internal drama, and a crisis in governance. SushiSwap continues to be one of the top decentralized exchanges, but it has fallen way behind Uniswap in terms of liquidity and usage.[9]

Another important component to the DeFi ecosystem is borrowing and lending platforms. These platforms allow users to deposit their funds into smart contracts from which other users can take collateralized loans. To bring more users and liquidity, DeFi protocols began offering rewards to users for holding their assets on these platforms. In December 2018, a derivative asset protocol called Synthetix was the first to launch with Yield Farming incentives, inspiring many other projects to do the same. Yield farming is basically locking up or lending out your crypto in exchange for rewards; you're farming yields, and the platform benefits from your liquidity, because it allows them to serve their other customers. A borrowing and lending platform called Compound caught on, and on June 16, 2020, started rewarding liquidity providers with their COMP governance token. This drove a ton of new users to the platform and brought even more attention to the yield-farming concept. The idea became so popular that it kicked off an era known as "DeFi Summer," where new yield farms and AMMs were being launched every single day.[10]

One of the most interesting things about DeFi summer was that some of the era's most successful projects were formed out of ICOs that had launched during the bull run of 2017. Up until that point, the crypto industry had mostly looked back on the ICO phenomenon as a mistake. There were so many failed projects and scams, and so many retail investors had gotten burned, that it appeared that no ICOs had made it – but some did. For example, Chainlink, which is a price oracle that is essential in keeping markets honest. Price oracles are tools that track prices and other information for assets across a variety of different platforms and exchanges, which keeps prices fair and in equilibrium. On September 18, 2017, Chainlink launched as an ICO and went on to become one of the foundational tools for DeFi. Another great example is AAVE – one of the leading lending and borrowing platforms on Ethereum – which initially launched on November 25, 2017, as an ICO under the name ETHLend.[11]

The Challengers

Fast-forward to 2020: DeFi began showing real value, and investors started to believe again. Maybe the dream of decentralizing the world was actually possible. There were a lot of new users flooding on to Ethereum to use these applications, which was putting strain on the network and raising fees, just as in the previous bull run. Ethereum has a very detailed road map that includes a variety of different strategies for scaling the blockchain throughput, both on the base layer and through layer-2 networks.[12]

In August 2021, an upgrade called EIP-1559 went live that improved the fee structure on the network while also implementing a burn mechanism, which "burned" a portion of each transaction fee, removing it from circulation forever so as to reduce the rate of inflation. The network was also in the process of switching from a Proof-of-Work (PoW) consensus mechanism to a unique Proof-of-Stake (PoS) design, which means that miners would no longer be needed to secure the network. Instead, a decentralized network of validating "stakers" could lock up some of their ETHs and secure the network from their home computers. (Over the years mining operations have become more industrialized and harder for the hobbyist to play a significant role because of the massive costs involved.) Like everything in crypto, this came with a series of trade-offs, with both advantages and disadvantages. On the plus side, this new Proof-of-Stake network for Ethereum is more accessible and removes sell pressure from the asset, because miners are no longer dumping their coins to cover costs of electricity. On the minus side, PoS lacks the competitive network effects of Proof-of-Work and tends to favor larger validators.

Given the fact that the minimum amount of tokens required to stake can be in the dozens or even thousands, this leaves a lot of node operations in the hands of the wealthy. For example, in order to run a validator node for Polkadot, you'd have to have a minimum of 5,000 DOT tokens. At the time of this writing, that's nearly $40,000 USD.[13]

There are billions of dollars at stake, so Ethereum developers are being extremely careful with their transition from PoW to PoS and the other significant changes that are being made to the network. This is probably the way it should be, but some users are getting impatient – which is also understandable, because Ethereum is too expensive for many in its current form. Ethereum's scaling challenges created an opportunity for competing projects to launch similar products with much lower transaction fees and capture a large portion of the retail market that wanted to participate in DeFi but was priced out of Ethereum.

The first "alternative layer 1" to find success with this strategy was Binance Smart Chain (BSC), an "EVM Compatible" smart-contract blockchain developed by the Binance exchange and launched in September 2020. "EVM Compatible" means that a blockchain is compatible with the "Ethereum Virtual Machine" – in other words, it uses the same programming language that Ethereum does. This makes it easy to port applications from one blockchain to another without creating a ton of extra work for developers. This also makes it very easy for competitors to fork the code of an original project and create their own copycat version. This happened a lot on BSC, which used Binance's exchange token "BNB" as its native currency in the same way that ETH is used on Ethereum. On BSC, there was a clone of Uniswap called "PancakeSwap," which allowed users to trade tokens for a fraction of the price they paid on Ethereum. Lower fees were possible on the BSC network because it was developed with a different architecture that made different trade-offs. The BSC network was significantly more centralized than Ethereum, with far fewer nodes – which allowed for a higher throughput but much less security. In late 2021, the BSC blockchain was unable to handle the amount of transactions coming through the network and suffered from major performance issues that caused many users and developers to flee the ecosystem.[14]

Around the same time that retail investors were losing faith in BSC, another contender began rising to prominence in March 2020: Solana. One of the most heavily VC-invested chains on the market, it had an incredible rally in 2021, rising from $1.84 on January 1 and peaking at almost $260 on November 6. Solana was created by a developer named Anatoly Yakovenko, who published his white paper on Solana in November 2017. But the person who is actually most associated with Solana is one of its main investors, Sam Bankman-Fried, or SBF, as he is often called among industry insiders. SBF quickly rose to become one of the richest people in crypto after launching his exchange FTX in May of 2019. SBF also earns a significant income through his trading firm, Alameda Research, which has a very close relationship with

FTX as well. Alameda was just one of many firms that were heavily invested in Solana early on, so the project was very well funded in time for the 2020–2021 bull run. The Solana ecosystem rolled out DeFi offerings similar to the ones seen on Ethereum – once again with a fraction of the prices and extremely fast speeds.[15]

For a time it really looked like Solana was fit to take on Ethereum, especially given how crazy the price was pumping, but after a while the blockchain started to show some signs of weakness. Throughout 2021 and 2022, the Solana network began suffering a series of outages where the blockchain was down and totally unable to operate for several hours. This is not acceptable for a blockchain network with billions of dollars of value, and these types of outages can result in serious consequences for users. In cases of market volatility, leverage traders and borrowers are unable to top off their collateral, and could be unnecessarily liquidated because they simply can't interact with the blockchain. Staying online 24/7 without any outages is a standard that has come to be expected of blockchains, so this was a major blow to the Solana ecosystem and to the confidence of many of its users. However, the Solana team continues to build and there is still a lot of money in that ecosystem, so they will likely still be in the conversation in future cycles.[16]

There are enough layer-1 smart-contract platforms in the market today to fill a whole book, so we'll only stick with the most important ones for this chapter. The most notable layer-1 blockchain that I've barely mentioned is Polkadot, and that's because we haven't really seen what this project is capable of yet. Polkadot is still worth paying attention to because Gavin Wood, one of the Ethereum cofounders, is behind the project.[17]

It's far too early in this race to pick a winner, but it doesn't seem like it will be a winner-take-all situation. Ethereum has a significant lead, with a high market cap, but other blockchains can still be extremely successful through serving a unique community or focusing on a specific use case.[18]

CHAPTER 13

Brave New World

Beyond Bitcoin

Just as the Hubble telescope opened our eyes to the depth of space, and the James Webb telescope magnified the details, the cryptoverse is expanding at a huge rate – and entirely new classes of technologies are being born like gas clusters ready to progress to the next step of stardom. At the time of this writing there are over 20,000 crypto projects, and more are coming online every day.[1] Bitcoin may be the center of the universe, but it's important not to get tunnel vision. There are quality projects out there that you should be aware of. Many of them will be category-defining businesses in the coming years.

I went over Ethereum and its place as a decentralized computer in the previous chapters, and you'll see that many of the projects are based on Ethereum. I've also covered true cryptocurrencies like XRP or XLM, and crypto assets like Bitcoin. But there is so much more to crypto. Let's adjust our focus and see what else is out there in the cryptoverse and how it relates to the future of crypto assets.

Stablecoins

On the surface a stablecoin is about as boring as they come, but don't let the word "stable" fool you. Stablecoins are the oil in the engine of crypto – as well as one of the most hotly regulated, scrutinized, valuable, and divisive technologies in all crypto.[2] Before we get into the drama, I'll set the scene.

All stablecoins serve one purpose: to be pegged to the value of another asset. They have lots of names, like USDT, USDC, GUSD, DAI, etc., etc. See a trend here? At the time of this writing, nearly all stablecoins are pegged to the US dollar – but that reality is already changing; in my view, stablecoins will encompass all the G8 currencies in the next five years. This is coming at the same time that the interbank messaging system is being updated to integrate blockchain into their cross-border payments and settlements.[3]

Stablecoins come in two flavors: asset-backed and algorithmic. The two dominant stablecoins – USD Tether (or USDT) and USD Coin or (USDC) – are asset-collateralized 1:1 with either dollars or assets of equivalent value that are stored off-chain. So, if you want to turn some regular dollars into USDT (or just "Tether," as it's commonly referred to in crypto) you do that on an exchange like Coinbase, where you purchase USDT from a giant Coinbase bucket that's filled with Tether. Coinbase purchases the Tether straight from Tether Operations Limited, who verified the transfer of assets. The process is the same for the other asset-backed stablecoins, like those backed by such currencies as the British pound, or even gold.

On the other side of the *coin* are algorithmic stablecoins. These fancy pieces of code are just that . . . code. They aren't backed by an off-chain asset but instead use algorithms to adjust their price and incentivize certain market behaviors to keep values afloat. And though this technology shows a lot of promise, it isn't ready for prime time. You may have heard of a crypto called Luna that had a spectacular crash in 2022. That was precipitated by a depegging of its algorithmic stablecoin UST from the dollar – after which it dropped to fractions of a penny.

Stablecoins are the lifeblood of crypto; without them crypto would grind to a halt. Stablecoins are the main on-ramp to buying crypto and especially trading crypto. Because politicians know this, stablecoins have become the primary target for regulation, censorship, and bans. Many from the Treasury Department, Securities and Exchange Commission, Office of Foreign Assets Control, and other agencies have taken aggressive stances toward crypto, especially stablecoins.[4] Some of this is warranted; bringing the right amount of regulation to stablecoins would be good for the industry. But, from the standpoint of many, myself included, a lot of the opposition comes from a fear of losing control of the money needed to finance wars, subsidies, kickbacks, and bailouts. Opponents also know they're behind the curve on crypto adoption and are clamoring to stop innovation before their monopoly is overturned. But I'll elaborate more on that in Chapter 20.

Oracles

Next we have the fascinating realm of blockchain oracles, which are built on the back of smart contracts. Tokens like XYO, VeChain, and ChainLINK are all projects currently delivering on the promise to be the next innovation in blockchain. A blockchain oracle is an interface for external systems putting real-world data onto a blockchain; in other words, they are the bridge from the real world to the blockchain. That means everything from weather data to football stats to supply-chain logistics can be decentralized and optimized. This offers an immense amount of value that has yet to be fully tapped into. Already oracles like Chainlink (LINK) are used across crypto to harvest price and contract data from various exchanges and other financial services.[5] Blockchain oracles are also what makes DeFi possible. And the technology is also revolutionizing policymaking by providing access to data across multiple departments that otherwise couldn't share across different technology platforms. VeChain (VET) is a logistics blockchain that will give unprecedented access and optimization to supply chains. It's taking manufacturing to the next level by collecting logistical data from multiple sources – such as shipping, trucking, warehousing, container owners, and point-of-sale devices – all on to one accessible stream of data. Any company using that oracle will enable all that data to be easily accessible to all concerned parties instead of being scattered across various servers, software, and operating systems.

Memecoins

We all love a good meme. It's been said that "He who controls the memes controls the universe,"[6] and there's a lot of truth to that. But a meme is just a compelling idea with a dash of virality, and crypto isn't immune to that kind of flash-in-the-pan popularity. Thanks to the fact that making a coin on Ethereum, and especially on Binance Smart Chain, can be done by anyone after watching a 30-minute YouTube video, Memecoins have taken a slice of the crypto market cap – and brought with them a bunch of FUD (Fear, Uncertainty, and Doubt), scams, and heartbreak. Memecoins don't have any utility besides being a meme. They have funny names like Dogecoin, Safemoon, Baby Doge Coin, and even Garlicoin. They usually have a price per coin that's in the millionths of a penny and a supply that can exceed quadrillions of coins. A lot of them pump by many thousands of percentages – only to have the developers (who hold a majority of the supply) rug-pull and leave everyone else holding a bag of worthless magic internet money. A few, like Dogecoin, have stuck around for a couple years only because of its continued meme status. Coins like ShibaInu, which is based on Ethereum, have attempted to make their own NFTs, Defi, and Rebase Tokens to become legitimate, but the ridiculous tokenomics and anonymous development team keep them from being considered by large VCs. It's mostly retail investors that get in to memecoins hoping to make a quick buck, but 99.9% of the time they get burned instead.

Community Coins

Meaningful shared experiences are a powerful way to create value. And though a meme is a shared experience, it's not particularly meaningful, which is why memecoins tend to dip in and out like wedding crashers at a reception buffet. But true shared experiences – those that are face to face and in person, with shared goals and charismatic participation – hold their value and can create their own economy. This is readily apparent with soccer teams – or "football," as it's known in most countries. Soccer teams have an intense global following that persist over generations. The global market cap of just one team – Real Madrid – is $5.1 billion USD. That would place it in the top 20 cryptos at the time of this writing. Sports entities like the UFC, E-Sports, American college football, and sports content creators; NFT Projects like Bored Ape Yacht Club; and traditional intellectual properties like Star Wars, Marvel, and even Disney itself are worth billions, have millions of followers, and, like a well-oiled machine, have already monetized their fan base.

And then there's blockchain. A way to unify the fan experience. To bridge the gap between the digital and physical, and to make the engagement that much more seamless while increasing the value of the products and experiences. It's no surprise that one of the biggest advances in blockchain development is happening in what I like to call "community coins." On the top of that list is Chiliz, which has partnered with dozens of professional sports teams – creating fan tokens that fund sales, merch, tickets, NFTs, and experiences for teams and brands. There's also Rally, which is a social-token project made for content creators and brands. Creators can make a branded coin that becomes the currency of their brand. Across platforms, creators can monetize their work and bring all their assets under their control instead of farming it out to big data and other businesses that take a large cut. Community coins are the tip of the spear for Web3, which is something I'll get into later in the book.

These are just some of the types of projects that have tremendous potential. And there are dozens of subcategories for each. There's a lot of profit to be made as these projects disrupt the technology and financial industries. But before you hop on Coinbase and YOLO[7] into a token, you need to learn the basics of crypto trading.

CHAPTER 14

Investment Prep

NOT Financial Advice

If you're reading this book, there's a great chance the first thing that piqued your interest in crypto was the idea of *significant* financial gain. I'm here to tell you . . . it is rare. I didn't write this book to help you make it rich quick in crypto. This is not an investment book. I'm certainly no financial adviser, and I can't tell you what is best for your situation, financial level, and risk tolerance amid a myriad of other things that are unique to you.

I wrote this book to boost your perspective and understanding of crypto so you can have confidence in your next steps. And though it's the hope for profit that draws many into this crazy crypto world, my hope is that somewhere along the way you'll hold a growing portfolio while also embracing the true message of crypto. What is the message of crypto? Well, it's a mix of decentralization, permissionless development, transparency, evolution of technology, and offering an antithesis to the broken fiat system. However, many people never make it long enough in the crypto markets to find those deeper ideals.

So if you're looking to put your first hard-earned, backed-by-nothing fiat into the crypto market, this chapter will show you what your options are – but then it's up to you to choose in which direction you want to go. This book will not hold your hand and tell you where you should be putting your money; these are your decisions, and you have to feel the weight of that responsibility.

Also, I couldn't possibly do a thorough enough walk-through on this topic in only one chapter. Even an entire book dedicated to these topics would still not be enough to set you up for long-term success. For you to master investing or trading, you need to spend countless hours going deep into books, courses, indicators, research tools, and much more. Active investing and active trading can be full-time jobs – not like you see in the movies, where day traders can hit a few buttons on a computer and make a bunch of money before they finish their first cup of coffee. That couldn't be further from the truth. Success in these markets, whether you're investing or trading, takes hard work and dedication.

First, you need to decide what's the best path for you: investing or trading. You might not think there's much of a difference between these two financial strategies, but there are many differences. For starters, though most traders are also investors, most investors are not traders. Trading is a beast of its own.

The biggest difference between investing and trading is the time horizon on which each strategy requires. When someone speaks of investments, these generally have long-term implications. You have money sitting in a bank earning .01% interest. That's not even close to enough return on investment (ROI) to make up for inflation over 20 years! So, leaving money in a bank account is a negative ROI based upon the actual historical inflation data. Investing would consist of taking some of the money out of the bank account and moving it somewhere that it can flourish and generate passive returns over time. Investing can often be a "set it and forget it" endeavor. If you had taken $1,000 and invested it into Amazon or Apple stock after the dot-com bubble collapse in 2001 – without lifting a finger, you would have made a fortune. The power of investing is letting the returns compound while you don't break a sweat. Investing can certainly have expiration dates where you move out of one position and into another, but generally you are not making moves on a regular basis. The bulk of investing work comes *before* you make the investments – not after. The hard part is deciding where to put your money, because investments can feel like jumping off a financial cliff. Once you make decisions it's harder to change direction, because that defeats the purpose of long-term investing.

Step One: Researching

A good investor knows that decisions must be made upon facts, historical data, market research, current market conditions, and many other factors. What should never be taken into consideration when choosing your race-horse? Emotion. Your feelings should never come into play when picking one asset or another. Gut feelings in investing are akin to calling psychics to get their opinions. Investments should be based upon parameters that you put together in a system. Some people invest only in tech stocks because tech stocks as a category consistently made large returns. Warren Buffett, on the other hand – one of the greatest investors ever (but a crypto hater!) – doesn't invest in too many tech stocks because he believes in investing in only things you understand. And the technology and crypto world have passed him by. Some investors only buy stocks that provide dividends to holders. There are baskets of assets some choose to invest in because they prefer a wide range of exposure to different industries. Creating an investment system and sticking to it is a great way to remove human emotion and make smart decisions.

Free coin-research sites like CoinMarketCap.com or CoinGecko are the most used tools in crypto for analyzing specific coins. You will find their market cap numbers, volume, tokenomics, supply details, exchanges those coins are found on and much more. If you are totally in the dark about the differences between different altcoins, these sites are very intuitive and you can easily navigate through the different information, charts, graphics, news, etc. in order to compare one coin to another. Paid coin-research sites like TokenMetrics.com (we have a promo code for you on the resources page in the back of the book) takes coin research to a deeper level by integrating Quant AI, aggregated predictions, rankings, sample portfolios, and much more.

Another investor guide is fundamental analysis, which takes into consideration data that affects an asset's fundamental value or perceived value in a marketplace.[1] Perusing the crypto news powerhouses CoinDesk.com, CoinTelegraph.com, and others can reveal breaking stories that could be favorable or detrimental to a crypto asset's price. For example, if a coin debuts on a major exchange, then traditionally that adds liquidity and interest, resulting in price increases. But if a project gets served a lawsuit from the SEC, then that's a good indicator the price may drop considerably. Taking on-chain fundamentals into consideration – like hashrate, amount of Bitcoin flowing in or out of exchanges, traditional bottom- or top-of-the-market indicators, and tons of others – can also help you determine how close a crypto is to a pump or a collapse. You can get access to many of the on-chain fundamentals through Glassnode.com.

A good investor uses as many of these tools as possible as frequently as possible to determine various factors: which projects to invest in, reasonable expectations of returns, levels to take profits out – basically any decision that needs to be made. The more information, the better the decisions. That's true in many aspects of life, but it's particularly true in investing where, over time, small edges can turn into big advantages.

In crypto, making good investment decisions can be more difficult than in traditional markets because crypto assets are so new. Even the oldest – Bitcoin, of course, created in 2009 – wasn't actively trading for the first few years. So there are barely 10 years of trading data for the longest-tenured asset in the space. Many of the top-performing altcoins have much less than 10 years of data, and new projects are popping up regularly with no trading history. So, since we can't analyze the 10-year history of a chart, it's daunting to forecast what that long-term investment can do over 20 years. That's three times its existing price history! Investors in the crypto market understand these risks . . . or at least they should.

Remember, nothing is guaranteed, so you should *never* invest money you *cannot* afford to lose. If you have $500 to pay your rent, but need $1,000 to cover other stuff, don't fall into the trap of thinking you can quickly double what you've got. This is a loser's mentality. You can't afford to lose your rent money; find an alternate way to make the additional $500 you need. Most successful investors use disposable income that they could do without if they lose it – such as disposable income they could spend on tickets to a ballgame or a trip. So, instead of putting that money toward an experience or an item, they risk the opportunity to increase those funds.

Repeatedly making wise decisions of calculated risk leads to compounded gains over time. Because each time the value of your investments grows, or you add more disposable income to your portfolio, you supercharge your investments to potentially increase your returns. If you make 100% profit on $100, you earn $100; if you make 100% profit on $10,000, then you earn $10,000. Let your money work for you. More money at risk means a higher possible ROI in literal dollars. While your ROI in dollars may drastically range based upon initial investment, your percentage gains or losses will be consistent no matter what you started with.

Step Two: Choosing

Investing comes in all shapes and sizes. If you believe crypto investing is right for you, and you understand that all investments contain risk, then there are several things you need to consider. The first determination is which crypto asset you want to invest in. Once you've chosen that, you'll need to select the exchange you want to work with. When you're buying in, you use we call a "fiat on-ramp"; conversely, a "fiat off-ramp" is where you'll later cash out – and these are often done at the same exchange.

Bitcoin ATM

Just as you can deposit or withdraw funds at a physical ATM kiosk, you can exchange crypto using a Bitcoin ATM. The first one started in Vancouver, Canada, in late October 2013,[2] followed by US debuts in 2014. Given that the transactions don't involve the internet, some people consider them more private. But note that most of the Bitcoin ATMs all over the country require "KYC" or Know Your Customer processes for which you must confirm your identity – the Vancouver one required a handprint – which negates the hope for privacy. In addition, they usually have higher fees than you find online. In my opinion, while Bitcoin ATMs are big business – as of August 2022, there are 39,000 ATMs worldwide, trading in more than one currency[3] – they aren't particularly useful to the average person looking to invest in crypto (and pay their taxes).

Centralized Exchanges (CEX)

Crypto transactions are usually conducted on crypto exchanges. One type is the centralized exchange, or CEX, which serves as a third party to which you entrust your investment. The most trusted centralized exchanges are Coinbase, FTX, and Binance – followed by Kraken, Gemini, and Crypto.com. How it works is you submit fiat currency to the CEX, which then purchases the crypto asset of your choice and credits your crypto account. Your cryptocurrency is kept in a digital "wallet" hosted by the exchange. They're called "centralized" because they are the central location of investors' funds. This is risky for two main reasons. One is they can be the targets of hackers infiltrating the network via bugs in the software and siphoning off funds. And we're talking a lot of money; according to Blockworks, the amount lost in 2022 is approaching $2 billion as of July 2022.[4]

The other risk is that even trusted exchanges can become insolvent – meaning they don't have enough money in assets to cover the amount of crypto they hold. In July 2022, Celsius, Vauld, and Voyager Digital all declared bankruptcy, and other exchanges are poised to follow.[5] Many people (including myself) can lose money from trusting a centralized third party to handle our funds for us – which is exactly what we do with the traditional banking system. We trade the convenience and security that banks offer in exchange for either quick access to our money or higher ROI on our investments. Let's face it: the .01% returns banks give you is an absolute joke and puts your wealth in a losing position. Unfortunately, centralized crypto exchanges look eerily like the traditional banking system crypto is meant to replace. And, so far, in the world of crypto there are few other options – especially for traders, who have to keep their trading funds on the exchange.

But as an investor, you can and should remove your funds from third-party exchanges as soon as possible. We call the way you manage and hold your funds "custodianship" or "crypto custody," and it's extremely important. To truly *own* your crypto, you and only you need to have access to your funds, so it's pivotal that you learn to self-custody your crypto. These places aren't going to honor your deposit if they get hacked or go bankrupt. This is the responsibility the crypto community has been so adamant about since its inception. We want independence; not an insecure nanny state that provides us with glorified solutions to problems that the state created. They want to keep citizens guarded for our own protection. That's always how they convince you to get back in the cage. For your own protection. I, for one, don't need the government to be responsible for my assets, my financial well-being, my career, or my protection. I've got all that handled.

Custody concerns both the wallet where you store your currency and the key to that wallet. So, once you've purchased your crypto on a centralized exchange, you'll want to move it off the exchange into your wallet of choice.

You can send your crypto assets to "hot wallets" or "cold storage wallets." A hot wallet is usually a desktop app or mobile phone app that connects you to your wallet while your phone is connected to the internet; that's what makes it "hot." Cold storage wallets are usually USB devices like the popular Ledger Nano S or the Trezor Wallet. These are said to be cold storage because, once you finish your transaction via an internet connection, you unplug it from your computer or device – making them closed off to hacks and thus the safest option.

Now for the key: with self-custody you, not a third party or custodian, possess the private key to your digital wallet. Only you have access to your private key; no one can open your wallet without you giving them permission by sharing the key. (A key is a very long string of either alphanumeric code or a string of either zeros or ones, called "bits." Bitcoin private keys are 256 bits.)

"Not your keys, not your crypto." This is the golden rule of crypto ownership. If someone finds your private keys, consider your crypto gone. So, how do you ensure self-custody? One pro tip is to always manually write down your private keys instead of keeping digital records. This is because the cloud is your enemy when it comes to protecting digital currency; even after you delete files from your computer, the cloud always has a version somewhere stored forever. Also, make sure to protect your manual version in a fire safe or disaster-safe location. It helps to store a backup, off-site copy as well – somewhere only you know about. You can never be too careful with storing your private keys. These strategies also work for other types of wallet access, such as what's called mnemonic phrases or seed phrases – basically passwords of your choosing that grant you access to your wallet.

Decentralized Exchanges (DEX)

The opposite of centralized exchanges are decentralized exchanges (or DEX for short). With a DEX you hold the crypto yourself and make a transaction directly on the blockchain without the need for a third party to handle your money. Examples of these include the platforms Uniswap, Balancer, PancakeSwap, and more. The idea behind DeFi – decentralized finance – stems from the original concept of digital currency: not having to trust an intermediary to exchange your funds for you.[6] One thing to keep in mind about decentralized exchanges is that very few of them provide fiat on-ramps and off-ramps, so in most cases to use a DEX you must first on-ramp fiat with a CEX.

While decentralized exchanges allow you to hold your own crypto during the transaction, they unfortunately lack the regulation to protect investors from what's called a "rug-pull scam." New types of coins pop up every day, and because no one knows in advance which coins are going to increase in value, it can be tempting to buy the newest thing when its price is lowest. But sometimes the sole purpose of a new product is to scam investors by pulling the liquidity of the coin after the supply is bought up. We refer to this as a "rug-pull" because the liquidity, or availability and access to a coin, is pulled out from under investors, leaving them the with virtually worthless coins.[7]

Step Three: Deploying Capital

So we've covered the nitty-gritty of getting started in crypto; you'll also want to determine *how* you want to deploy your capital. Many people simply decide to allocate for an initial crypto investment an amount of disposable income that makes sense for their goals and budget: this could be $10, $1,000, or $10,000. The important part is to choose an amount that you can stomach to lose in a worst-case scenario. Or, you may have a diversified portfolio that consists of a mix of investments – such as stocks, bonds, real estate, etc. – and you decide to allocate a specific percentage of your portfolio to crypto. Freeing up capital by moving around or selling some of your existing portfolio also makes sense, and is the most common ways people begin investing in crypto.

But what if I told you there's a tried-and-true method of investing that sets you up for long-term success *and* negates some of your risk, even in the volatile crypto markets? This strategy does exist and even Warren Buffett stands by it.[8] I'm talking about the strategy "Dollar Cost Averaging," or DCA for short. With this approach, you consistently invest the same amount over a predetermined time interval. For example, you might DCA by investing $100 per week into Bitcoin on a permanent basis. Remember what I said about keeping emotion out of investing? The method works well because it negates getting caught up in the volatility and drastic swings a market can go through. By buying the same amount of Bitcoin each week, you are, for all intents and purposes, buying Bitcoin at its average yearly price every week – without regularly calculating whether your latest purchase made you a quick profit or left you with unrealized losses. In short, when using the DCA strategy you don't focus on the current value of the asset. When done over long periods of time, this is a powerful and tested investment method many pro investors use to hedge their risk while still accumulating profit.

You may hear people in crypto talk about "Buying the Dip," a phrase frequently regurgitated by the crypto community every time an asset drops in value. It's a rallying cry for those looking for the opportunities that lower prices present: buy when the price is low, and sell when the price is high. We also call this strategy "Buying in the red and selling in the green." Sounds simple, right? Well, simple and easy are two different things. It's hard to keep your wits when you are seeing red candles. In the following chapters, I'm going to give you some pointers on how to get set up for success.

CHAPTER 15

Tips of the Trade

Charting, Trendspotting, and Leveraging

Most of the basic concepts, principles, tools, and indicators of traditional investing also apply to cryptocurrency, and investing and trading are the most common bridges between the two. The first lesson to learn in both investing and trading is that you won't get optimal results every time. To put it bluntly, sometimes you lose everything. So learning how to stomach the realities of losses is an absolute necessity. Some people who are very risk averse find that even relatively safe investments give them anxiety because they aren't completely in control. Good investors and traders know that nothing is guaranteed, and losses happen. Handling those losses like a champ and focusing on learning a lesson from each loss will keep you humble. You need to stay in the market if you want to gain enough experience to tilt the odds of success in your favor. You can't beat the market if you aren't in the market.

If investing is more your style, then there are several steps you can take next to get started on this journey. There is a list of resources in the Appendix to assist you in making some of these decisions. What follows in this chapter is about trading. But before you do any trading, I want you to be prepared for everything that comes along with professional trading. As I've said before, just reading this book isn't enough. You're going to need to really commit to learning everything you can. But I can get you started, and I can tell you that trading is not always glamorous. It's a steady grind that doesn't always have a big payday at the end. But if you keep at it you might find you enjoy the journey.

Many believe that if you want to become a trader, starting with paper trading is ideal. Paper trading is where you keep a ledger of your overall bankroll, trades, wins, and losses without putting a dime in the market. If you can prove to be a profitable trader on paper, then in theory you should be able to do it with real money.[1] Well, I disagree. I don't think people can operate the same way with real money as they do when they're not actually liable for their mistakes on paper – because there is no money and therefore no real risk or gain involved. Sure, it's easy to take profits when you're up 10% with fake money, but it's a whole different ballgame to take real profits on an active trade. It's easy to start thinking about what would happen if the price continues to move up, and so be reluctant to sell and get a small profit now for fear of losing your chance at a bigger profit. This is what we call Fear of Missing Out, or FOMO: being afraid that selling now means you'll miss out on what would have happened down the road.

Well, I'm here to tell you, a very simple rule to live by if you are a trader is this: it is *never* a bad time to take profits.

If you keep that on the forefront of your brain, it makes it easier to cash in on a green trade. Every time your trade goes green instead of red then you win (unless you're shorting the market, which I'll discuss later). The more green trades you make, the more profit you are realizing. It sounds easy enough, but why is it so difficult to become a winning and profitable trader over time? After all, the stats say that most traders lose and are never consistent winners. Sure, they may get a lucky trade here or there, but most end up on the losing side. The reason trading is hard is because it takes much practice and experience to be able to dissect a chart and pick out the *best* spots to commit to. Recognizing the optimal trade setups from the just good trading setups is the single biggest factor that separates pros from the pack. You're going to need to get that practice and experience on your own, but I can tell you about what you can trade.

Trading Tokens

One type of coin traders and investors alike should become familiar with is the stablecoin. Stablecoins maintain a consistent value, such as $1 for stablecoins backed by dollars. USDC (USD Coin, or Circle) and USDT (Tether) are two examples of dollar stablecoins. Theoretically they'll remain pegged to a value of $1, though they may fluctuate by fractions of a penny. If you want to lock in profits when moving in and out of trades, exchanging your volatile crypto assets (that fluctuate in value by the moment) for stablecoins can achieve this.

One important note is that dollar-backed stablecoins supposedly have a 1:1 ratio of dollars or assets (like precious metals) per each stablecoin. Tether and Circle back USDT and USDC respectively, and for now both seem to have sufficient reserves on hand – but the exact ratio of which assets back which parts of their supplies always remains in question. Many believe USDT is a ticking time bomb that will eventually collapse, in part because the company hasn't been transparent about confirming its backing. It is the oldest stablecoin, however – first minted in October 2014, on a Bitcoin second-layer protocol called Mastercoin, now Omni blockchain – and continues trucking along, with only the rare instance of momentarily losing its peg to due to extreme market conditions. Because of the transparency concern, I use only USDC because they are backed by traditional finance giant Circle. Tether also has some sketchy history. In 2019 the New York State Attorney General accused it and its sibling (and supposed "partner"), the crypto exchange Bitfinex – they're both owned by iFinex – of fraud for attempting to hide massive losses from hacks, in part by transferring funds between Tether and Bitfinex. I'd say Tether has been mired in scandal since the beginning. It's now available on many different chains such as Ethereum, BNB, Tron, and more.[2]

Stablecoins can be a trader's best friend because they allow you to park money on the sidelines that retains its value in the case of a crypto crash – whereas many crypto assets would quickly lose their value. Stablecoins allow you to reallocate that parked capital at a more opportune time when you can get more bang for your buck. To visualize this, imagine you bought one Bitcoin at $20K in 2020. When Bitcoin hit $60K in 2021, you decide to take profits and trade in your one Bitcoin for stablecoins – specifically, 60,000 USDC tokens valued at $60K. You now have three times what you started with. You keep your stablecoins and remain patient. In 2022, the value of Bitcoin went back down below $20K – at which point you decide it's the perfect time to redeploy your capital. (This is an example of "Buying the Dip" mentioned in the previous chapter.) And that, ladies and gentlemen, is how you could turn one Bitcoin into three with just a few simple trades and two years of patience.

An exception to the dollar-backed stablecoin is the algorithmic stablecoin, in which the value of the coin is tied to a crypto asset with an elastic supply. Coins are created or burned (destroyed) on a daily basis, dependent upon the market cap of the backing asset. Though that's generally how they work, the different chains have different rules and nuances that determine each coin's peg and "tokenomics."[3] These algorithmic stablecoins are experimental and I don't advocate trading these because we have yet to see one stand out as successful. You may have heard about the Terra Luna crash that rocked the crypto world in May 2022. The brainchild of Do Kwon, the founder of Terra Labs, the UST algorithmic stablecoin backed by Terra lost its peg by dramatically falling to zero from what seems to have been a coordinated liquidity attack attributed to hedge funds Blackrock and Citadel. Both funds denied involvement. In any case, this easily exploitable vulnerability in the supply and structure of Terra and UST's relationship ultimately brought down what was once considered the sixth best overall coin in crypto and the third-largest stablecoin, when it held $18 billion in market cap. Terra and UST investors lost virtually everything in a matter of days.[4] This is one reason why it's always important to create a balanced and diversified portfolio. If one coin could break your entire net worth, you're not diversified enough.

Some Trading Caveats

Trading isn't a super entertaining job outside of the exhilaration when you win (or the devastation when you lose). Looking at lines and bars on charts and making decisions based upon the narrative you glean from it isn't the sexiest way to spend your days – and your nights, since we're talking about the crypto market, which is 24/7. Trading can take up all your free time and can overwhelm you easily if you let it – especially if you take some big hits and start chasing after the lost portion of your bankroll. And keep this in mind: if you trade and invest as different strategies, *keep your portfolios separate*. Don't borrow from your investment portfolio if you lose all your trading funds. That probably means you need to take a long break, polish up on your skills, and determine whether trading is for you. Trading can quickly turn into gambling for many people.

Many attempt to become professional traders and, as with most things in life that require hard work, many people fail a lot before they see a breakthrough. The high rate of failure and the pressure of consistently producing profits, combined with the inevitable pain from losing streaks and big losses, can take traders to extremely vulnerable positions. The point is: trading is not for everyone. I've seen many traders achieve success and then lose everything in short periods of time. Trading can take an extreme toll on your physical, mental, and emotional well-being. Just like price charts, our emotions can go up and down at sometimes breakneck speeds. To traverse those challenges you need a plan.

Part of that plan includes ensuring you have a trusted person to talk to – a friend, family member, counselor, colleague, etc. – for the times when you're struggling. I would suggest someone other than your spouse because the last thing you want is both your emotional well-being and security being contingent upon your success in the market. For me personally, I chose to bear the weight of my trades and investments alone to free my wife of sharing that burden. She has no idea how to trade, so it would be unfair for me to have her worry about things she couldn't control. Maybe for some that approach would make sense, but it wasn't the right decision for my family.

The hard truth is that some people are not cut out for the stress many professional traders live with. When you have an open trade, you'll likely carry anxiety until you close it. If you go to sleep with an open trade, that sleep might not be restful: you may dream about it, have nightmares where you lose it, or wake up several times, sweating heavily, and check your phone to see how close you are to liquidation. These are real things that I've dealt with as an extremely profitable trader to the tune of seven figures. I decided to slow down my trading when I found myself constantly staring at my phone when I should have been spending time with my family. I couldn't enjoy anything while I had open trades and I lived constantly stressed. But there are some ways to reduce the stress:

- Close most of your trades before you go to sleep.
- Set stop losses and take profit targets while you sleep so you never have to wake up to liquidation. (More on this to come.)
- Significantly reduce your amount per trade and/or your leverage. Low leverage over long time frames is not much more stressful than simple spot trading.
- Maintain control over your trading. If trading starts to control your life, then take a break and regroup.

Trader Training

Okay, let's say you've considered everything you've read so far and you've decided to try your hand at becoming a serious trader. Here's some pointers to get you started.

Charting

Of particular value to both traders and investors are the financial charts that show the historical data of an asset. Studying these charts is fundamental to successful trading. "Charting" – also known as performing technical analysis – is much more than just math, geometry, and seeing patterns. Technical analysis is, at its core, finding patterns within chart-organized data to determine (or make an educated guess) the patterns' next direction or variation – in other words, if and how an asset's value will change next. Most of the time, a correct choice means you win a trade and an incorrect one means you lose a trade. But sometimes a chart can move so quickly that you could lose a trade even if you initially guessed correctly. Trading is not a 50/50 scenario – where you have an equal chance of winning or losing – like many would have you believe.

Trading calls for taking into consideration a variety of time horizons, all of which are much shorter than most investors prefer. The time horizons discussed next indicate that each bar (known as "candles" on a financial chart) represents an asset's movement during that denomination of time. Each candle on the hourly chart is one hour, while on the three-day chart each candle represents three days. Swing traders use long time frames like the weekly or monthly charts to take advantage of slow-grinding uptrends or downtrends.

Day traders will use the four-hour or eight-hour charts to determine shorter, compact moves of assets where they can usually make small, quick profits. There are even traders who make tons of trades in a day using the fifteen-minute, five-minute, or even one-minute charts. The shorter time horizon you trade, the more trades you'll have to make to remain profitable.

Trendspotting

The next step is to learn how to read the data – or, more specifically, how to make sense of the patterns in the data. How do you spot these patterns, read them, and identify the right moves these patterns reveal? Each pattern will have a corresponding set of data that trends one way or another. For example, let's look at long-term uptrends and downtrends. With an uptrend, a chart is showing the asset is consistently outperforming its recent history. Though this is not guaranteed – nothing is guaranteed, since it hasn't hit any level on the chart that has pushed price action back down. The inverse also is true. If an asset is on a downtrend and continually moving lower than it has in some time, then it is most likely going to continue down further. On the charts, we call this looking for higher highs to show strength or lower lows to show weakness and fear.

To really learn how to read the market you must look deeper. You're not tracking ambiguous lines on charts without meaning – markets are purely about human psychology. At their core, charts measure human psychology. They reveal the choices of humans who based financial decisions on price movement. Over time, if you tracked a particular person's trades, you'd see patterns representing that person's willingness to buy or sell an asset as a direct result of an asset going up or down in value at a particular pace.

Candlesticks and Pennants

A bullish pennant pattern breaks up most of the time, whereas a bearish pennant indicates a continuation of a down pattern. When you play the odds based on what the pattern is telling us about history, that means you should win most of the time when using that indicator.

Visit Investopedia.com for some really helpful info presented in bite-sized portions:

Candlesticks (#26 of 55 mini lessons in technical analysis): **https://www.investopedia.com/articles/active-trading/092315/5-most-powerful-candlestick-patterns.asp#toc-how-to-read-a-candlestick-pattern**
Pennant (#37 of 55 mini lessons in technical analysis): **https://www.investopedia.com/terms/p/pennant.asp**

Technical Analysis Indicators

A technical indicator is simply a measurement of market data. Any type of data associated with an asset can become an indicator: time, price, quantity, volatility, supply, etc., etc. Specific technical analysis indicators that I see many people using are the basic ones many chart websites like TradingView provide to integrate within your chart of choice. These different indexes or indicators provide info like trade volume (rises and falls), trade ranges, divergence (divergence is when there is a discrepancy between price action and a momentum indicator like volume), the strength and momentum of a trend, etc. To learn more about these individual indicators and how to use them, please visit the Frankie Candles YouTube Channel, where he details each indicator and shows examples.[5]

Also, visit Investopedia: **https://www.investopedia.com/top-7-technical-analysis-tools-4773275**

Types of Trading

A common phrase in trading is that the trend is your friend. Many traders find the best results when they "long" assets in uptrends and "short" assets in downtrends. "Longing an asset" means betting the price will go up during a certain period, and "shorting an asset" means betting an asset will go down over a certain time. I'm not talking about making a harmless prediction; I'm talking about placing a monetary bet that something or other will happen. That's right! You can make money when the value of an asset goes down. There are many ways to play the market and tons of investment types you can choose from. These consist of things like calls and puts, trading on margin, futures contracts, and more.

Spot Trading

The simplest way of trading is known as "spot trading," where you literally buy in to the market at one price or "spot" on the chart and then sell the asset at a different spot on the chart. If you bought low and sold high, you make a profit; if you bought high and sold low, you took a loss. You're either profiting or losing the difference between your buy and sell points. This is the most elemental form of trading assets and it's a concept you should be comfortable with before moving on to leveraged trading. Most financial institutions offer spot trading to their customers and you may already be familiar with this from trading stocks or commodities. But there is a saying in crypto that you must always remember and that is: "Crypto Never Sleeps." The cryptoverse is open

24/7/365. There are no bells. There are no holidays. Spot trading in crypto is a different animal entirely from your daddy's day trading.

Leveraged Trading

Earlier I said trading is not a 50/50 scenario, where you're equally likely to win or lose. Well, this is especially true of leveraged trading. Trading with derivatives can offer high rewards at a high risk. Leveraged trading is a type of derivatives investment where you make determinations of price direction with someone else's capital. If the price moves too quickly in the opposite direction of your entry point into the trade, you risk liquidation. "Liquidation" means if the price moves a certain percentage, you forfeit all the capital you had in the trade. This is also called "trading on margin" because a buffer exists between your trade and your liquidation point. We call this buffer your "margin."

Leveraged trading can also be known as margin trading. There is a slight difference between the two – determined by collateral you risk – but they're essentially the same concept. Your risk and liquidation points can range wildly based upon how much capital you borrow – or "leverage" – against the market. Borrowing more means your liquidation price will be closer to your entry point. This is called "high leverage." If you borrow two times your capital, it's called trading on 2 × leverage. In extreme cases, some exchanges will let you borrow up to 150 times your capital. But 150 × leverage is irresponsible and shouldn't exist. It's simply a marketing technique that exchanges use to excite people. Your margin between entry and liquidation is so razor thin that you could be liquidated in seconds.

WARNING: Leverage trading is not for beginners! You can lose everything in your account in one violent bitcoin move!

Here's a quick example of the difference between spot and leverage trading. Imagine you bought one Bitcoin on the spot market at $25,000. If the price of Bitcoin drops to $20,000, you still have one Bitcoin – you've simply lost $5,000 of its value as an "unrealized loss." But if you sold the Bitcoin at a loss, it would be a "realized loss" of $5,000. In the high-risk world of leveraged trading, you can place $25,000 at risk on a trade. If you choose to long Bitcoin (betting price will go up, remember!) on high leverage – let's say 10 × leverage – and the price goes down to $17,000, you'd get "margin called" and would face liquidation. This means your entire $25,000 would be gone even though the price of Bitcoin only dropped $8,000. But if instead the price went up to $30,000 on your 10 × leverage, you'd make a small fortune. The problem is, you're always going to win some and lose some. Continually using high leverage without mitigating risk through proper risk-management techniques will almost always eventually result in liquidation and suffering a 100% loss – literally all your money. Again: not for beginners.

Risk Management

Many believe leverage trading is pure gambling, but it doesn't have to be if you do it the right way – using proper risk-management tools, like these that follow:

Stop-Loss Orders: With a stop-loss order you establish in advance to sell if an asset drops to a certain point in order to minimize your loss. So, if the price of Bitcoin dropped dramatically, you'd have established in advance that you want to cut bait and take a small loss instead of hanging onto the hope it'll bounce back before it hits your liquidation point.

Diversify Your Trades: You should also never deploy all your trading capital into one trade because eventually you will go bust. Choose a percentage of your portfolio you are willing to lose on any single trade and you can absorb many losses without going broke.

Auto-Closing: Many exchanges also have features where you can set an amount of profit you are comfortable auto-closing your trade. You can set it so that anytime your trade is at a 20% profit, the contracts are closed, and you realize the earnings. Manually deciding when to close a trade high in profit is a very difficult decision to make. Sometimes using the automated tools helps you remove emotions.

Swim *with* the Whales: Follow the charts that have the biggest volume increases over a certain amount of time to make sure you are working with the big money, not against them.

Use Social Intelligence: Follow what is trending on social media for deep research. It keeps your head steady so you are not buying into community hype and also gives you clues on what is gaining momentum.

Nothing Ventured, Nothing Gained

The high-risk, high-reward nature of leveraged trading means that all it takes is one unbelievable win or one devastating loss to make or break your profitability. In crypto, leveraged trading is often vilified because many beginners try it and get "rekt," as we say. They quickly take one gigantic loss on the chin and write the whole thing off as a scam. But the reality is that those traders didn't take the time to study risk management, and instead treated trading like gambling. Blaming others for their financial loss helps them avoid taking personal responsibility for their own decisions; winning traders, however, take responsibility for even their losing trades, and use them as lessons to study and improve their skills.

Remember, this is only a high-level look at these tools; the complete advice breaking down leveraged trading has filled volumes. Beginners: *stay away* from leveraged trading until you've mastered spot trading. Then spend countless hours understanding this type of trading more in depth before jumping in. (Again, in the Appendix are resources – tips, tools of the trade, and research sites – to help you on your journey.)

The more resources and tools that traders acquire and keep at their fingertips, the more likely they are to be successful. Using a wide array of tools helps traders bring things into focus and choose not just good spots but the best spots. The most common website in crypto that enthusiasts use for charting, technical analysis (TA), and just overall price checking is TradingView.com. It allows users to create customized dashboards for viewing charts and an assortment of tools and indicators that easily integrate into any chart you choose. You can also buy custom indicators that integrate with your TradingView charts. I've used the infamous Market Cipher indicator created by my friend CryptoFace for well over three years now and have had great success with it. Market Cipher combines many different trading indicators into one easily digestible tool that helps you shortcut learning-class technical analysis. (There's a discount code for Market Cipher in the Resources section in the Appendix.) But note: reliable fast-tracking indicators are just excellent tools to add to your experience. *Nothing* replaces learning technical analysis in depth.

A few last pointers. Taking a balanced approach is almost always best. If you find yourself making extreme decisions, take a long break. Always remember: no financial loss is ever worth considering harming yourself. You must be determined and serious to make optimal decisions, but you also can't take everything too seriously. And be sure to maintain your mental health and manage to have a little fun.

CHAPTER 16

Non-Fungible Tokens (NFTs)

So far I've talked about a variety of crypto assets. And though many of these assets have had different properties or utilities, and served different use cases, all of them had one thing in common: fungibility. You might remember this term basically means that all the units in a particular asset are identical and interchangeable, like dollars or Bitcoin. Not all assets are fungible – some of them are unique. For example, stocks and real estate are common examples of nonfungible assets. A one-of-a-kind Bugatti or a Basquiat painting are nonfungible assets as well. In crypto, nonfungible assets are called "Non-Fungible Tokens," or NFTs. (We need to come up with a better name for this if we want to achieve mass adoption.) NFTs can be art, collectibles, membership passes, keys, digital identification, certifications, and more.

It's hard for many people to imagine how real-world assets can fit into the digital world of blockchain, but that's what they used to say about money too. Stock trading is already mostly digital on the surface, but under the hood the system runs on outdated technology, and could really benefit from a blockchain upgrade. As for the idea of reducing real estate and cars to tokens, it's not the actual items that get into the blockchain but the titles, deeds, and proof of ownership that are currently on paper and in the centralized servers of local, state, and federal governments. Ownership of these assets can be proven and verified on the blockchain far more efficiently than in the current system. There are some cases where the digital world can overlap with the physical as well. For example, we're now seeing virtual real estate in the form of metaverse land, and for the past several decades digital art has been some of the most visible art on the planet, from special effects in movies to billboards, advertisements, and item packaging.[1]

NFTs first started to get media attention in 2017, but I can remember this topic being discussed among early adopters for as long as I've been in crypto. In fact, back in the early days of the industry, there was hope that NFT functionality could be added on top of Bitcoin. There were even projects that were working to do just that. The most popular NFT project on Bitcoin was Colored Coins, and it was designed to bring representations of real-world assets on to the Bitcoin blockchain. The project was focused mostly on things like equities and commodities; art and collectibles were not part of the conversation.[2] Oddly enough, Vitalik Buterin, who would later make NFTs possible with Ethereum, helped write the whitepaper for Colored Coins. In the end, this project didn't work because Bitcoin's infrastructure didn't allow for this type of functionality – and the Bitcoin community was set on keeping the network the same, and not taking any risks with adding new features. As covered in Chapter 9, Vitalik went on to create a blockchain where these features and more were possible, and a vast majority of the development in NFTs moved over to Ethereum.

Historical NFTs

However, there is one art-based project that launched on Bitcoin as this transition was happening: the Rare Pepes. These NFTs were based on the Pepe the Frog meme and were launched using a platform called Counterparty, one of the numerous projects hoping to build NFT functionality into Bitcoin at the time. The Rare Pepes have come to hold value because they are what collectors deem "historical." Speculators believe that the oldest NFT collections will hold the most value simply because of their historical significance. The only problem here is that the goalpost keeps on moving as NFT archeologists continue to dig up new projects. Because many of these projects went unnoticed at the time they launched, they aren't a part of the historical record until they're later found by researchers. Old projects continue to be discovered – like Curio Cards, Ether Rocks, and Immortal Player Characters – and they typically explode in value once they're classified as historical.[3]

CryptoPunks

The grail of historical NFTs is without a doubt the CryptoPunks collection, which was first launched by Larva Labs in June of 2017. They don't look like much; they're simply a collection of 10,000 pixelated images that were randomly generated to have different styles and traits. This created a genre of crypto art known as "generative profile picture collections." When these avatar collections are launched, they're released through a minting process: buyers send ETH (Ethereum's native asset) to a smart contract in exchange for a randomly generated NFT image. To create these types of collections, artists will draw an assortment of traits – like skin color, hair color and style, or wearing glasses or goggles, or smoking a cigarette or pipe, etc. – and upload these images into a program that will randomly put these traits together when someone clicks the MINT button. The result is an army of unique characters with various combinations of traits – though there are a few NFTs that look almost identical. The CryptoPunks were the inspiration for the creation of a new token standard, ERC-721, which was designed specifically for nonfungible tokens – just like ERC-20 is the standard for fungible tokens. The collection sold out in less than a month and had decent trading volume on the secondary market, but the only people who were really paying attention were your hardcore blockchain hobbyists. Very few people had even heard of NFTs back then.[4]

CryptoKitties

The mainstream didn't start to take notice until a project called CryptoKitties, which launched just a few months after the CryptoPunks but managed to break through and go viral, grabbing headlines around the world. Crypto-Kitties were so popular that they actually clogged the Ethereum blockchain, becoming the most popular application on the network. They're similar to CryptoPunks in that each one is unique, unreproducible, and sellable. And given that there are likely hundreds of "cattributes or traits or gene expressions" to work with, their possible combinations run in the billions, according to Bryce Bladon, one of the CryptoKitties founding team members. But they also can be bred, which means that their supply is essentially unlimited. (It took less than a year before the one-millionth CryptoKitty was born in September 2018.) Their popularity slowed down the network, and their prolificacy flooded the market and diluted the supply, reducing the value of the collection as a whole – despite the fact that CryptoKitties have huge historical significance. They also launched at the peak of the bull market, so it was hard to maintain traction when most of the retail investors had left the industry.[5]

The Next Generation

NFTs went into hibernation during the crypto winter of 2018, but teams continued to build, and a small group of hobbyists continued to pay attention. The team behind CryptoKitties, Dapper Labs, was able to leverage their reputation to raise $39 million from venture capitalists to build their own blockchain. Since CryptoKitties had tested the limits of what Ethereum could handle, the Dapper Labs team wanted to build a blockchain made specifically for NFTs to create a better user experience. In order to achieve this level of scale this quickly, the blockchain would need to be more centralized – but that was a trade-off the Dapper Labs team was willing to take. Their blockchain was called Flow.

NBA Topshot

Dapper Labs's first big project was called NBA Topshot. As the name implies, these are collectible professional basketball NFTs. They are essentially sports trading cards that offer fans short clips of memorable games called "moments." Some of these "moments" have sold for as much as $200,000. Think of them as collectible trading cards for the digital age, complete with video highlights. NBA Top Shot brought in over $1 billion in less than two years for Dapper Labs, but it suffered from the same problems as their previous project CryptoKitties. The supply of Top Shot's "moments" grew way too fast for the demand, and the prices crashed.[6]

Art Blocks

Art Blocks, a popular generative art project, suffered a similar fate. Generative Art is essentially art that was generated by a computer. The artist or coder gives the computer certain inputs – and the artist has no idea how the final product will look – and the computer spits out art. It doesn't seem like much, but it takes a lot of skill to have these things turn out well, and there can be a special type of beauty in work that was created by a program. A lot of high-value collections came out of the Art Blocks project, including the Fidenza collection, some pieces of which sold for over $3 million at their peak.[7] Though Fidenza and other grail Art Blocks collections have retained their value over time, most of the project's other collections have suffered major price declines because multiple weekly drops diluted the supply.

Beeple

In 2020 and 2021, digital artists began experimenting with NFTs and finding that they could monetize their work better than ever before. Mike Winkelmann, an artist who goes by Beeple, was one of the biggest success stories from this new class of NFT users. Beeple was among a growing group of artists who began minting their work on the Ethereum blockchain and selling it to their social media followers. Before diving into NFTs, Beeple had amassed a large following for his strange, graphic, and sometimes gruesome works of art, which were often shared widely across the internet. Beeple has been prolific throughout his career, posting a new design on his social media every day for 15 years – regardless of how he was feeling or what he had going on at the time – and he did it entirely for free, surviving mostly on commission work that came from his viral reputation. After making a name for himself with NFTs, Beeple would go on to sell a collection of these pieces on March 11, 2021, for over $69 million at the prestigious Christie's auction house.[8]

Drift

There were also photographers who began selling their work as NFTs, which allowed them to build communities around their work. One standout is Isaac Wright, or Drift, who is sometimes also known as "driftershoots" due to his website and Twitter handle. Drift is an Army veteran with PTSD who keeps his mind at peace by climbing the tallest buildings in different cities and taking incredible photos and videos of the climb and the skyline. In 2021, Drift became the subject of a manhunt when authorities were convinced he was some sort of terrorist. Unbeknownst to him, he was wanted for various crimes, including "unlawfully entering" secure areas (of tall buildings) in various cities across the country. A highway was shut down in Arizona, with 20 police officers, dogs, and helicopters hunting down a guy who was just taking pictures, and didn't even realize what was happening. The NFT community rallied to his defense and made the case national news, which gave him the benefit of public support in court.[9] Drift continues to climb and create his art, which is consistently some of the most high-value photography in the space.

Bored Ape Yacht Club

With so many artists and speculators making a lot of ETH with NFTs, they started looking for creative ways to flaunt their success and signal that they were a part of the NFT community. This is when CryptoPunks made their grand resurgence. Since their launch in 2017, the CryptoPunk collection has had a small but enthusiastic community, many of whom were Ethereum developers who used punks as their profile picture. After the NFT boom, CryptoPunks became a hot commodity, and the ultimate symbol of success in crypto. The popularity of CryptoPunks inspired a new wave of profile picture projects intended to reach everyone who was priced out of the CryptoPunks. The best-executed profile picture collection to launch after the CryptoPunks was Bored Ape Yacht Club, whose creator, Yuga Labs, cast the collection as the scrappy underdogs fighting for a seat at the CryptoPunk table. Yuga Labs also gave Bored Ape holders something not offered by anyone else: licensing rights to the Apes artwork they owned, including using their character as the mascot for their business or in any form of media. Yuga Labs also had a very smart and aggressive strategy of using celebrities to promote their brand. It's not entirely clear how they onboarded dozens of high-profile celebrities so quickly, but a law firm called Scott+Scott filed a suit claiming that many of these endorsements were paid and undisclosed. Whether the growth was organic or not, the Bored Ape Yacht Club became a viral phenomenon in a very short amount of time. Over the course of just a few months, celebs like Ben Simmons, Eminem, Jimmy Fallon, Justin Bieber, Kevin Hart, Lil Baby, Madonna, Paris Hilton, Post Malone, Snoop Dogg, and Steph Curry had switched their profile photos to Bored Apes. All of this celebrity attention made the Bored Ape Yacht Club one of the most talked about developments of 2021, both inside and outside crypto. Yuga Labs continued to provide value to its community in the form of airdrops and new collections. Less than a year after launching BAYC, Yuga Labs bought the IP rights to the CryptoPunks from Larva Labs – at which point they granted licensing rights to the holders of all CryptoPunks NFTs.[10]

The Next-Next Generation

Traditional markets and crypto are both heavily influenced by whales, and the NFT market is no different. Whales will mint hundreds of NFTs of many of the top collections, then use their significant portion of the entire supply to control the price and market sentiment. Sometimes these whales can be benevolent: Their purchase invigorates the market, and then they profit from selling slowly over time without dumping on the community. Pranksy, one of the richest NFT collectors in the space, has been partly credited with maintaining the floor price of Bored Ape Yacht Club in its early months before it caught on, because they owned so much of the collection and refused to sell. However, Pranksy also famously sold much of their Bored Ape collection below 10 ETH – which is far lower than the all-time high or average price range. This is an example of how whales often capture early gains and large profits on the way up, leaving them with only a few NFTs when the prices really start to run. There are dozens of different "legendary" wallets owned by whales like Pranksy that are tracked and followed by a variety of different services like Nansen, for example. Through these applications, traders are able to watch what all of the big holders are buying. The fact that people follow their trades so closely gives these whales even more control over the markets. This is really only possible because the space is so new; as these markets mature and grow, they will be too big for whales to control. But institutions can always pose this kind of threat, in pretty much every market.[11]

It's important to note that we're still at the first stage of this technology. Art and collectibles are essentially a proof-of-concept for NFTs, a use case that shows what this technology is capable of while giving developers opportunities to experiment. As the space continues to grow, I predict that art and collectibles will make up a smaller and smaller percentage of total NFT activity. Digital art and collectibles will still continue to trade and be popular among a core group of hobbyists, but NFTs will also be used for everyday functions in the form of property deeds, diplomas or certifications, concert tickets, passports, and more.

Though we're still a few years away from this level of NFT adoption, the technology will start to go mainstream much sooner – and more than likely through video games. Gaming is a perfect medium for NFTs, because there are already in-game assets and virtual currencies built into the mechanics of some games. Some of the most popular multiplayer games of all time – like Warcraft, Counterstrike, and Everquest – all had virtual assets that ended up being worth real-world money. For example, popular items like weapons, clothes, pets, and cosmetic customizations enabled players to personalize their gaming experience. Unfortunately, these secondary markets were typically not approved by the game publishers, so many were shut down. But when crypto assets with real value are encouraged, players can earn an income with their time in the game in a model known as "play to earn" or P2E. We're seeing the first attempts at this model play out now, giving us a sense of how this could work.[12]

Gamers have expressed strong resistance to NFT by being some of the most vocal critics of the technology. But why? Most recent estimates suggest that 65% of people in the United States play video games, and you'd think they'd be excited for an opportunity to make some side money with one of their hobbies. Well, it turns out that gaming companies have a bad reputation for squeezing every last penny out of players with aggressive microtransactions and extra fees. With companies in the gaming industry having this type of track record, it's understandable that people are suspicious about the new financial features these companies are starting to roll out. There are also some hard-core gamers out there who hate anything to do with crypto because miners have made their graphics processing unit (GPU) – which enables high-resolution screen imagery – more expensive and difficult to find.[13] But I predict that these objections will be dropped once gamers can earn money and valuable assets for playing their favorite games. This will be the "killer app" for NFTs that will demonstrate why this technology is here to stay.

Ticketing will be another early use case that will help bring NFTs to the masses, in part because NFT tickets for concerts, sports, and other events would solve the perennial challenges of counterfeits and scalpers. The fact that NFT ownership could be verified on a blockchain would prevent counterfeits, and smart contracts would allow the ticketing company to prevent resale altogether – or ensure they got a cut every time a ticket is resold. Large festivals like Coachella have already started to experiment with NFT tickets, and some artists are even using NFTs to create exclusive fan clubs for their biggest supporters. In 2022, Method Man treated holders of his "Mefaverse" NFT to a private intimate show at the iconic Sotheby's art auction house, complete with staff in tuxedos serving free food and champagne. NFTs could infiltrate the music industry in various ways, even acting as a medium for the music itself. Artists can release NFTs of their songs so their large base of fans can listen for free, but a small group of special fans can actually pay for the bragging rights of owning the song, which could also entitle them to a percentage of the royalties in some cases. This is a good deal for the artists because they'd be giving a small percentage of their earnings to their fans – instead of a large percentage of their earnings to their record companies, as they currently do. NFT music platforms like Royal are seeking to do just that.[14] With these kinds of use cases serving as testing grounds, the technology will mature to the point that people will readily use NFTs to access their medical records, birth certificates, and property deeds.

CHAPTER 17

Web3 and the Metaverse

The internet has gone through a few different stages in its development since reaching mainstream markets in the 1990s. It started with simple web pages that displayed text, photos, and sometimes videos. Designing web pages required some level of technical skill, but it was something that anyone could try. This is how the internet was for over a decade, with a small number of highly skilled content creators and a much larger number of internet consumers. Researchers will often call this the "Web 1.0" era of the internet. Over the years, it slowly became easier to create content online. Social media platforms like MySpace, Facebook, Twitter, and YouTube allowed anyone to distribute their own content on the internet, even if they didn't know how to code or build a website. Around the time these platforms were rising to prominence, there was a series of tech conferences called the Web 2.0 Summits, which were hosted by the tech publisher O'Reilly Media. These summits and the Web 2.0 branding were intended to illustrate how the internet was going through an important transformation.[1]

The term "Web 2.0" was first coined in 1999 by the author and programmer Darcy DiNucci, but it didn't really catch on until the first O'Reilly Web 2.0 Summit in 2004. After the first summit, "Web 2.0" quickly caught on as a popular way to describe the new social media era of the internet. Soon enough social media was just a regular part of life and it no longer needed a catchy buzzword to help people understand what it was. And though individual internet users have been given incredible power by social media, these platforms are far from perfect. Their algorithms intentionally create division in society just to keep us arguing on their apps as much as possible. And instead of focusing their moderation policies on the scammers ruining the lives of many of their users, they engage in petty censorship to keep their corporate advertisers happy, an issue that seems baked into the Web 2.0 business model of "surveillance capitalism."[2]

The internet has reached a plateau and needs a fresh injection. We need a new business model, one where the power is more evenly distributed, and where the users have a financial stake in the platform. As you may have gathered by now, this is one of the core values in Web 3.0.

Ethereum cofounder Gavin Wood is credited with coining the term "Web 3.0" in 2014 when Ethereum was just getting started. The term didn't really catch on at the time because there weren't any blockchain applications that looked anything like web applications yet, and people were already overwhelmed with new terms like "blockchain" and "cryptocurrency." And, in early 2019, Crystal Stranger, CEO of PeaCounts, wrote in *Cryptoweek* how "much of the hatred of blockchain today stems from cryptocurrencies losing 80–95% of their value during [2018] amidst U.S. Securities and Exchange investigations and billionaires tearing the markets apart through the Bitcoin Cash hashwar."[3] Unfortunately, it seems to me that media coverage of the crypto industry led to widespread confusion among the public about what this technology is and what it can achieve. The media talks a lot about the speculation, along with the scams and crimes, but I rarely hear them talk about the underlying technology. The journalists are not to blame for this, though; overnight successes and multimillion-dollar hacks are more interesting to read about than the nuts and bolts of a weird new technology. But this dynamic has definitely created some optics problems for the industry; it's difficult to help people understand this new and complex technology if the word "crypto" conjures up only visions of a Dogecoin millionaire or a teenager with a Lambo – and they just tune out.

This is how "Web 3.0" became a useful tool for winning the PR war of words. The terminology has none of the negative baggage associated with "crypto" and it implies that this developing technology is as significant as the social media revolution. Also, somewhere along the way the ".0" was dropped from "Web 3.0," and industry insiders started calling it a fresher and hipper "Web3." And, interestingly, now that we have Web3, companies that weren't technically a part of the social media revolution, such as Amazon and Google, are now considered Web2 companies. So the meaning (and proper name) of "Web 2.0" have changed a bit from what they were 10 years ago; now it's called Web2, and it is used to describe established internet applications that don't use blockchain.

Web3 is more than just a gimmick or a buzzword, though; it represents an entirely different philosophy and infrastructure for the internet. Web3 is defined by decentralization, censorship resistance, and user ownership of platforms, which sets this vision apart from the internet that we use today.

Starting with user ownership: Decentralized Autonomous Organizations, or DAOs, make it possible for platforms to be owned and controlled by their users, and most Web3 platforms will be governed by DAOs. In Chapter 9 I described DAOs as cooperatives or "co-ops" that are powered by blockchain technology. This description highlights how DAOs are more horizontal in organizational structure – with power distributed across a wide network of individuals – instead of centralized with one figurehead. This governance model is the main thing that separates Web2 from Web3. Think about what Facebook would be like if all of the users were airdropped company stock that allowed them to vote on the direction of the company, with the total weight of the users being much heavier than the single vote of Mark Zuckerberg or the board of directors. This is the model that is being adopted for Web3, and we're already starting to see some early experiments with this concept. For example, Audius is a music-streaming platform that pitches itself as a decentralized Spotify. Popular streaming platforms like Spotify are notorious for underpaying musicians – while the owners of the company bring in billions. Audius is promising to cut out the intermediary and connect musicians directly with their fans so they can earn a higher percentage of the streaming revenue.[4] This same logic can be applied to applications like Uber, AirBnb, or any other service that uses a centralized platform to facilitate a trade of goods or services.

Web3 is still a very new concept, and the ecosystem of applications is still slowly materializing. Today, Web3 consists mostly of NFT and crypto gaming communities, but I believe it will eventually consume the whole internet just like Web2 did. The Web3 philosophy has stirred up a ton of excitement – but not everyone is sold. For example, Jack Dorsey, founder of Square and Twitter, has been especially critical of Web3 – but his criticisms should be taken with a grain of salt, considering that he's a Bitcoin maximalist who attacks everything in crypto that isn't Bitcoin. In a 2021 Tweet, Dorsey said, "You don't own 'web3.' The VCs and their LPs do. It will never escape their incentives. It's ultimately a centralized entity with a different label. Know what you're getting into."[5]

Some of the concerns raised about the current state of Web3 are legitimate. Not much has been built yet, and many of the projects that have launched so far have been heavily controlled by VCs who own a large percentage of the token supply. Fortunately, this increasing influence from VCs is something that can be solved by the industry. Instead of depending on a few VCs, crypto projects could crowdfund their seed money using Initial Coin Offerings (ICOs) to kickstart their projects. However, regulators in many jurisdictions – including the States – have not made it easy for these projects to raise funds directly from retail investors. In order to make early-stage investments in companies or ventures that aren't registered and regulated as securities, you need to be an "accredited investor" – according to the definition the SEC specifies in Rule 501 of Regulation D – which lists a few requirements. Until recently, one had to earn at least $200,000 per year or have a net worth exceeding $1 million. (In August 2020, the SEC widened its guidance to include registered brokers and investment advisors.) According to the SEC's own estimates, only 13% of the US population can qualify as an accredited investor. Apparently the premise of these guidelines is that accredited investors are "deemed financially sophisticated enough to bear the risks" of this kind of investing[6] – but I can't help but think that this is just another example of how those born with money are set up to succeed, leaving the rest of us with yet another barrier to entry.

This is why crypto is so promising: in addition to offering a decentralized store of value and medium of exchange, crypto also promises to decentralize investing by allowing anyone with an internet connection to make an early-stage investment in a project – with basically no barrier to entry aside from capital. As you may remember, these ICOs were the first major use case for Ethereum. With smart contracts on Ethereum, teams were able to easily launch tokens and crowdfund their projects with small contributions from retail investors around the world. This entirely bypassed accredited investor laws and allowed the average person to get good entry points on promising projects regardless of how much money they had in the bank. As a result, a lot of people who never had the opportunity to build wealth were able to get rich very fast. Of course, a lot of people lost money too – but that happens in the traditional stock market as well.

Unfortunately, the SEC has taken the position that pretty much every token that launched as an ICO is an unregistered security, which technically means that many of the initial investments were illegal – because they weren't made by so-called accredited investors. After the SEC started cracking down on projects for selling tokens to people who weren't accredited investors, teams have been pushed right back into the arms of the VCs, and retail investors have suffered as a result.[7] Now the crypto markets are starting to look a lot more like the traditional markets, where VCs get in early and then dump on us when we try to buy a token the first day it's listed on an exchange. VCs also have an oversized share of platform governance in this arrangement, as there is a system where one token = one vote in the governance process. This framework is often called "Token Based Voting" or "Token Governance." Right now it appears that the only way to solve this problem and create a true level playing field for investors is to get rid of the accredited investor rule and lower the barrier to entry for the working class. Fortunately, there are numerous efforts underway to change these laws, including one that the Bitsquad is currently working to advance in the state of California, California Senate Joint Resolution 16: Financial services: investor certification examination process. This resolution would urge the US Congress to replace the current accredited investor standards with a free online investor certification test. We are joining other efforts too, including H.R.4753: The Accredited Investor Self-Certification Act, which was introduced to Congress in 2021.[8]

I think some of the criticisms of token-based voting in Web3 are also fair, but this is another problem that the industry is taking very seriously. Vitalik Buterin regularly speaks out against the token-voting model, and different teams are starting to take new approaches that make it more difficult for whales to control the governance of their platforms. Optimism and Gitcoin are great examples of this. The Optimism network launched with a unique governance system that involves multiple branches, similar to what you would find in a parliamentary system, while Gitcoin uses a method called "quadratic funding," where the platform is able to match the donations of smaller contributors. But it's unfair to paint the Web3 ecosystem with a broad brush, judging it by its worst participants – a tactic I've seen maximalists use to dismiss developments happening on other blockchains.[9] Besides, even if all of the criticisms of Web3 were entirely accurate, it would still be a far better system than we see in Web2.

The Metaverse

Web3 will end up providing the infrastructure for the next step in the evolution of the internet: the Metaverse. The Metaverse is a concept that has been imagined by technologists and science fiction authors for decades, but it still doesn't have a clear and agreed-upon definition. Most people understand the Metaverse as a digital world that people connect to using virtual reality (VR), but it goes much deeper than that, and VR isn't always a requirement either. In its most basic form, a metaverse is a digital space that people from all over the world can tap into at the same time and share the same experience. A proper metaverse will also have its own culture and economy that are totally independent from the outside world. It's the culture and the economy that ultimately set the metaverse apart from other games or shared online experiences.

Launching in 2000, Habbo Hotel was one of the first major metaverses on the internet. In the pixelated Habbo universe, users – mostly teens and young adults – could create avatars styled to their liking and design their own rooms. They might also be tasked with taking care of virtual pets and completing various quests. For a few years Habbo Hotel developed a cult following, which rose to roughly 9 million users at its peak in 2012 before running into some trouble that's too much to go into here (but check out the *TechCrunch* article in the citation to follow). It's still in action today, though renamed just Habbo. At its 20-year anniversary it was reported as having 316 million registered avatars and 500 million rooms.[10]

Another early virtual world to gain mainstream notoriety was Second Life, which is also still operational today. Second Life initially launched in 2003 and peaked around 2013 with about one million regular users. Second Life also had its own virtual currency, the Linden Dollar, which could be exchanged for fiat currency. Second Life was geared more toward adults, and major corporations like Amazon, Cisco, and IBM used the platform to bring workers together, in both small meetings and large conferences. It was a revolutionary concept that seemed to have the potential to change the future of work, but these hopes vanished as soon as the trend fizzled out.[11] There were also several online games during this era that became virtual worlds for their users, even developing in-game economies by accident in some cases. A few great examples of this were World of Warcraft, Eve Online, and Everquest.

Online multiplayer games were some of the most popular virtual worlds, and many of them had the same characteristics of a metaverse, including in-game economies. This was especially true for MMOGs (Massively Multiplayer Online Games). However, there were a ton of limitations with these economies because they were often changed by the centralized companies that published the games. Unauthorized economies were also easy for these companies to eliminate or sanction. This frustrated many players, including a young Vitalik Buterin, who in 2010 quit playing World of Warcraft after the company behind the game made the devastating decision of "nerfing" (weakening) his favorite spell. This transgression began Buterin's long battle against centralization. Buterin once wrote that he cried himself to sleep over the incident and said, "On that day I realized what horrors centralized services can bring."[12] This is the nerdiest thing I've ever heard of, but it needed to be in this book. You're welcome.

If you aren't a gamer you might have a hard time wrapping your mind around why this was such a tragic event, but think about how dangerous this type of power could be if a significant portion of our everyday lives moves into the metaverse. If we're working, banking, socializing, and engaging in activism in the metaverse, we wouldn't want someone to have the power to shut down our voice or freeze our account at will, as we see today in Web2.

The Metaverse might seem like a strange topic in a book about crypto but, as mentioned, the Metaverse will be a fundamental part of Web3. If a virtual world doesn't have an open economy that you can be a part of, it's basically a virtual dictatorship, where all of the power and control flows to a single entity. People may be willing to accept that in Web2, but that's because, in my opinion, they don't know any better – and they don't know better because they literally don't see any viable alternatives. When people have access to platforms where they can earn money for playing games or sharing their content, they will have no interest in building some nerd king's fortune on a closed platform. That doesn't mean that the nerd kings won't try; Mark Zuckerberg has already dedicated billions to building a Facebook metaverse, in a desperate attempt to recapture some of the younger Facebook users that have been slipping away in recent years. Despite the massive user base of Facebook and the billions of dollars in capital, the Zuckerverse will probably fail because it will be boring and uninspiring compared to its open and decentralized counterparts where users can take ownership of the platforms. We already know that the Facebook "Social Metaverse" will be a closed system, but even this system will still incorporate tokens and NFTs into its infrastructure on some level. Zuckerberg wants everyone to think that Facebook is the Metaverse, which is why in October 2021 he literally changed the name of the company to Meta.[13] When Zuckerberg did that he was effectively planting his flag in a space that others have already been building in for decades.

Not a New Idea

The term "Metaverse" was first introduced by Neal Stephenson, author of the 1992 novel *Snow Crash*, which describes a future where people spend most of their time in a digital world controlled by corporate mobsters. In the story, it was normal to work and hang out with your friends in the metaverse, and the things that took place there had a huge impact on the outside world. This was by no means a positive future, though; this was a dystopian novel, so it paints a pretty bleak picture of what the metaverse would be like. From my experience, most futuristic stories about digital worlds are not optimistic, with most rooted in fears that an evil corporation will have total control of the metaverse and, ultimately, total control of humanity. These are legitimate concerns considering what we have seen from Facebook, but this dystopian future is not guaranteed. Facebook's biggest competition in this race is the entirety of the Web3 ecosystem, which has the power to create a much better future than the one that Zuckerberg is offering. A free and open metaverse enabled by crypto and blockchain technology could actually be a positive thing that brings new opportunities to people all over the world. The crypto builders have had a head start as well, as many projects had been in development for several years when Facebook's metaverse ambitions began. There are even some crypto metaverse projects that are already working as a beta version at the time of this writing.

The State of the Metaverse

The most popular and furthest along in development is a project called The Sandbox, a large pixelated world that is sectioned off into small pieces of land. Each piece of land in The Sandbox is represented by an NFT that can be bought and sold on secondary markets. The intellectual property of the game is owned by Animoca Brands, which is one of the most powerful companies behind the crypto industries' push into the Metaverse. Animoca managed to acquire rights to The Sandbox after buying out its developer Pixowl for just under $5 million. In total, Animoca Brands has a portfolio of over 150 different blockchain projects, and the list of partners seems to be growing every day.[14]

Animoca's portfolio also includes many projects that would be considered competitors to The Sandbox, including Decentraland and The Otherside. Decentraland is similar to The Sandbox, but whereas The Sandbox has more options for gaming, collecting, and exploring, Decentraland currently just offers a shared virtual space with a few casinos. But Decentraland has some very powerful backers, including Digital Currency Group,[15] so it's continued to stay in the conversation and remain among the top metaverse projects.

Even though Otherside is one of the most recent entrants to the race, it's already a serious contender. Otherside is the Bored Ape Yacht Club metaverse, and everything that this community is involved with seems to be a success. Yuga Labs is also incredibly well funded and has hired an experienced team to build out their virtual world.[16] Their community is also one of the strongest in crypto, so they're going to keep everyone talking about Otherside.

As noted, virtual reality is just one aspect of the metaverse, and that's the angle that Facebook has chosen to pursue – which makes sense considering that they own the VR company Oculus. But most of these crypto metaverse projects are not heavily focused on virtual reality, although some may offer it as an additional option. Instead, they allow users to participate in the game with a relatively basic computer setup. People are also free to participate in the speculation by buying and selling land or other NFTs. Blockchain-based metaverses tend to be more focused on building robust cultures and economies, while allowing for some level of user ownership or profit-sharing. Building the cultural and economic infrastructure first will probably be the winning strategy, in part because virtual reality is still several years away from mainstream adoption, and we are living in a time when people are in desperate need of a side hustle and a place to belong. And though virtual reality headsets have come a long way, they're still clunky and buggy, and a significant number of users still experience motion sickness, even during shorter sessions. Longer sessions are still not recommended – some recommend a 15-minute break after 30 minutes – so spending a full work day plugged into VR goggles probably won't be happening any time soon.[17] However, sitting in front of your computer at home and completing different tasks for various apps in exchange for crypto seems far more realistic at this point. The fully immersive VR version of the metaverse will happen in the coming decades, but we're going to need to scale up to that, just as we've done with every other technological advancement. Aside from a few exceptions, the next generation of full-scale metaverses will likely be experienced through a keyboard and a computer screen. Slowly, a hybrid model will develop where some people use VR headsets and others don't. Some virtual worlds may become exclusive and closed off to anyone who doesn't have the equipment, but most projects will want to have as many players in their metaverse as possible – and it will be quite a while before a VR headset is in every home, especially in the developing world.

In the past few years, we've seen the beginning stages of this primitive metaverse starting to emerge. Remote work has become more common and young people are starting to take an entirely different view of work. Nowadays, kids are hoping to grow up to become influencers and YouTube stars – and for many of them, finding their niche to create content online is a better option than working for a job that may become obsolete or outsourced to robots within a few years. We'll probably have a very rough transitional period, but this seems to be the direction that the economy is headed. Content creation won't be the only way to make a buck in the metaverse; I believe that gaming will also be a core component of the metaverse economy. The play-to-earn model of gaming discussed in the previous chapter on NFTs will increasingly fill gaps in the global economy as more sectors of the workforce are automated. We've already seen play-to-earn gaming play a significant role in the economies of developing countries. For roughly a year, a simple play-to-earn game called Axie Infinity was paying out enough tokens that some players in the Philippines were making more money in the game than they were at their day jobs. Roughly 40% of Axie Infinity's player base lives in the Philippines, but it's also very popular in places like Thailand, Indonesia, Venezuela, and Malaysia.[18] Though this early attempt didn't last, the idea stuck. I predict that thousands of other gaming experiments will launch over the next several years, each with their own unique mechanics and tokenomics. Many of these projects will fail, but the few that succeed could change the world, and possibly employ millions of people.

Other aspects of our life that are currently shifting into Zoom calls will eventually transition into the metaverse. Things like business meetings, college courses, or even court cases could be conducted in the metaverse – and to some extent they already are, now that Zoom and other virtual meeting services have become so popular.[19]

The technologies that make the metaverse possible are just tools, and they can be used responsibly or they can be misused. There's no doubt that plenty of people will use these tools too much, and powerful people will try to use them as tools for control. But ideally most of us can find a balance that allows us to take advantage of the opportunities that this new technology offers without letting the negative aspects of it impact us too much. This is a balance that we're already learning to manage with smartphones and social media. These new devices and platforms have introduced new challenges to society, and they definitely have some negative externalities, such as fueling depression in young people and deepening our political divide.[20] But they've also empowered billions of people all over the world by providing tools for finding work, making friends, and just making life easier. Technology is often a double-edged sword that can be used for both creation and destruction, and the metaverse will be no different.

CHAPTER 18

Crypto FUD

Fear, Doubt, and Uncertainty

E very new era of technological innovation faces extreme ridicule and scrutiny because humans fear change on a very deep level. We become comfortable in our environments and routines, and can feel threatened by new technologies that have the potential to disrupt our habits, our careers, and our way of life. These fears are widespread – even in our technological age of constant innovation. When American homes first started plugging into the internet in the mid-1990s, there was a lot of media coverage focused on stock price speculation and FUD – otherwise known as Fear, Uncertainty, and Doubt. As we covered in Chapter 17, these are the kind of stories that get attention, and it wasn't any different back then. Most of the news coverage I remember from those days were stories about nerds getting rich or creeps corrupting children in chat rooms. It seemed like a lot of people developed an idea that this new technology was weird, dangerous, and possibly a scam. There were also articles warning about the disastrous environmental impact that would be brought on by basic activity on the internet like e-commerce. At best, the internet was seen as a novelty that had no chance of disrupting the long-established brick-and-mortar stores that dominated the economy.[1] However, there was an enthusiastic group of believers who could tell that the internet would have a profound impact on the world, and, eventually, of course, they were proven right.

A similar atmosphere of FUD has surrounded the crypto industry since its inception, and many of the talking points have been the same. The original crypto FUD revolved around concerns about Bitcoin and crime. Considering that Bitcoin's original claim to fame was undermining the government with an online drug marketplace, it's hard to blame people for associating crypto with crime back in the early days. In the years since the fall of Silk Road, blockchain technology has developed to support a wide variety of different use cases, which now represents the vast majority of the activity in the crypto market. Nowadays, crime represents an extremely small percentage of the activity that takes place on Bitcoin and other blockchain networks. According to data from Chainalysis, the top company working to monitor blockchains for law enforcement and other government agencies, illicit activity accounted for only .15% of all blockchain transactions in 2021. That's a little more than a tenth of 1%. To be fair, there is still a ton of crime taking place on the blockchain, mostly with hacks, scams, and stolen funds. Despite accounting for much less than 1% of total transactions, crypto crime still hit an all-time high in 2021, with illicit addresses receiving $14 billion, up nearly double from $7.8 billion in 2020.[2]

It's important to put these figures into context, though. Crime happens everywhere, and the amount of criminal activity that is facilitated by fiat is many magnitudes larger than we see with crypto. This is largely because cash is much more widely used, but it's also harder to trace and easier to launder than crypto. No source publishes accurate annual reports on how much cash is changing hands between criminals as Chainalysis does with crypto. As we will explore in the next chapter, hackers and scammers are definitely a concern on blockchain networks – but scammers have been around forever, using any method they can to separate people from their hard-earned money.

Outside of scams and hacks, what constitutes a "crime" often varies in different countries and jurisdictions. Some governments are criminal themselves[3] – in which case the privacy that crypto offers gives citizens freedom from tyranny. It seems to me that many governments are extremely suspicious of the crypto industry because it gives citizens more autonomy and self-sovereignty, taking away some of the governments' ability to surveil and control the population. To some extent, this control gives governments a better handle on crime, but it comes at the cost of our freedom. But taking this control away from the government does not put power in the hands of criminals – it puts power in the hands of the average person. As a side effect, criminals have another tool at their disposal – but so do the police, who can use the blockchain just like the criminals do.

The Long Arm of the Law

The tension between the crypto industry and the governments of the world has been a constant source of FUD over the years as well. Many of the mainstream institutional investors and the talking heads on TV have predicted that governments would eventually rein in crypto before it became too much of a threat – for example, Ray Dalio, a legendary investor and founder of Bridge Associates, has predicted on numerous occasions that the government will try to ban Bitcoin – despite being a supporter in the technology himself. And Robert Kiyosaki, the author of *Rich Dad Poor Dad*, has gone so far as to predict that the government will seize all crypto assets. But these pundits were putting too much faith in the system that gave them their fortunes.[4] Bitcoin in particular has proven time and again that it's pretty much unstoppable, even from nation-state-level attacks and bans. For years, there was FUD circulating in the media that China was going to ban crypto at any moment. These fear campaigns were recycled once or twice every year, usually referring to nothing more than a small tightening of regulations. After a while many of us thought that a ban of crypto would never happen in China, but the CCP called our bluff in September 2021 with a widespread ban of Bitcoin trading and mining across the country. The China ban did end up happening but it was still FUD – because it was nowhere near as catastrophic as had initially been predicted. The Bitcoin network remained strong during the ban, despite some price volatility, which is not unusual for these markets anyway. One effect was that the hashrate (mining power) migrated away from China and into other countries – which helped to decentralize mining away from China, which held a significant portion of the hashrate at the time. The ban wasn't even entirely effective in China, as citizens are still able to access crypto services using VPNs.[5]

In addition to FUD about crypto bans, there's also plenty of FUD about crypto regulation. It's entirely rational to have fears about government regulators because of issues like regulatory capture, which we covered in Chapter 7. But just as we have seen with bans, I predict that the actual results of crypto regulation will be far less catastrophic than many traders imagine. There may be some short-term negative impacts from regulation, and there may be some cases where regulators attempt to protect the legacy banking system by stalling certain aspects of the industry. But, overall, I believe that regulation will help mainstream this technology and bring trillions of dollars into the crypto markets. Regulation will change the industry in ways that will make many cypherpunks and crypto anarchists cringe – but they'll be cringing all the way to the bank, because it will make the industry more successful. Just in the past few years, as lobbying dollars start to flow in from the industry, opinions about crypto among politicians in the United States have begun to improve.[6]

A major turning point came in 2021 when the US government attempted to sneak measures into the country's infrastructure legislation that would put new restrictions on the crypto industry in an attempt to extract more taxes from crypto holders. The industry responded with internet outrage and lobbying dollars, the only two languages that politicians understand. The campaign was a massive success, and made Washington take notice that crypto holders were a voting block of their own, not some fringe community that could be ignored. Crypto founders like Charles Hoskinson and Sam Bankman-Fried have testified before Congress about the industry,[7] and seemed to get more respect than Jack Dorsey and Mark Zuckerberg did when they went to Washington. The FUD is that crypto will be regulated out of existence, but we have already seen that this is impossible. Governments and institutions have no choice but to join it. Regulation will not be perfect, but it's also true that the industry is currently being held back by regulatory uncertainty. A plethora of institutional funds and more conservative investors are interested in the space but are waiting for regulatory clarity before they start allocating their capital. A large section of the market has been sitting on the sidelines ready to go, just waiting for any regulation.[8]

Energy Use

With institutions waiting in the wings, it has become obvious to many investors that the space has matured, so narratives about government bans and regulation have given way to new FUD about the environment and Bitcoin's energy-intensive proof-of-work mining algorithm. Similar concerns were raised about all of the power used by the internet when it was just getting started, but that narrative died as soon as people saw how useful the internet was – and we're seeing similar attitudes toward crypto. Nearly everything we use requires energy, from Christmas lights to washing machines. The energy used by the Bitcoin blockchain is protecting and securing a trillion-dollar financial network, which has the potential to be worth much more. Protecting assets in the traditional financial world is energy intensive as well – but it's much more opaque, as its statistics aren't recorded on an open-source blockchain for all to see. (According to a 2021 research report from Galaxy Digital, Bitcoin uses less than half of the energy that is consumed by the traditional financial system. Of course, because Galaxy Digital is a crypto fund, they have an obvious bias, but there will likely be further research in this area.) Armored trucks, aircraft carriers, armies, and all sorts of energy-intensive, carbon-emitting strategies are used to defend the US dollar – and with gold the business gets even dirtier. Gold miners contribute to deforestation by "slashing and burning" miles of rainforest so it's easier for them to work. This also kills the local wildlife and displaces some of the last remaining native tribes on earth. Many of the devastating forest fires that we see around the world can be traced back to gold mining, including some of those seen in the Amazon Rainforest in recent years.[9]

Another point is that energy usage doesn't automatically result in negative consequences for the environment. A survey published by the Bitcoin Mining Council suggests that many Bitcoin miners are already using renewable energy, a trend that will ideally increase with awareness and access.

Volatility, Centralization, and Quantum Computing

There is also plenty of FUD about Bitcoin's volatility, with critics suggesting that an asset with such wild price swings should not be taken seriously as an asset. Bitcoin is definitely volatile, but this is normal for an emerging asset that is still growing in use and adoption. Ethereum founder Vitalik Buterin predicts that crypto will eventually trade with the same volatility as "gold or the stock market" once it becomes more established. He says: "In my view, a lot of the volatility early on had to do with *existential* uncertainty." This is a new technology and people aren't sure how to price it – and so some have doubts it will work out. But it will.[10]

Another popular FUD angle concerns the centralization of large Bitcoin wallets. There's no doubt that some whales bought in early and held through all these years, such as Max Keiser or Roger Ver. This is problematic because having such a large share of the supply gives them the power to move markets. But it's also true that the data often cited on this topic can be misleading; sources will point to the fact that a large percentage of the Bitcoin supply is held by only a few wallet addresses. This piece of data is correct, but it isn't telling the whole story: many of these massive whale wallets are actually exchange wallets that hold assets for thousands of different people.[11] In general, the FUD about centralization of wallets is caused by a misunderstanding of how custodial services operate on the blockchain.

Let's get one thing clear about centralization and your private keys: It can be dangerous for users to have their funds on a custodial service. Even the most trusted centralized exchanges can go down during times of extreme volatility, which leaves their users unable to access their funds for a period of time. This is a routine occurrence, with exchanges going offline for maintenance for hours at a time, but unplanned outages can occur too. During a market crash in 2021, Binance and Coinbase, two of the top exchanges in the industry, were down unexpectedly for several hours.[12] But, as it happens, this is precisely the type of bad user-experience that this technology aims to avoid. And there are protective measures built into the process, such as hardware wallets and seed phrases (for more, see the next chapter). When it comes to Bitcoin, Ethereum, and Cardano, the supply has become widely dispersed over time. Also, note that not all of the whale wallets visible on the blockchain are active. It's estimated that at least 20% of all BTC in circulation is actually lost and unrecoverable, which makes the remaining supply rarer and thus more valuable.

But, keep in mind: regarding many of the lesser-known projects on the market, especially meme coins – most of the tokens are actually held in a single wallet belonging to just one person or group of people that can dump at any time. So anyone considering the more speculative projects should thoroughly research the risks.

The most complex FUD about crypto is the theory that quantum computing will break cryptography.[13] However, Bitcoin would be the least of our concerns if modern cryptography is hacked – things like banking records, government secrets, and even nuclear codes would all be compromised. The smartest minds in the world are working in cryptography; I believe they'll be able to keep up with the quantum era.

FUD often has a grain of truth to it, which is why it's so effective, but it blows things out of proportion. Remember Y2K? FUD often makes catastrophes out of issues that will either never come to pass or will be nothing more than a blip that's quickly forgotten. That's not to say that there is no danger in this industry – there is plenty that you need to be careful about, which we'll cover next. But these risks should not prevent you from taking advantage of the opportunities that crypto has to offer.

CHAPTER 19

Crypto Warnings

Hackers, Scammers, and Contagion

B ehind the FUD, there are legitimate concerns in this industry that you should be aware of. Aside from user error, the most serious dangers that users face on the blockchain are hackers and scammers – and these dangers are everywhere.

Hackers

Hackers are a major threat because they can compromise trusted exchanges or smart contracts even without you giving them any access to your account. If you have your money on a centralized exchange or locked up in a yield farm, staking service, or other smart contract, it will be lost if a hacker compromises that platform. This is a risk that you need to consider whenever you're storing funds on a third-party service or locking up tokens in a smart contract. Even wallets have attack vectors that can be compromised by hackers, so keeping your funds in a cold storage hardware wallet is the best first step to improving your crypto security. A hardware wallet is a USB device that holds your keys so they are never stored anywhere online, while a hot wallet is your average mobile or browser extension wallet. Hot wallets are less secure because your keys are stored in the application, so if a hacker gains control of your computer, that hacker could also gain access to your keys.[1]

If you're holding onto a significant amount of crypto, it is essential for you to learn how to use a hardware wallet. This is important because it allows you to keep the keys for your wallet in a device that is not connected to the internet, which will prevent hackers from accessing your seed phrase if your computer, phone, or email address is somehow compromised. However, a hardware wallet will not prevent you from losing your funds if you are locked up in a yield farm or staking platform that gets hacked, or if you approve a signature that gives other users control of your assets. So always make sure you know what you're approving.

Bridge Hacks

Bridges between blockchains are also popular targets for hackers. A bridge is a smart contract that allows you to transfer assets from one blockchain to another. Bridges can contain hundreds of millions of dollars, and they're very common targets because this is a new and highly complex technology, and there are still plenty of gaps in the markets to exploit for those who know how to do it.[2]

Because bridges hold such large honeypots of money, bridge hacks typically result in much heavier losses than the average security breach. In August 2021, a hack of the Poly Network captured $611 million – though fortunately the team was able to negotiate with the hacker to get the funds returned. In March 2022, the bridge into the economy for the game Axie Infinity was hacked, resulting in upwards of $617 million in lost funds, perhaps the largest hack to date. The attack on Axie Infinity's Ronin Bridge was carried about by a group of North Korean hackers called the Lazarus Group (also known as "advanced persistent threat 38" (APT38). According to Chainalysis, North Korean hackers also stole nearly $400 million worth of crypto in 2021.[3]

If you think that North Korean hacker gangs are interesting, wait till you hear about the criminal duo who pulled off the Bitfinex heist of August 2016, in which 119,756 Bitcoin was stolen, worth about $72 million at the time. For a while it seemed the hackers would get away with it. But in early 2022 Heather Morgan and her husband, Ilya Lichtenstein, were arrested for laundering billions of dollars from the hack. (It's not clear if they worked alone or not.) After the pair was arrested, the Department of Justice said it seized $3.6 billion in stolen funds – which makes sense given that the increased value of Bitcoin in the years since the heist boosted the value of the original theft to $4.5 billion. The most interesting thing about this case was the identity of the hackers, especially Heather Morgan, who had a very loud public persona. Morgan had been a tech writer for popular websites like *Forbes*, and had even written articles about how businesses can stay safe from hackers. She was also a wannabe rapper who went by many names, including the "Crocodile of Wall Street" and "Razzlekhan," which, according to her bio, likened her to Genghis Khan but with more "pizzazz."[4] Morgan's music was a unique style that was branded as "cringe rap," which is actually a great description.

Not all hackers are criminals, though; there are some people who hack for good. These ethical hackers test the code for popular applications to detect vulnerabilities, and sometimes they're awarded for their efforts in the form of "bug bounties," which are sometimes worth millions of dollars. In one such case, Aurora Labs paid a $6 million bounty to an ethical hacker who detected a vulnerability in their code. If the vulnerability had been exploited by an unethical hacker, it could have cost Aurora Labs over $200 million.[5]

Scammers

In addition to hackers, you also need to watch out for various types of scammers looking to separate you from your crypto. There are two different types of scammers, the "anon" (anonymous) scammers and the public-facing charlatan scammers. The anon scammers will often pose as popular influencers – having created spoofed accounts or websites – and message fans to pull them into fake investment deals that turn out to be scams. (This is why many popular influencers or Discord moderators include statements like "I will never DM you" [Direct Message you] in their bios.) Sometimes scammers will send emails with phishing links, or set up fake airdrops or NFT mints that are actually designed to drain your wallet. Hackers will incorporate these strategies as well. For example, hackers will take control of discord moderator accounts, or social media profiles for popular influencers. Once they hack into the account, they share links to malicious smart contracts with promises of some type of incentive, such as an airdrop.[6]

Fortunately there are some red flags to look out for so you can identify scams before falling victim to them:

- When a social media channel is hacked and being used for this purpose, the hacker usually turns off comments so that more knowledgeable community members aren't able to warn newcomers unfamiliar with this tactic.
- They will also instill a sense of urgency and make you feel like you're missing out if you don't click on the link immediately.
- As a result of these types of hacks, many serious projects have entirely stopped doing any surprise airdrops or "stealth" NFT drops – so if you see any surprise launches be extremely careful.
- Any links should be approached with utmost caution, and you should always double-check to make sure that you're on the correct URL and not mistakenly on an imposter website.
- Sometimes scammers will buy domains that are misspellings of popular crypto services to catch people who aren't paying attention. For example, a scammer might buy the domain "conbase.com," to catch users hoping to visit "coinbase.com." Users will see a screen that looks just like the one where they always sign in, but as soon as they enter in their usernames and passwords, the scammer will have their login info and be able to access their accounts.[7]

Even more dangerous than the anon scammers are the public-facing charlatans, and there is sadly no shortage of them in this industry. It can be hard to spot them too, because the industry is filled with loud and charismatic figures – all of whom have been called a "scammer" at one point or another. The term is thrown around constantly in this industry, even at projects that are entirely legitimate. For example, on December 27, 2018, entrepreneur and author Chris Burniske tweeted, "One of the biggest scams in crypto is the number of people that call non-scams scams."[8] With all the maximalism and tribalism that takes place in crypto, these separate tribes will often accuse one another of scamming investors; influencers will try to label their rivals as scammers to cast themselves as the heroes. If a project fails, the founders are called scammers even if they had entirely honest intentions. But once someone reveals their face and true identity to the world, that earns a certain level of trust and respect because it implies the person is willing to take some responsibility for the impact their product has on the market. So, who should you trust? Looking at a team's background and track record is often a good strategy when investing in crypto projects, and teams with doxxed identities are usually a bit easier to trust than anonymous teams, especially if they don't have a proven track record under a pseudonym.

Doxxing

When you've been "doxxed," that means some of your private data or identification has been put online, usually without your consent. The term comes from an old hacker abbreviation for "documents," shortening it to "dox" as in "I'm dropping the dox today."

However, in both crypto and the worlds of traditional tech and finance, there are some very brazen charlatans who readily engage with the public while operating scams. Although these scams take many different forms, the most popular are probably rug-pulls, vaporware, exit scams, and Ponzi schemes.

Rug-Pulls

Rug-pulls are common, and happen most often in low-liquidity projects and memecoins. Rug-pulls will usually have anonymous founders, but a large number of public founders have also pulled the rug on their community. When a project founder "pulls the rug" it means that they pull the liquidity out of the market, making it effectively impossible for anyone to trade, and driving the price of the asset straight to zero. This is possible because they hold such a large percentage of the supply that they are the sole market-maker for the asset. This is an important red flag to look out for when doing research on projects: be sure to find out how much of the total supply is controlled by the team, VCs, and other market makers.

Vaporware

Vaporware is a product that doesn't exist and will probably never exist, but people raise money for it anyway. In crypto this usually comes in two forms: far-out and ridiculous ideas that aren't physically possible, and phony competitors for popular projects. These phony copycats launch in droves every time a new trend comes around.[9] For example, if a DeFi project named after a food gains popularity, hundreds of DeFi tokens named after food will launch in hopes of capturing some of that hype. But oftentimes only a small number of these projects will be legitimate competitors; many of them will be vaporware, designed to make a quick buck off speculators looking for the "next best" of a trend-setting project.

Exit Scams

One of the most interesting scams in crypto is the exit scam, which is basically when someone builds a platform that users entrust with their money – then they close the exchange or claim they've been hacked and make off with everyone's money.

One of the most notorious exit scams of all time was the wild case of the early Canadian crypto exchange QuadrigaCX. The exchange was founded in November 2013 by Gerald Cotten and Michael Patryn. Cotten, the public front man, was a regular at crypto meetups and conferences, and was always happy to appear on camera or speak with journalists. The exchange ran for several years without incident, and seemed to have a bright future – until December 9, 2018, when Cotten mysteriously died at the age of 30. He reportedly passed away from Crohn's disease while on his honeymoon in India, where he was also opening an orphanage – which was an incredibly suspicious story. Crohn's disease is not typically fatal, especially for people in their thirties, and the timing was suspect as well. Within weeks after Cotten's death was announced in January 2019, it was also revealed that the QuadrigaCX customers were owed $250 million CAD ($190 million), and that the company had filed for "creditor protection." At first, the story was that Cotten had the only private keys to the company's treasury, with all of the customer's funds, but it was later discovered that the exchange had been insolvent for a long time. According to *Newsweek*, an investigation by the Ontario Securities Commission found Cotten had created "fake Quadriga accounts, used fake funds, and made real trades, betting on the value of cryptocurrency." These circum-stances have led many to speculate that Cotten staged his death after he lost his customer's money on his own trades.[10] This mystery was never solved, and after Quadriga's downfall Patryn went off the grid, but he left evidence on the blockchain that would eventually expose him.

Years later, the silent cofounder Michael Patryn would resurface again. Prior to cofounding Quadriga with Cotten, Patryn had been convicted of being involved with an identity theft ring. He's basically a career scammer, which is probably why he mostly stayed behind the scenes. Over the years, Patryn had worked for different DeFi projects as an anon, using the name 0xSifu. He managed to manipulate his way into key positions with billion-dollar pro-tocols where he was in control of the multisig keys that gave access to the treasuries. The biggest of these projects was called Wonderland (its token was called TIME), and it had a market cap of $2 billion at its peak.

Wonderland investors first became suspicious of 0xSifu after he took money from the project's treasury to cover his own leveraged positions – to protect his personal positions from getting liquidated. After further investi-gation, blockchain sleuth ZachXBT discovered that 0xSifu's wallet was con-nected to wallets used by Patryn on Quadriga. This revelation ultimately resulted in the downfall of the project, which seemed to be unsustainable to begin with. But despite all this, Patryn has not suffered any consequences for the crimes he's committed against crypto holders.[11]

Ponzi Schemes

In a Ponzi scheme, a scammer promises investors high returns for a nonexist-ent investment, and then pays fake earnings with the funds of newer inves-tors. These can work for a while, especially in bull markets, but they fall apart when a large number of investors decide to cash out, which happens often in bear markets. There have been plenty of Ponzi schemes throughout crypto history – a few so large they significantly impacted the market. The first one worth mentioning is BitConnect.

BitConnect launched in 2016 promising to offer the types of borrowing and lending services that we see in DeFi today, but the platform was entirely centralized. Users were able to lock up their funds on the BitConnect platform to earn daily interest, and the project became extremely popular during the bull run of 2017. The platform claimed to have proprietary trading bots that would supposedly generate income for users. But when the bull run came to an end at the beginning of 2018, US regulators charged BitConnect with run-ning a Ponzi scheme, after it was discovered that the team was paying back old investors with money that was recently deposited by new investors. It took a few years, but BitConnect founder Satish Kumbhani was finally indicted in

February 2022 and charged with defrauding investors out of $2.4 billion – but he went missing before he could be legally served. He was later booked in August by police in Pune, India, after being pursued for separate charges.[12]

Sometimes, legitimate businesses can turn into Ponzi schemes. That's what happened with a large lending service called Celsius in 2022. Celsius was one of the biggest centralized platforms in crypto throughout 2020 and 2021 because it gave users access to the types of services and yields that were happening in DeFi, but with a user interface that was much more user friendly. There are a lot of crypto traders who are afraid of managing their own private keys because the process is complicated and overwhelming, and there's no recourse if something goes wrong. Some people want to entrust that responsibility to a centralized service like Celsius – and we've already seen that centralized services come with the risks of mismanagement or fraud. Somewhere along the way, Celsius CEO Alex Mashinsky began gambling with the money that investors trusted on his platform, and started losing badly. Rumors began to swirl about the platform's insolvency and impending liquidations, but Mashinsky remained defiant, making public statements insisting that Celsius was fine, and that all of the criticism was nothing more than FUD. Just one day after mocking his critics and claiming that Celsius would not be preventing anyone from taking their money off the platform, Mashinsky sent out another statement announcing that Celsius was halting withdrawals. A few weeks later, Celsius declared bankruptcy, leaving its customers wondering if they would ever see their money again. A court filing in July of 2022 showed that Celsius had a $1.3-billion hole in its balance sheet – which means that it is totally unsalvageable.[13]

This sort of thing can happen because centralized crypto platforms are not transparent like blockchain protocols are. This is even true for hedge funds in the crypto space. Three Arrows Capital, more commonly known as 3AC, was a crypto hedge fund that was thought to have between $10 billion and $15 billion under management at its peak. 3AC founders Su Zhu and Kyle Davies became very popular on Twitter, and used their public reputations as influencers to borrow large sums of money from anyone who would lend to them, including crypto exchanges, other hedge funds, and even crypto start-ups.

3AC had such a stellar track record for making money that everyone just trusted them with millions of dollars. Meanwhile, behind the scenes, Zhu and Davies had no risk management and were using their customers' funds to place their own bets. When the bull market hit and many of their big investments fell apart, 3AC faced major liquidations and was unable to pay back many of their debts. One exchange in particular, Voyager, let 3AC borrow $675 million without taking any collateral. Voyager never got any of their money back, and the loss forced them into bankruptcy. In July 2022, Zhu and Davies fled Singapore and went on the run.[14]

Contagion

This is a perfect time to bring up another serious risk in crypto: contagion. Celsius and Three Arrows Capital were doing plenty of shady business behind the scenes, but what ultimately brought them down was their over-investment in the Terra Luna ecosystem, which horrifically collapsed in 2022, as covered in chapter 15. Terra and Luna were the first dominos to fall, but then hedge funds, exchanges, and lending services that were invested in the ecosystem also began to fall, which caused smaller platforms underneath them to fall as well. This causes prices on the market to fall across the board, causing further losses and liquidations for individuals and institutions alike. The interconnected nature of the crypto markets helps accelerate building – but it can also accelerate disasters as well, as we saw with the contagion from the collapse of Terra Luna.[15]

There's another type of risk to share concerning regulation. In the previous chapter I laid out how most of the regulatory concerns about the industry are overblown FUD. Though the industry as a whole doesn't currently face existential threats as a result of regulation, regulators can cause serious problems for individual projects and platforms that they decide to target. For example, take the asset XRP, which was delisted from numerous major exchanges after the SEC announced its case against Ripple. This case will not be the end of Ripple, and in the long run it might even benefit the company, but XRP holders suffered major losses as a result of the delistings.[16]

CHAPTER 20

The Future of Crypto

Equities, ReFi, and UBI

W e have come a long way from the genesis block and Silk Road, but we are still so early. What we're seeing now is merely the foundation for what this industry will become. No one can predict the future with precision, especially in crypto, but there are a few major trends that I see developing in the next few years.

Crypto Grows Up

One thing we're almost guaranteed to see is more regulation. Regulation will be a double-edged sword that will have both negative and positive consequences, but overall it will likely be good for the industry. Some aspects of the cypherpunk vision will be watered down as regulators crack down on privacy applications, but the permissionless nature of blockchain networks will make it difficult to ban these applications entirely. The debate about privacy on blockchains is very tricky, and it's one of those issues where there are points on both sides that make a lot of sense. On the one hand, I hate to see terrorists, scammers, and rug-pullers using this technology to avoid the consequences of their crimes. This narrative has brought a lot of negative attention to the industry, and it would be nice to see that narrative change. It's not that simple, though. There are legitimate reasons to want to stay anonymous on the blockchain, especially for people in countries that are corrupt and oppressive.[1] I don't favor giving dictators a complete view of every citizen's financial records. So it's not a cut-and-dried issue – and one we'll probably be debating for decades.

One thing is for sure: Regulation will be very positive when it comes to price and mainstream adoption, even if the laws aren't entirely perfect. The lack of regulatory clarity from some governments has been one of the main things both holding back mainstream adoption and suppressing the prices.[2] There are so many institutional investors, corporations, and large organizations that have been sitting on the sidelines for years, afraid of getting involved in crypto out of worry that the technology will be regulated out of existence. For these investors regulation will be the green light that they need to start buying crypto. If regulations are especially harsh in the United States it would be very bad news for the US economy, but it wouldn't stop crypto. Builders would just move to other countries where regulations are more favorable, and the States would miss out on all the wealth created from crypto, including jobs and tax revenue.

Soon enough, institutions and governments will begin either using or imitating crypto in their day-to-day activities. They have already begun to dip their toes in, but in the coming years this trend will accelerate as the industry becomes more regulated. Many institutional players will begin to take advantage of the "DeFi mullet" strategy – which means they have Web2 fintech in the front, with an easy interface for users, and DeFi as the back-end infrastructure, with the platform's algorithms or employees doing all the hard work behind the scenes.[3] With this setup users can log in with a normal username and password and take advantage of DeFi even without knowing how to use blockchain technology. However, this does come with a certain level of risk, as these are third-party platforms (as I highlighted in chapter 19), but third-party services will always exist, because there will always be people who don't feel comfortable managing their own private keys. As the industry matures, these centralized actors will become more regulated, which will lower the counterparty risk. There will also be plenty of people who feel comfortable taking custody of their own assets, so the industry will not be entirely dominated by centralized services.

Stablecoins

There will be certain sectors in crypto that the establishment will fight to gain control of. Stablecoins are especially of concern for governments because they have the potential to displace the current system of fiat money. To prevent this possibility, governments are rushing to launch digital versions of their fiat currencies before crypto stablecoins achieve mainstream adoption. These digital versions of fiat currencies are called Central Bank Digital Currencies (CBDCs). China has already been experimenting with the Digital Yuan, but it's unfortunately the opposite of a cryptocurrency. It is digital, but the government has total control over individuals' funds and can track all their transactions; they can also inflate it just like they do with paper fiat. Meanwhile, officials in the United States have said they're looking into the potential of a CBCD but have not announced any formal plans. Hopefully, a CBDC will look much different in the States than it has in China. Many of the US officials who support the crypto industry are pushing to have a stablecoin from the private sector adopted as the US CBDC – which would most likely end up being USDC, the stablecoin favored by most politicians and regulators. USDC would be much better than China's Digital Yuan, but if the US government took a few more steps toward authoritarianism, they could force Circle, the company behind USDC, to do whatever they wanted. Circle has proven in the past that they will comply with any government order they're given, which does present a potential censorship risk.[4] Ideally, Circle would be forced to engage in censorship only in extreme situations like crime or terrorism – but governments have been known to use their powers against political enemies, so the control that Circle has over USDC is not to be taken lightly.

Blockchain Equities

It will take a while, but eventually we'll start to see entire stock markets transferring over to blockchain rails. In recent years it's become extremely obvious that our financial system is running on obsolete technology. The faults in the system were laid bare during the Wall Street Bets Saga of 2021, where an army of Reddit degenerates drove up the price of Gamestop's stock for the sole purpose of liquidating some evil hedge funds. They were actually successful for a short time, but their party was cut short when numerous brokers halted trading in the stock – thereby shutting down the rally. Speculation about corruption was rampant, and brokers were suspected of not having enough liquidity to facilitate the trades. Nobody wanted to admit this, though, because then they'd have to admit how narrow their margins are and how they operate on the edge of insolvency at all times.[5]

But if these stocks were being traded on a public blockchain, the liquidity would be transparent. In other words, users would be able to look at how much stock and cash brokers like Robinhood had on hand to determine if they were telling the truth about why they shut down trading. (Opaque shutdowns would be possible on centralized exchanges, but not on decentralized blockchain protocols.) Blockchains are just so much more efficient and secure than the technology currently used to operate stock markets around the world.

The Flippening

The next few years will bring some power shifts in the crypto markets as well, the biggest of which is the potential for Ethereum's market cap to surpass that of Bitcoin. I think it's highly likely that Ethereum will flip Bitcoin in the coming years. This is not to say that Ethereum is better than Bitcoin. Bitcoin and Ethereum serve totally different purposes, so comparing them is like comparing football with chicken wings: they're both amazing inventions – and if you ask me to pick a favorite, I'll just say they go great together. When it comes to revenue, though, chicken wings dominate over football. The NFL provides a very specific purpose in organizing and broadcasting games for football fans. For the 2021 season, this business model generated $347.3 million – which is certainly respectable, but it's hard to compete with food. On Super Bowl Sunday in 2021, Americans ate a record 1.42 billion chicken wings, which at an average price of 30 cents per wing comes out to $426 million – and that's just one night.[6] Of course, there are some overhead costs that need to be deducted from that figure, so this math is not perfect, but this example shows how a general-purpose product has a larger surface area than does a product designed for a very specific purpose.

The Flippening

Crypto people use this term as a shorthand for the moment Ethereum's market cap becomes more than Bitcoin's, hence *flipping* the dominance in the crypto space in favor of Ethereum.

Economists call this surface area the Total Addressable Market (TAM) of the product. Bitcoin is digital gold, and the current market cap for gold as of this writing is just over $11 trillion. A digital store of value like Bitcoin could be more accessible and provide more utility than gold, which means that it could far exceed gold's current market cap – but the TAM is still limited when compared to Ethereum. The Ethereum network threatens to disrupt the entire stock market of every country, which as of 2021 has a total estimated market cap of $124.4 trillion. It's also possible that Ethereum could be the new layer to the internet that most tech companies build on top of, which would create even more value. I've made some enemies among Bitcoin maximalists for my perspective on this, but they're losing power and credibility anyway. People are learning that you don't need to be a maximalist in order to be a Bitcoiner, and now the maximalists are outnumbered. Many Bitcoiners are invested in other projects, and they want the industry as a whole to succeed. It is only a very few influencers and out-of-touch whales who are really driving this maximalist narrative.[7]

Regenerative Finance

As the industry matures, I really hope we see an end to the tribalism and infighting that has become so common between different crypto communities. It's normal for businesses to be competitive with one another, but the hostility in crypto is on a whole other level, and it needs to calm down so the industry can truly grow. There is one small but growing corner of crypto that has already figured this out, and that's the Regenerative Finance sector (ReFi).

Regenerative Finance is commonly known as ReFi. This is a play on the term "DeFi," which also calls back the "degenerate" label often given to crypto traders. The idea is to use the greed of the degenerate crypto traders for good and funnel their money into social or environmental causes – while allowing them to profit in the process. "Regenerative Finance" is a broad term used to describe projects that are harnessing the power of markets to provide public goods,[8] which are products and services that are provided for free to anyone who needs them. Throughout most of history, public goods have been handled by governments, churches, and charities – because in most cases it was physically impossible to generate a profit while giving away things for free. This has resulted in a deficit in public goods. The masses are motivated by money, and the vast majority of people out there are struggling financially, so they have legitimate reasons to focus on their own finances and leave the bigger problems to someone else. With everyone so worried about keeping themselves fed, important goals and problems get neglected because there isn't a clear path to profit. From what I've observed, projects in the ReFi space are oddly cooperative when compared to the rest of the crypto industry. Even competitors seem to be rooting for each other, and that's because they all want to create the same positive change in the world. That's exactly how all of us in crypto should be approaching this path we're on together, but not everyone sees it that way yet.

Now with crypto it's actually possible for developers to generate a profit for themselves, give away the product for free, and then share some of their earnings with their users to top it all off. This is what we have seen happen with play-to-earn games, and this same business model can be applied to all sorts of different applications from social media to fitness apps. This simple change could radically shift the incentives in our economy – to the point where finding solutions to poverty could make someone a fortune, or where preserving rainforests is more profitable than cutting them down. This may sound crazy, but there are numerous crypto projects – like Toucan, Solid World DAO, Open Forest Protocol, Klima DAO, and others – that were built with the specific intention of funding environmental causes like rainforest restoration.[9] There are countless environmental projects that are now being made possible thanks to blockchain technology – which is yet another point against the FUD that says the crypto industry is destroying the planet.

There are also plenty of other subsectors within the ReFi ecosystem aimed at funding open-source development or alleviating poverty. One of the original crypto ReFi projects is Gitcoin, which funds open-source development on the Ethereum blockchain. On Gitcoin, developers submit proposals about open-source projects that they want to build, and the community decides what gets funded. Gitcoin also matches donations using a unique mechanism called quadratic funding, where the number of contributors has more weight than the dollar value of the contributions – which prevents whales from gaming the system.[10]

Universal Basic Income

There are also projects like Proof of Humanity (PoH), which is working to develop ways users can prove they're human without revealing their identity. This system is being used to distribute a Universal Basic Income (UBI) token to help people make ends meet. UBI is a concept that governments around the world have been slowly starting to consider over the years. The general idea is that people are given a guaranteed minimum income to cover basic necessities so they have a bit more financial flexibility and don't have to live paycheck to paycheck – as 59% of Americans do, according to Charles Schwab's 2019 Modern Wealth Survey. Other studies have shown that UBI can improve well-being and actually increase employment.[11] Unfortunately, the idea has always sounded unrealistic because UBI is a massive expense that few governments could handle, and it would likely result in huge tax increases and other negative consequences. Besides, it rarely turns out well when the government is in charge of these kinds of things, so state-sponsored UBI programs aren't very interesting to me. What is interesting is the possibility that crypto projects could use this technology to create new value and give money and valuable services to some of the people who need help the most.

Former US presidential candidate Andrew Yang made a name for himself during the 2016 election cycle advocating for UBI; he's now one of the most recognized advocates for the idea in the States. And though most of his attention these days might seem to be on crypto and Web3, what he's saying demonstrates his goals haven't changed at all. In August 2021, Yang tweeted that "Cryptocurrency is one path to universal basic income." In February 2022 he elaborated in another tweet on Twitter: "My goal is simple – eradicate poverty. Web3 technologies represent the biggest anti-poverty opportunity of our time. Millions of lives are being transformed and creators empowered by new ways to exchange and generate value on the blockchain. It's bottom-up not top-down."[12]

This is the kind of narrative that crypto needs. Instead of news stories about people getting rich on dog coins, we should be seeing coverage about how this technology can improve life for people who don't have money to spare – let alone money to invest. This includes ReFi of course, but it also includes things like gaming and Web3 social media. Investments seem like a luxury to most people who live paycheck to paycheck, scraping together quarters and dimes for gas or a bus ticket, which is why many people think crypto is pointless and frivolous. But their perspective could change if they learn they could earn crypto just by playing games or using apps similar to Facebook, Google, YouTube, Uber, or Fitbit. Web3 applications that pay their users could potentially provide that base level of financial subsistence that people need to cover basic necessities. P2E refers to gaming; earning money in a Web3-enabled app like Facebook, Uber, or Fitbit would not be considered P2E.

We still have a long way to go before we can make this possibility a reality, but the industry is certainly building in that direction. It looks like gaming will be the first sector to start dishing out large volumes of free crypto to mainstream users. Between 2020 and 2022, VC firms poured billions into the development of play-to-earn crypto games,[13] which indicates that countless teams will be funded to work on these games throughout the next decade. The quality of these games and their economies continue to improve with each major release, and soon they will be able to compete with some of the top gaming studios. As the automation of manual labor jobs continues to increase, I believe that jobs like gaming and online content creation will start to take up a larger percentage of the economy, and crypto will play a huge role in that. In the future, blockchains, cryptography, and digital assets will be a part of the infrastructure for most of the applications that we use in our day-to-day lives.

The fact that you're reading this book shows that you are forward-thinking and ready to take on the challenges ahead. With each challenge comes a great reward, and being in a position to understand the next asset class is a once-in-a-millennium opportunity.

CHAPTER 21

Where Do You Go from Here?

N ow that you have an overhead view of what I think the industry is going to look like over the next few years, let's take a deeper look at the markets and leave you with some actionable information that can help you navigate this new frontier. Let's do a bit of a review first. Some of the most dominant crypto assets on the market at time of writing, are Bitcoin (BTC), Ethereum (ETH), Binance Coin (BNB), Cardano (ADA), Ripple (XRP), and Polygon (MATIC), as they tend to spend a lot of time in the top 10 or 20 of the market cap list. I believe that these assets have had tremendous staying power in the crypto markets because they have strong communities, offer legitimate utility, and have skilled developers. Bitcoin and Ethereum have both established themselves as pillars of the industry, and we have covered them at length in these pages, but there are a few other projects that have also shown that they are here to stay. Binance is the leading exchange in the world, and it has its own token BNB, which has a variety of different utilities.[1] BNB can be used for transaction fees on the Binance Smart Chain network similar to gas on the Ethereum network, but it can also be used for trading discounts on the Binance exchange and it can even be spent using a Binance credit card.

Community Is Key

As you may have gathered so far, crypto assets are driven by communities, and Cardano has proven to have one of the most powerful communities in crypto. In the 2022 "Brand Intimacy Study," Cardano was listed as #26, ranking higher than both Bitcoin and Ethereum, but also beating out companies like IKEA, BMW, and Nestle.[2] Despite catching flack for their slow and methodical development schedule, Cardano has established itself as a serious player in the blockchain world.

Polygon is another popular project that I believe will have continued growth in the years to come. Polygon's growth has been relatively recent as compared with other assets that we have covered in this book. For years, Polygon has been serving as an overflow network for Ethereum, hosting faster and cheaper versions of popular Ethereum applications such as Uniswap, Open Sea, AAVE, and others. Polygon is its own blockchain, so it is not technically a "layer-2" like Optimism and Arbitrum, which are secured by the Ethereum blockchain. This is where things start to get interesting, though. Optimism, Arbitrum and other layer-2 networks for Ethereum were not able to launch until the layer-2 infrastructure was ready. Instead of waiting, Polygon simply launched their own chain and began onboarding users. I remember seeing some pushback from the Ethereum community about this over fears that Polygon would attempt to become an Ethereum competitor. These fears were ultimately unfounded, because in 2021, Polygon announced that it was working on becoming an official layer-2 network for Ethereum. Even more exciting was the fact that their layer-2 solution would be using innovative cryptography called Zero Knowledge proofs.[3] This is far more advanced than the current technology used by other layer-2 networks. Zero Knowledge (ZK) technology makes it possible for individuals to prove certain things to other parties without revealing unwanted information, which can help make blockchain transactions more private.[4] ZK technology can also make it possible to verify financial, medical, or educational credentials without revealing your entire personal history. Think about how much personal information you give to strangers every time you show them your ID to prove your age or confirm your name. Every time you show someone your ID, you are also showing your personal address, even if that information is not pertinent to them, just because it is included on the ID. This is a potential security risk, but in a world with zero knowledge proofs, you could prove your identity and other important information, without revealing other details that might be sensitive.

Polygon is a dark horse in the layer-2 race because it is still not officially considered a layer-2 by developers at time of writing, but it has a larger community and market cap than all its layer-2 competitors and it will soon have the technical capabilities to be considered in the same conversation.

Last, but not least, for the big caps is Ripple (XRP), which is locked in a bitter trial with the SEC at time of writing. I hope that by the time you're reading this, the case is closed and Ripple has won, but I believe that they will have a bright future regardless of the outcome that we see from their case. All through the litigation, Ripple has been making deals with banks around the world to establish its cross-border payment solution "On Demand Liquidity" ODL to various countries around the world, including Brazil, Australia, Japan, Philippines and Singapore.[5] Ripple's ODL service uses the XRP asset to provide liquidity to the network, so banks can use it as a bridge currency to streamline settlement times for international payments.

While the winners mentioned here continue to perform, one coin that deserves an honorable mention is Stellar (XLM), a payments blockchain that has managed to win the favor of the International Organization of Standardization, which sets global standards for financial instruments, as well as technology, scientific testing, and working conditions. Stellar was among five crypto assets that were deemed to be compliant with the organization, which could lead to potential deals in the future.[6]

Mainstream Takes Time

Getting involved in some of the riskier and less-established assets can pay off big but remember the vast majority of the crypto projects that launch will fail. This is not an indictment of the industry – this is actually not a problem that is unique to the crypto space. 80% of restaurants fail in the first five years, 90% of startups fail within the first ten years of their launch,[7] so this is something that you need to consider when making any investment, but considering how volatile crypto is, you need to be especially careful about where you park your money. You'll also need to keep a close eye on the projects you're invested in, to make sure that the team is following through on their promises and continuing to build. Patience is key in these markets as well. As much as it pains me to quote Bill Gates, he really nailed it when he said that "We always overestimate the change that will occur in the next two years and underestimate the change that will occur in the next ten."[8] This quote is fitting for the crypto markets, where dreams are big and progress is often way slower than we expect it to be. People also have unrealistic expectations about the speed at which this technology will be adopted by the mainstream. I think this has a lot to do with the fact that we have seen applications on the internet advance so quickly, but people forget that we are building an entirely new infrastructure. People seem to be comparing blockchain development to application development, but I think it is more like the creation of the internet, which was a much slower and more gradual progression. It took 20 or so years for the internet to go mainstream, and then another 20 for it to mature into the internet that we know today, and it's probably nowhere near done advancing. I believe that we will see a similar timetable with crypto. We are already about 10 years deep, and maybe about 10 years out from full mainstream adoption. Then after that we still have a way to go before we see a mature crypto market.

Embrace Change

The future of finance is, without a doubt, set up for some serious and far-reaching changes. It will be a paradigm shift in not just how we put money to work, but how we are able to pursue life, liberty, and happiness. But there is a struggle happening between those on the side of freedom and those on the side of centralization. It's a continuum, always drifting to one side or another, but thankfully for the past 300 years it's been ending up more on the side of individual freedom. But that trend started to diverge over the last 50 years. A technocracy has formed at the highest levels of governments and corporations. The two are merging together and their focus is to have total control. Their goal is for you to own nothing, and be happy about it. You can see this in the numbers when fiat currency replaced gold-backed money in 1971. It's been a backwards regression since then with a shrinking middle class, stagnant wages, and a money printer that only benefited those closest to the spigot.[9] Everything was going the way the Technocrats wanted, and it all seemed inevitable. The real test to their system came in 2008 with the Great Financial Crisis (GFC). The central banks, in concert with elected officials, used tax payer money to wipe away the transgressions of their greed. They did it in full view of everyone, bailing out the ruling class all while telling us it was the only way to save institutions that were so critical to society that they were "too big to fail." To this day only one person from the United States has gone to jail for all the swindling and greed that led up to the GFC.[10]

But Bitcoin was their black swan. Something they never saw coming. It's something they still don't fully understand. But if human nature keeps doing what it does it's inevitable that two things will happen: (1) The Keynesian debt experiment will collapse in on itself; and (2) the future of finance will be built on top of hard assets. Some of those assets will be made of atoms and others made out of code – Bitcoin being the chief among them. This won't happen overnight. Disentangling decades of mismanagement and toxic debt is going to be a long and painful process, but I can see a world in the next 50 years where the fiat currency system will be long dead and Bitcoin will sit as a world reserve currency.

But by then people won't care what the dollar price of Bitcoin is – it could be in the millions of dollars or more – because the dollar will be a meme coin at that point. Instead, Bitcoin will be the base layer of the digital economy, the bedrock of value. Yes, there will be centralized monies and CBDCs, but those will be just a means of exchange. It's also likely that the smart-contract blockchains end up replacing banks entirely. Each one would be its own hybrid exchange, bank, lender, and creditor. Defi would be the norm and Cefi would be the exception. I think Ethereum will most likely be the biggest, and would hold trillions in assets, securities, and derivatives – but so would Cardano, and even other blockchains that have yet to be made.

You have a chance to be part of this revolutionary change that is coming to finance. A disruption that will shake up the establishment and give more people the opportunity to find financial freedom, not just for themselves but for generations to come. Congratulations, you've taken the first step. You are now caught up to crypto.

Appendix: Essential Resources and Tools of the Trade

Now that you are caught up to crypto, I wanted to point you in the direction of some of the tools of the trade to help you on your crypto journey. These are just some of the tools that I personally use to make trades, hold my crypto, and do research. You can follow all of these QR codes to get exclusive sign-up bonuses.

First off is the Bitlab Academy, a series of online courses that allows anyone to dive into the complexities of crypto in a fun and entertaining way. It's great for anyone on their journey to financial freedom through crypto assets. There is a wealth of information for newbies, hard-core traders, Web3 builders, NFT junkies, and even the casual investor.

Bitlabacademy.com

First and foremost, you MUST keep assets you are holding long term in a cold wallet. This keeps their private keys your possession and is the most secure way to store your crypto. I personally use the Ledger cold wallet. It's the industry leader in security and asset management innovation.

bitboycrypto.com/deal/ledger

For Crypto trading these are the best tools of the trade:

- Kucoin – for general trading in the United States

bitboycrypto.com/deal/kucoin

- Binance – for general trading outside the United States

bitboycrypto.com/deal/binance

- Phemex – for leverage trading in the United States

bitboycrypto.com/deal/phemex

- ByBit – for leverage trading outside the United States

bitboycrypto.com/deal/bybit

Doing research should be second nature to any crypto investor and these invaluable tools are used throughout the industry:

- TokenMetrics – Deep research powered by AI that looks at the entire crypto industry and scores various altcoins based on a dozen different metrics

bitboycrypto.com/deal/tokenmetrics

- TradingView – Industry leading technical analysis for crypto, stocks, and more

bitboycrypto.com/deal/tradingview

- LuxAlgo – High level TA indicators and tools

bitboycrypto.com/deal/luxalgo

- MarketCipher – Top-tier TA indicators that tracks on-chain analytics and plugs directly into Tradingview

bitboycrypto.com/deal/marketcipher

And finally you can use CoinStats as your all-in-one portfolio tracker across multiple platforms.

bitboycrypto.com/deal/coinstats

Notes

Chapter 1

1. John Carney, "America Lost $10.2 Trillion in 2008," *Insider*, updated February 3, 2009, 11:57 a.m., **https://www.businessinsider.com/2009/2/america-lost-102-trillion-of-wealth-in-2008**; Colleen Shalby, "The Financial Crisis Hit 10 Years Ago. For Some, It Feels Like Yesterday," *Los Angeles Times*, September 15, 2018, 10 a.m., **https://www.latimes.com/business/la-fi-financial-crisis-experiences-20180915-htmlstory.html**; Oliver Burkeman, "US Tent Cities Highlight New Realities as Recession Wears On," *The Guardian*, March 26, 2009, 15:18 EDT, **https://www.theguardian.com/world/2009/mar/26/tent-city-california-recession-economy**.

2. Jordan Major, "Economist Who Predicted 2008 Financial Crisis Says 'U.S. Economy Is About to Shut Down,'" Finbold, May 10, 2022, **https://finbold.com/economist-who-predicted-2008-financial-crisis-says-u-s-economy-is-about-to-shut-down/**; Stephen Mihm, "Dr. Doom," *New York Times Magazine*, August 15, 2008, **https://www.nytimes.com/2008/08/17/magazine/17pessimist-t.html**; Reuters Staff, "Bernanke Sees No Spillover from Mortgage Woes," Reuters, May 17, 2007 5:41 a.m., **https://www.reuters.com/article/us-usa-fed-bernanke/bernanke-sees-no-spillover-from-mortgage-woes-idUSWBT00698520070517**.

3. Jim Cramer, "Bear Stearns Is Fine!," Mad Money with Jim Cramer, **CNBC.com**, March 11, 2008, **https://www.youtube.com/watch?v=gUkbdjetlY8**.

4. Matthew Ericson, Elaine He, and Amy Schoenfeld, "Tracking the $700 Billion Bailout," *New York Times*, accessed August 4, 2022, **http://archive.nytimes.com/www.nytimes.com/packages/html/national/200904_CREDITCRISIS/recipients.html?source=post_page**.

5. Sean Illing, "The 'Deep State' is Real. But It's Not What Trump Thinks It Is," *Vox*, May 13, 2020, 11:00am EDT, **https://www.vox.com/policy-and-politics/2020/5/13/21219164/trump-deep-state-fbi-cia-david-rohde**.

6. Davey Alba and Sheera Frenkel, "Medical Expert Who Corrects Trump Is Now a Target of the Far Right," *New York Times*, March 28, 2020, **https://www.nytimes.com/2020/03/28/technology/coronavirus-fauci-trump-conspiracy-target.html**.

7. "Fiat Currency Graveyard: A History of Monetary Folly," Gini Foundation, accessed August 7, 2022, **https://ginifoundation.org/kb/fiat-currency-graveyard-a-history-of-monetary-folly/**.

8. Jared Krebsbach and Eric Lambrecht, "What Role Did Inflation Play in the Collapse of the Roman Empire," **DailyHistory.org**, accessed September 3, 2022, **https://dailyhistory.org/What_Role_Did_Inflation_Play_in_the_Collapse_of_the_Roman_Empire**; Douglas Broom, "These Are the Countries with the Highest Inflation," World Economic Forum, August 13, 2019, **https://www.weforum.org/agenda/2019/08/inflation-deflation-venezuela-global/**.

9. Jon R. Moen and Ellis W. Tallman, "The Panic of 1907," Federal Reserve History, December 4, 2015, **https://www.federalreservehistory.org/essays/panic-of-1907**.

10. Thomas E. Woods Jr., "The Great Gold Robbery of 1933," Mises Institute, August 13, 2008, **https://mises.org/library/great-gold-robbery-1933**; Larry Elliott, "Rise of Cryptocurrencies Can Be Traced to Nixon Abandoning Gold in 1971," *The Guardian*, August 15, 2021, 07:20 EDT, **https://www.theguardian.com/business/2021/aug/15/rise-of-cryptocurrencies-can-be-traced-to-nixon-abandoning-gold-in-1971**; Chris Colvin and Philip Fliers, "How the US Government Seized All Citizens' Gold in 1930s," The Conversation, May 21, 2020, 10.32am EDT, **https://theconversation.com/how-the-us-government-seized-all-citizens-gold-in-1930s-138467**.

11. Kenneth Rogoff, "America's Endless Budget Battle," Project Syndicate, October 1, 2013, **https://www.project-syndicate.org/commentary/kenneth-rogoffwhat-a-us-default-would-mean-for-america-and-the-world**.

12. Serkan Arslanalp and Chima Simpson-Bell, "US Dollar Share of Global Foreign Exchange Reserves Drops to 25-Year Low," IMFBlog, May 5, 2021, **https://blogs.imf.org/2021/05/05/us-dollar-share-of-global-foreign-exchange-reserves-drops-to-25-year-low/**.

Chapter 2

1. Tyler Winklevoss, "Gemini Now Supports Dogecoin. Much Wow," Gemini Blog, May 4, 2021, **https://www.gemini.com/blog/gemini-now-supports-dogecoin-much-wow**.

2. Amy Tikkanen, "A Brief (and Fascinating) History of Money," *Encyclopedia Britannica*, January 31, 2020, **https://www.britannica.com/story/a-brief-and-fascinating-history-of-money**.

3. Amy Tikkanen, "A Brief (and Fascinating) History of Money," *Encyclopedia Britannica*, January 31, 2020, **https://www.britannica.com/story/a-brief-and-fascinating-history-of-money**; Andrej Kapcar, "Tally Sticks of the Stone Age," May 2011, **https://www.academia.edu/18709816/Tally_Sticks_of_the_Stone_Age**.

4. Julija A., "Paper or Plastic? The Definitive List of Cash Versus Credit Card Spending Statistics," Fortunly, updated February 11, 2022, **https://fortunly.com/statistics/cash-versus-credit-card-spending-statistics/**.

5. Julie Pitta, "Requiem for a Bright Idea," *Forbes*, November 1, 1999, 12:00 a.m. EST, **https://www.forbes.com/forbes/1999/1101/6411390a.html?sh=6aaf4ac2715f**; Anonymous, "How DigiCash Blew Everything," NEXT, January 1999, **https://cryptome.org/jya/digicrash.htm**; see also David Chaum, "ECASH," accessed September 4, 2022, **https://chaum.com/ecash/**.

6. Poorvi Vora, "David Chaum's Voter Verification using Encrypted Paper Receipts," George Washington University School of Engineering & Applied Science, accessed September 4, 2022, **https://www2.seas.gwu.edu/~poorvi/Chaum/chaum.pdf**.

7. Pelle Braendgaard, "How the Man Finally Brought E-gold Down," Stake Ventures, July 22, 2008, **https://blog.stakeventures.com/articles/the-man-finally-brought-e-gold-down.**

8. Stephen Foley, "Bitcoin Needs to Learn from Past E-Currency Failures," *Financial Times,* November 28, 2013, **https://www.ft.com/content/6d51117e-5806-11e3-a2ed-00144feabdc0.**

9. Pelle Braendgaard, "How the Man Finally Brought E-gold Down," Stake Ventures, July 22, 2008, **https://blog.stakeventures.com/articles/the-man-finally-brought-e-gold-down.**

10. Julie Pitta, "Requiem for a Bright Idea," *Forbes,* November 1, 1999, 12:00 a.m. EST, **https://www.forbes.com/forbes/1999/1101/6411390a.html?sh=6aaf4ac2715f.**

11. Brian O'Connell, "History of PayPal: Timeline and Facts," TheStreet, August 26, 2019, updated January 2, 2020 12:48 p.m., **https://www.thestreet.com/technology/history-of-paypal-15062744;** "PayPal Surpasses 100 Million Account Mark," PayPal Newsroom, February 13, 2006, **https://newsroom.paypal-corp.com/2006-02-13-PayPal-Surpasses-100-Million-Account-Mark;** Shelly Banjo, "PayPal Once Worried No One Would Buy Stuff Online," Quartz, July 20, 2015, last updated July 20, 2022, **https://qz.com/458716/paypal-once-worried-no-one-would-buy-stuff-online-it-was-wrong/;** Tomio Geron and the Fintech team, "PayPal Changed The World. Now the World Is Changing PayPal," Protocol, February 2, 2022, **https://www.protocol.com/newsletters/protocol-fintech/paypal-payments-economy?rebelltitem=3#rebelltitem3;** Sam Cook, "Identity Theft Facts & Statistics: 2019–2022," Comparitech, August 1, 2022, **https://www.comparitech.com/identity-theft-protection/identity-theft-statistics/#:~:text=Fraud%20losses%20up%2045%25%20between,and%20%245.8%20billion%20in%202021.**

12. Donell Holloway, "Explainer: What Is Surveillance Capitalism and How Does It Shape Our Economy?," The Conversation, June 24, 2019, 11:34pm, **https://the-conversation.com/explainer-what-is-surveillance-capitalism-and-how-does-it-shape-our-economy-119158;** Shoshana Zuboff, "Facebook, Google and a Dark Age of Surveillance Capitalism," *Financial Times Magazine,* January 24, 2019, **https://www.ft.com/content/7fafec06-1ea2-11e9-b126-46fc3ad87c65;** Shoshana Zuboff, *The Age of Surveillance Capitalism: The Fight for a Human Future at the New Frontier of Power* (New York: Public Affairs, 2019).

Chapter 3

1. Alexander Klimburg, *The Darkening Web: The War for Cyberspace* (New York: Penguin, 2018), 46.

2. Stephen Levy, *Crypto: How the Code Rebels Beat the Government Saving Privacy in the Digital Age* (New York: Penguin, 2002).

3. Gareth Halfacree, "Cryptography Whizz Phil Zimmermann Looks Back at 30 Years of Pretty Good Privacy," *The Register,* June 8, 2021, 17:01, **https://www.theregister.com/2021/06/08/pgp_at_30/.**

4. For an example see Adam Back, "Munitions T-shirt," **Cypherspace.org**, accessed September 4, 2022, **http://www.cypherspace.org/adam/rsa/uk-shirt.html**.

5. Ian Goldberg and David Wagner, "Randomness and the Netscape Browser," Dr. Dobb's Journal, January 1996, **http://people.eecs.berkeley.edu/~daw/papers/ddj-netscape.html**.

6. Robert Manne, "The Cypherpunk Revolutionary," *The Monthly*, March 2011, **https://www.themonthly.com.au/issue/2011/february/1324596189/robert-manne/cypherpunk-revolutionary#mtr**.

7. Eric Hughes, "A Cypherpunk's Manifesto," **Activism.net**, March 9, 1993, **https://www.activism.net/cypherpunk/manifesto.html**; Samuel Falkon, "The CypherPunks Ten Prophets: John Gilmore," LinkedIn Pulse, January 5, 2018, **https://www.linkedin.com/pulse/cypherpunks-ten-prophets-john-gilmore-samuel-falkon/**; Jamie Bartlett, "Cypherpunks Write Code," *American Scientist* 104, no. 2 (March–April 2016): 120, **https://doi.org/10.1511/2016.119.120**; Jose Rey, "What Is a Cypherpunk?," Bitnovo.Blog, April 4, 2021, **https://blog.bitnovo.com/en/what-is-a-cypherpunk/**; Michelle Delio, "Hackers Lose a Patron Saint," *Wired*, July 22, 2003 2:00 a.m., **https://www.wired.com/2003/07/hackers-lose-a-patron-saint/**; Timothy C. May, "The Cyphernomicon: Cypherpunks FAQ and More," Version 0.666, September 9, 1994, Nakamoto Institute, **https://nakamotoinstitute.org/static/docs/cyphernomicon.txt**.

8. Timothy C. May, "The Cyphernomicon: Cypherpunks FAQ and More," Version 0.666, September 9, 1994, Nakamoto Institute, **https://nakamotoinstitute.org/static/docs/cyphernomicon.txt**; "What is the Cypherpunks Mailing List?," cryptoanarchy.wiki, accessed September 4, 2022, **https://cryptoanarchy.wiki/getting-started/what-is-the-cypherpunks-mailing-list**; Robert Manne, "The Cypherpunk Revolutionary," *The Monthly*, March 2011, **https://www.themonthly.com.au/issue/2011/february/1324596189/robert-manne/cypherpunk-revolutionary#mtr**.

9. Cynthia Dwork and Moni Naor, "Pricing via Processing or Combatting Junk Mail," accessed August 5, 2022, **https://www.wisdom.weizmann.ac.il/~naor/PAPERS/pvp.pdf**.

10. Wei Dai, "B-Money," **WeiDai.com**, accessed September 4, 2022, site last updated January 10, 2021, **http://www.weidai.com/bmoney.txt**; Gregory Snelgar, "History of Blockchain Part 3: Wei Dai (1998)," *Altcoin Magazine*, November 7, 2018, **https://medium.com/the-capital/history-of-blockchain-part-3-wei-dai-1998-1195ab5a4e08**; Samuel Mbaki Wanjiku, "Wei Dai: What Is His Influence in the Crypto Sector?," crypto.news, April 8, 2022, 2:24 p.m., **https://crypto.news/wei-dai-what-is-his-influence-in-the-crypto-sector/**.

11. Bram Cohen, "BitTorrent: A New P2P App," Yahoo eGroups, Monday July 2, 2001, 11:30 p.m., archived from the original on January 29, 2008; retrieved April 15, 2007, **https://web.archive.org/web/20080129085545/http://finance.groups.yahoo.com/group/decentralization/message/3160**.

12. "Julian Assange: What Is Happening to the WikiLeaks Founder?," The Week, October 28, 2021, **https://www.theweek.co.uk/101031/julian-assange-timeline-what-has-happened-to-wikileaks-founder**; Steve Butcher, "Assange Helped Our Police Catch Child Pornographers," The Age, February 12, 2011, 3:00am, **https://www.theage.com.au/national/victoria/assange-helped-our-police-catch-child-pornographers-20110211-1aqnl.html**; Nikki Barrowclough, "The

Secret Life of WikiLeaks Founder Julian Assange," *Sydney Morning Herald*, May 22, 2010, 3:00 a.m., **https://www.smh.com.au/technology/the-secret-life-of-wikileaks-founder-julian-assange-20100521-w1um.html;**

13. Julian Assange with Jacob Applebaum, Andy Müller-Maguhn, and Jérémie Zimmermann, *Cypherpunks: Freedom and the Future of the Internet* (New York: OR Books, 2012), 141.
14. "**marca@mcom.com** (Marc Andreessen)," cryptoanarchy.wiki, accessed September 5, 2022, **https://mailing-list-archive.cryptoanarchy.wiki/authors/marca_at_mcom_com_marc_andreessen_by_way_of_marca_at_mcom_com_marc_andreessen_/.**

Chapter 4

1. Satoshi Nakamoto, "Bitcoin P2P E-cash Paper," October 31, 2008, **https://satoshi.nakamotoinstitute.org/emails/cryptography/1/.**
2. Jamie Redman, "The Many Facts That Indicate Bitcoin's Creator Satoshi Nakamoto Won't Ever Come Back," **Bitcoin.com** News, October 27, 2021, **https://news.bitcoin.com/the-many-facts-that-indicate-bitcoins-creator-satoshi-nakamoto-wont-ever-come-back/.**
3. Nathaniel Whittemore, "13 Years On, the Meaning of 'Chancellor on the Brink of Second Bailout for Banks,'" CoinDesk, January 3, 2022, **https://www.coindesk.com/podcasts/the-breakdown-with-nlw/13-years-on-the-meaning-of-chancellor-on-the-brink-of-second-bailout-for-banks/.**
4. halfin (@halfin), "Running Bitcoin," Twitter, January 10, 2009, 7:33 p.m., **https://twitter.com/halfin/status/1110302988.**
5. Shaurya Malwa, "The First Bitcoin Transaction Was Sent to Hal Finney 12 Years Ago," Decrypt, January 12, 2021, **https://decrypt.co/53727/the-first-bitcoin-transaction-was-sent-to-hal-finney-12-years-ago.**
6. Liam Frost, "Hal Finney's Idea Now Sees $18 Million Bitcoin Price Prediction," Decrypt, January 13, 2020, **https://decrypt.co/16494/hal-finneys-idea-now-sees-18-million-bitcoin-price-prediction.**
7. Mark Rees, "Hal Finney – We Salute You," *Bitcoin Magazine*, September 2, 2014, **https://bitcoinmagazine.com/culture/hal-finney-salute-1409690363.**
8. vladusatii, "Is Hal Finney Satoshi Nakamoto? Evidence Thus Far," **teddit.net, https://teddit.net/r/Bitcoin/comments/pe2frp/is_hal_finney_satoshi_nakamoto_evidence_thusfar/?sort=confidence.**
9. Michael Kapilkov, "Twitter Evidence May Prove Hal Finney Is Not Satoshi," Cointelegraph, May 28, 2020, **https://cointelegraph.com/news/twitter-evidence-may-prove-hal-finney-is-not-satoshi.**
10. Dara Kerr, "Dorian Nakamoto Thanks Bitcoiners for Donating $20,000," CNET, April 22, 2014, 7:46 p.m., **https://www.cnet.com/tech/services-and-software/d-satoshi-nakamoto-thanks-bitcoiners-for-donating-20000/.**
11. Nick Szabo (@NickSzabo4), "@socrates1024 Not Satoshi, But Thank You," Twitter, July 6, 2014, 7:15 p.m., **https://twitter.com/nickszabo4/status/485970285254815745?lang=en;** Olga Kharif, "Latest Satoshi Nakamoto Candidate

Buying Bitcoin No Matter What," Bloomberg, June 2, 2020 at 7:39 a.m., **https:// www.bloomberg.com/news/articles/2020-06-02/latest-satoshi-nakamoto- candidate-buying-bitcoin-no-matter-what**.

12. Thomas Brewster, "Time to Call a Hoax? Inconsistencies on 'Probable' Bitcoin Creator's PhD and Supercomputers Revealed," *Forbes*, December 11, 2015, 04:55 a.m., **https://www.forbes.com/sites/thomasbrewster/2015/12/11/bitcoin- creator-satoshi-craig-wright-lies-hoax/?sh=9cb109f67947;** Elle Hunt and Paul Farrell, "Reported Bitcoin 'Founder' Craig Wright's Home Raided by Australian Police," *The Guardian*, December 8, 2015, 22:40, **https://www .theguardian.com/technology/2015/dec/09/bitcoin-founder-craig- wrights-home-raided-by-australian-police;** Josh Kenworthy, "Did the Real 'Satoshi Nakamoto' Just Stand Up?," *Christian Science Monitor*, May 2, 2016, **https://www.csmonitor.com/Technology/2016/0502/Did-the-real-Satoshi- Nakamoto-just-stand-up**.

13. Jordan Major, "Vitalik Buterin Calls Craig Wright a Scammer, Dares Self- proclaimed Nakamoto to Sue Him," Finbold, June 9, 2021, **https://finbold .com/vitalik-buterin-calls-craig-wright-a-scammer-dares-self- proclaimed-nakamoto-to-sue-him/;** Daniel Palmer, "Craig Wright Called 'Fraud' in Message Signed with Bitcoin Addresses He Claims to Own," CoinDesk, May 25, 2020, 7:44 a.m., updated September 14, 2021, 1:44 a.m., **https://www .coindesk.com/policy/2020/05/25/craig-wright-called-fraud-in-message- signed-with-bitcoin-addresses-he-claims-to-own/**.

14. Pete Rizzo, "7 Surprising Facts About Bitcoin Pizza Day," *Bitcoin Magazine*, May 21, 2022, **https://bitcoinmagazine.com/culture/beyond-the-bitcoin-pizza- price-surprising-facts-about-bitcoin-pizza-day**.

15. Kai Sedgwick, "Bitcoin History Part 9: Mt. Gox Is Born," **Bitcoin.com** News, January 26, 2019, **https://news.bitcoin.com/bitcoin-history-part-9-mt-gox-is- born/?preview_id=281310;** mtgox, "New Bitcoin Exchange (**mtgox.com**)," Bitcointalk, July 18, 2010, 01:57:19 a.m., **https://bitcointalk.org/index.php? topic=444.0**.

16. Alec Liu, "What Satoshi Said: Understanding Bitcoin Through the Lens of Its Enigmatic Creator," VICE, January 16, 2014, 2:30 a.m., **https://www.vice.com/ en/article/vvbm43/quotes-from-satoshi-understanding-bitcoin-through- the-lens-of-its-enigmatic-creator**.

17. KUSI Newsroom, "Economist Peter Schiff Warns Against Investing in Bitcoin," KUSI News, October 20, 2021, **https://www.kusi.com/economist-peter- schiff-warns-against-investing-in-bitcoin**.

18. Larry White, "A World Currency – Not a New Idea," *Bitcoin Magazine*, February 25, 2014, **https://bitcoinmagazine.com/culture/world-currency- new-idea-1393319726;** "Get Ready for the Phoenix," *The Economist* 306 (January 9, 1988): 9–10, **https://altcoopsys.org/wp-content/uploads/2017/01/ ArticleEconomist1988GetReadyforthePhoenix_001.pdf**.

19. Mat Di Salvo, "Bitcoin's Privacy Problem – And What Cypherpunks Are Doing to Solve It," Decrypt, August 12, 2022, **https://decrypt.co/107376/bitcoin- privacy-problem-what-cypherpunks-are-doing**.

Chapter 5

1. Daniel Phillips, "The Bitcoin Genesis Block: How It All Started," Decrypt, February 10, 2021, **https://decrypt.co/56934/the-bitcoin-genesis-block-how-it-all-started;** "Block Hash" [@2012-11-07 03:01:58], **BTC.com** Bitcoin Explorer, November 7, 2012, **https://explorer.btc.com/btc/block/206860;** "Block Hash" [@2021-11-02 19:10:46], **BTC.com** Bitcoin Explorer, November 2, 2021, **https://explorer.btc.com/btc/block/707957;** "Bitcoin Blockchain Size: 425.76 GB for Sep 07 2022," YCharts, **https://ycharts.com/indicators/bitcoin_blockchain_size.**
2. Bybit Learn, "Who Is Satoshi Nakamoto?," **Bybit.com,** May 11, 2021, **https://learn.bybit.com/crypto/who-is-satoshi-nakamoto/.**
3. Jake Frankenfield, "51% Attack," Investopedia, updated July 14, 2022, **https://www.investopedia.com/terms/1/51-attack.asp.**
4. "Bitcoin Hashrate Historical Chart," accessed September 8, 2022, **https://bitinfocharts.com/comparison/bitcoin-hashrate.html.**
5. "Proof-of-stake," Golden, accessed September 6, 2022, **https://golden.com/wiki/Proof-of-stake-8Y9VVJ.**
6. Jake Frankenfield, "Litecoin (LTC)," Investopedia, updated March 25, 2022, **https://www.investopedia.com/terms/l/litecoin.asp;** "What Is Ravencoin?," **Ravencoin.org,** accessed September 5, 2022, **https://ravencoin.org/about/.**
7. "Center for Sustainable Energy Walmart Supercenter Site Characterization Report," EPC-17-008, Center for Sustainable Energy, March 1, 2018, **https://sites.energycenter.org/sites/default/files/images/site/bigbox/pdf/EPC-17-008%20Final%20Walmart%20Draft%20Site%20Characterization%20Report%203-28-2018.pdf;** "ASIC Miner Profitability Ranking," WhatToMine, accessed September 8, 2022, **https://whattomine.com/miners;** Annika Feign, "How Much Energy Does Bitcoin Use?" CoinDesk Latest Headlines RSS, CoinDesk, August 18, 2021, **https://www.coindesk.com/business/2021/08/18/how-much-energy-does-bitcoin-use/;** "Make Crypto Green," Crypto Climate Accord, accessed September 8, 2022, **https://cryptoclimate.org/.**

Chapter 6

1. Timothy C. May, "Untraceable Digital Cash, Information Markets, and BlackNet," University of Miami School of Law website, February 24, 1997, **http://osaka.law.miami.edu/~froomkin/articles/tcmay.htm.**
2. "Ludwig von Mises argues that monopolies are the direct result of government intervention and not the product of any inherent tendency within the capitalist system (1949)," from *Human Action: A Treatise on Economics, vol. 2,* edited by Bettina Bien Greaves (Indianapolis: Liberty Fund, 2007), **https://oll.libertyfund.**

org/quote/ludwig-von-mises-argues-that-monopolies-are-the-direct-result-of-government-intervention-and-not-the-product-of-any-inherent-tendency-within-the-capitalist-system-1949; Jeff Riggenbach, "Samuel Edward Konkin III: Jeff Riggenbach," Mises Institute, July 20, 2010, **https://mises.org/library/samuel-edward-konkin-iii**; Vladimir G. Treml and Michael V. Alexeev, "The Second Economy and the Destabilization Effect of Its Growth on the State Economy in the Soviet Union: 1965–1989," Duke Economics Working Paper #95-33, April 27, 1997, **http://dx.doi.org/10.2139/ssrn.15546.**

3. C4SS, "Smashing the State for Fun and Profit Since 1969," Center for a State-less Society, accessed September 8, 2022, **https://c4ss.org/content/40129**; Dr. Paul J. Ennis, "Welcome to Bitcoin Country: Silk Road and the Lost Threads of Agorism," CoinDesk, September 23, 2017, **https://www.coindesk.com/markets/2017/09/23/welcome-to-bitcoin-country-silk-road-and-the-lost-threads-of-agorism/.**

4. Jesse Walker, "Sam Konkin, RIP," *Reason*, February 24, 2004, 12:29 p.m., **https://reason.com/2004/02/24/sam-konkin-rip/.**

5. Adrian Chen, "The Underground Website Where You Can Buy Any Drug Imaginable," *Gawker*, June 1, 2011, 3:20 p.m., **https://www.gawker.com/the-underground-website-where-you-can-buy-any-drug-imag-30818160.**

6. Andy Greenberg, "Collected Quotations of the Dread Pirate Roberts, Founder of Underground Drug Site Silk Road and Radical Libertarian," *Forbes*, January 29, 2014, **http://www.forbes.com/sites/andygreenberg/2013/04/29/collected-quotations-of-the-dread-pirate-roberts-founder-of-the-drug-site-silk-road-and-radical-libertarian/?sh=260c68361b0c.**

7. Colin Harper, "The Long and Winding Story of Silk Road, Bitcoin's Earliest Major Application," *Bitcoin Magazine*, October 1, 2020, **www.bitcoinmagazine.com/culture/the-long-and-winding-story-of-silk-road-bitcoins-earliest-major-application.**

8. Adrian Chen, "The Underground Website Where You Can Buy Any Drug Imaginable," *Gawker*, June 1, 2011, 3:20 p.m., **https://www.gawker.com/the-underground-website-where-you-can-buy-any-drug-imag-30818160**; John Edwards, "Bitcoin's Price History," Investopedia, updated July 02, 2022, **https://www.investopedia.com/articles/forex/121815/bitcoins-price-history.asp**

9. Matthew Guttenberg, "Open Letters to Ross Ulbricht: A True Libertarian Hero," *Bitcoin News*, November 28, 2015, **https://news.bitcoin.com/open-letters-ross-ulbricht-true-libertarian-hero/**; Meghan Ralston, "'Silk Road' Was Safer Than the Streets for Buyers/Sellers," Drug Policy Alliance, February 9, 2015, **http://www.drugpolicy.org/blog/silk-road-was-safer-streets-buyerssellers**; Kari Paul, "Ross Ulbricht Trial: Internet Libertarians Agree Their Dealer Is 'a Good Guy,'" VICE, February 6, 2015, **https://www.vice.com/en/article/8qxkxa/ross-ulbricht-groupies.**

10. "Manhattan U.S. Attorney Announces Seizure of Additional $28 Million Worth of Bitcoins Belonging to Ross William Ulbricht, Alleged Owner and Operator of 'Silk Road' Website," US Attorney's Office, Southern District of New York, October 25, 2013, **https://archives.fbi.gov/archives/newyork/press-releases/2013/manhattan-u.s.-attorney-announces-seizure-of-additional-28-million-worth-of-bitcoins-belonging-to-ross-william-ulbricht-alleged-owner-and-operator-of-silk-road-website.**

11. altoid, "anonymous market online?" #13860995, January 27, 2011, 03:28 p.m., Shroomery Message Board, **https://www.shroomery.org/forums/showflat .php/Number/13860995;** Vitalik Buterin, "Silk Road Shut Down, Alleged Owner Arrested," *Bitcoin Magazine*, October 2, 2013, **https://bitcoinmagazine.com/ culture/silk-road-shut-down-alleged-owner-arrested-1380753284;** Gary Alford, *Silk Road: Drugs, Death and the Dark Web*, documentary directed by Emily James and Mark Lewis, 2017, 23:35–25:25, **https://watchdocumentaries.com/silk-road-drugs-death-and-the-dark-web/.**

12. Alex Winter, *Banking on Bitcoin*, documentary directed by Christopher Cannucciarim, 2016, 38:38-39:33.

13. "Ross Ulbricht, A/k/a "Dread Pirate Roberts," Sentenced in Manhattan Federal Court to Life in Prison," Drug Enforcement Administration, US Department of Justice, May 29, 2015, **https://www.dea.gov/es/node/6592.**

14. Aaron Katersky, "El Chapo conviction upheld," ABC News, January 25, 2022, 12:27 p.m., **https://abcnews.go.com/US/el-chapo-conviction-upheld/ story?id=82463233.**

15. Silk Road Indictment Criminal No. CCB-13-0222 *(US v. Ross Ulbricht)*, Count Two, pages 6–12, **https://libertyunderattack.com/wp-content/uploads/2015/ 06/131001-Silk-Road-Indictment-Criminal-No.-CCB-13-0222-US-v.-Ross-Ulbricht.pdf;** John Hollenhorst, "Utah Man Forced to Fake Death After Dark Net Entanglement," KSL TV, updated December 7, 2018, 8:42 p.m., **https:// ksltv.com/404643/twists-turns-fake-death-darknet/;** Lisa Vaas, "Corrupt ex-DEA Agent Carl Force Gets 6 Years for Extorting Silk Road," Naked Security, Sophos, October 21, 2015, **https://nakedsecurity.sophos.com/2015/10/21/ corrupt-ex-dea-agent-carl-force-gets-6-years-for-extorting-silk-road/;** Lee Munson, "Secret Service Agent Pleads Guilty to Stealing Silk Road Bitcoins," Naked Security, Sophos, September 1, 2015, **https://nakedsecurity.sophos .com/2015/09/01/secret-service-agent-pleads-guilty-to-stealing-silk-road-bitcoins;** Nate Raymond, "Ex-agent in Silk Road Probe Gets More Prison Time for Bitcoin Theft," Reuters, November 7, 2017, 5:22 p.m., **https://www.reuters. com/article/us-usa-cyber-silkroad/ex-agent-in-silk-road-probe-gets-more-prison-time-for-bitcoin-theft-idUSKBN1D804H.**

16. "Motion to Dismiss Indictment," Case 1:13-cr-00222-CCB, Document 13, Filed July 26, 2018, **https://freeross.org/wp-content/uploads/2018/07/ Doc_14_Dismissal_Indictment_7-26-2018.pdf;** "Smeared with False Allegations," **FreeRoss.org,** accessed September 8, 2022, **https://freeross.org/false-allegations/.**

17. Andy Greenberg, "The Silk Road Creator's Life Sentence Actually Boosted Dark Web Drug Sales," *Wired*, May 23, 2017 10:00 a.m., **https://www.wired. com/2017/05/silk-road-creators-life-sentence-actually-boosted-dark-web-drug-sales/.**

18. Wang Wei, "More Than 400 Underground Sites Seized by FBI in 'Operation Onymous,'" *The Hacker News*, November 10, 2014, **https://thehackernews. com/2014/11/more-than-400-underground-sites-seized_10.html.**

19. Cyrus Farivar, "Before Sentencing, Ulbricht Begs for Leniency: 'Please Leave Me My Old Age,'" Ars Technica, May 24, 2015, **https://arstechnica.com/ tech-policy/2015/05/before-sentencing-ulbricht-begs-for-leniency-please-leave-me-my-old-age/;** "Art4Giving," FreeRossorg, accessed September 8, 2022,

https://freeross.org/art4giving; "Clemency for Ross Ulbricht, Serving Double Life + 40 Years for an E-Commerce Website," accessed August 6, 2022, **https://www.change.org/p/clemency-for-ross-ulbricht-condemned-to-die-in-prison-for-an-e-commerce-website.**

Chapter 7

1. Matthew O'Brien, "Everything You Need to Know About the Cyprus Bank Disaster," *The Atlantic*, March 18, 2013, **www.theatlantic.com/business/archive/2013/03/everything-you-need-to-know-about-the-cyprus-bank-disaster/274096/**; European Commission, "The Economic Adjustment Programme for Cyprus – First Review: Summer 2013," Economic and Financial Affairs, last updated November 27, 2014, **https://ec.europa.eu/economy_finance/publications/occasional_paper/2013/op161_en.htm#:~:text=The%20programme%20aims%20to%20address,Board%20on%2015%20May%202013.**
2. Maureen Farrell, "Bitcoin Prices Surge Post-Cyprus Bailout," CNN Business, March 28, 2013, 6:25 a.m., **https://money.cnn.com/2013/03/28/investing/bitcoin-cyprus/.**
3. Abbey Ellin, "Cyprus Crisis Boosting Unique Currency, the Bitcoin," ABC News, March 22, 2013, 1:26 p.m., **www.abcnews.go.com/Business/cyprus-crisis-boosting-unique-currency-bitcoin/story?id=18792763**; Maria Bustillos, "The Bitcoin Boom," *New Yorker*, April 1, 2013, **www.newyorker.com/tech/annals-of-technology/the-bitcoin-boom.**
4. John Edwards, "Bitcoin's Price History," Investopedia, updated July 2, 2022, **https://www.investopedia.com/articles/forex/121815/bitcoins-price-history.asp.**
5. "'Legitimate' Bitcoin's Value Soars After Senate Hearing," BBC News, November 19, 2013, **www.bbc.com/news/technology-24986264**; Steven Perlberg, "BERNANKE: Bitcoin 'May Hold Long-Term Promise,'" Insider, November 18, 2013, 9:20 a.m., **https://www.businessinsider.com/ben-bernanke-on-bitcoin-2013-11.**
6. John Edwards, "Bitcoin's Price History," Investopedia, updated July 2, 2022, **https://www.investopedia.com/articles/forex/121815/bitcoins-price-history.asp.**
7. Jake Frankenfield, "Mt. Gox," Investopedia, updated July 17, 2022, **https://www.investopedia.com/terms/m/mt-gox.asp**, citing Christian Decker and Roger Wattenhofer, "Bitcoin Transaction Malleability and MtGox," arXiv, March 24, 2014, Cornell University, **https://arxiv.org/pdf/1403.6676.pdf**; Robert McMillan, "Bitcoin Exchange Mt. Gox Goes Offline Amid Allegations of $350 Million Hack," *Wired*, February 24, 2014 11:57 p.m., **www.wired.com/2014/02/bitcoins-mt-gox-implodes-2/.**
8. Cyrus Farivar, "Original Mt. Gox Founder: 'I Lost Around $50,000' in Site's Collapse," Ars Technica, May 1, 2014, 11:15 a.m., **https://arstechnica.com/tech-policy/2014/05/original-mt-gox-founder-i-lost-around-50000-in-sites-collapse/**; Wolfie Zhao, "Mt Gox Founder Hit with Lawsuit over Alleged

Fraudulent Misrepresentation," CoinDesk, updated September 13, 2021 at 2:21 a.m., **https://www.coindesk.com/markets/2019/06/26/mt-gox-founder-hit-with-lawsuit-over-alleged-fraudulent-misrepresentation/**; Kevin Helms, "Mt Gox CEO Mark Karpelès Found Not Guilty of Embezzlement," **Bitcoin .com**, March 15, 2019, **https://news.bitcoin.com/mtgox-ceo-mark-karpeles-not-guilty-embezzlement/**; Yuri Kageyama, "Japan Court Backs Karpelès Conviction for Data Manipulation," ABC News, June 11, 2020, 9:10 p.m., **https:// abcnews.go.com/Technology/wireStory/japan-court-backs-karpeles-conviction-data-manipulation-71211400**.

9. Andreas Antonopoulos coined this phrase. stakefish, "Not Your Keys, Not Your Coins," Medium, May 21, 2020, **https://medium.com/stakefish/not-your-keys-not-your-coins-fad3d43c2713**.

10. Jon Southurst, "Roger Ver Pledges $20k in Bitcoin to **Antiwar.com** Campaign," CoinDesk, November 25, 2014, 3:24 a.m. PST, **https://www.coindesk .com/markets/2014/11/25/roger-ver-pledges-20k-in-bitcoin-to-antiwarcom-campaign/**; Roger Ver, "Bitcoin Venture Capitalist Roger Ver's Journey to Anarchism," *Daily Anarchist*, November 12, 2012, **https://dailyan-archist.com/2012/11/12/bitcoin-venture-capitalist-roger-vers-journey-to-anarchism/**.

11. "Did Mark Zuckerberg Steal Facebook? (Explained)," The Cold Wire, accessed September 6, 2022, **https://www.thecoldwire.com/did-mark-zuckerberg-steal-facebook/**; Ben Mezrich, *Bitcoin Billionaires: A True Story of Genius, Betrayal, and Redemption* (New York: Flatiron Books, 2019); Michael del Castillo, Susan Adams, and Antoine Gara, "Revenge of the Winklevii," *Forbes*, May 31, 2021, **https://www.forbes.com/sites/michaeldelcastillo/2021/04/05/revenge-of-the-winklevii-facebook-winklevoss-bitcoin-nft-billionaire-revenge/?sh=f9b84a11572a**.

12. Department of Justice, U.S. Attorney's Office, Southern District of New York, "Manhattan U.S. Attorney Announces Charges Against Bitcoin Exchangers, Including CEO of Bitcoin Exchange Company, for Scheme to Sell and Launder over $1 Million in Bitcoins Related to Silk Road Drug Trafficking," January 27, 2014, **https://www.justice.gov/usao-sdny/pr/manhattan-us-attorney-announces-charges-against-bitcoin-exchangers-including-ceo**; Shawn M. Carter, "What a 20-something Bitcoin Millionaire Learned from Going to Prison and Starting Over," CNBC Make It, updated December 8, 2017 9:07 p.m., **https:// www.cnbc.com/2017/12/08/what-bitcoin-millionaire-charlie-shrem-learned-from-going-to-prison.html**; Samuel Haig, "Charlie Shrem: BitInstant Was the Netscape of Crypto," Cointelegraph, May 2, 2020, **https://cointelegraph. com/news/charlie-shrem-bitinstant-was-the-netscape-of-crypto**.

13. Benjamin Bain, "From Goldman to SEC: Gensler's Next Stop Worries Wall Street," Bloomberg, January 13, 2021, 11:00 p.m., **https://www.bloomberg.com/news/ articles/2021-01-14/from-goldman-to-sec-gensler-s-next-stop-worries-wall-street#xj4y7vzkg**.

14. Sheppard Mullin, "BitLicense Regulations and the August 8, 2015 Deadline," Venture Law Blog, August 6, 2015, **https://www.venturelawblog.com/other/ bitlicense-regulations-and-the-august-8-2015-deadline/**; Daniel Roberts, "Behind the 'Exodus' of Bitcoin Startups from New York," *Fortune*, August 14, 2015,

8:19 a.m., **https://fortune.com/2015/08/14/bitcoin-startups-leave-newyork-bitlicense/**.

15. Pete Rizzo, "Gemini Exchange Moves Toward Launch with Twin NYDFS Approvals," CoinDesk, October 1, 2015, 2:10 p.m. PDT, **https://www.coindesk.com/markets/2015/10/01/gemini-exchange-moves-toward-launch-with-twin-nydfs-approvals/**.

Chapter 8

1. Jonathan Bier, *The Blocksize War: The Battle Over Who Controls Bitcoin's Protocol Rules* (Self-published, 2021).
2. Satoshi Nakamoto, "Satoshi's Last Email" (April 26, 2011), Satoshi's Archive, **Bitcoin.com**, accessed September 6, 2022, **https://www.bitcoin.com/satoshi-archive/emails/gavin-andresen/1/**; Kai Sedgwick, "Satoshi's Final Messages Leave Tantalizing Clues to His Disappearance," **Bitcoin.com**, October 30, 2019, **https://news.bitcoin.com/satoshis-final-messages-leave-tantalizing-clues-to-his-disappearance/**.
3. Tom Simonite, "The Man Who Really Built Bitcoin," MIT Technology Review, August 15, 2014, **www.technologyreview.com/2014/08/15/12784/the-man-who-really-built-bitcoin/**.
4. Jean Nichols, "What Is the Maximum Size of a Bitcoin Block?," Supply Chain Game Changer, August 10, 2022, **https://supplychaingamechanger.com/what-is-the-maximum-size-of-a-bitcoin-block/**; Jonathan Bier, "The Blocksize War–Chapter 1: First Strike," BitMEX Research, March 22, 2021, **https://blog.bitmex.com/the-blocksize-war-chapter-1-first-strike/**; see also note 1.
5. Till Musshoff, "The Bitcoin Block Size Wars Explained," bitrawr, June 23, 2021, **www.bitrawr.com/bitcoin-block-size-debate-explained**.
6. Jonathan Bier, *The Blocksize War*.
7. Joseph Young, "Coinbase CEO Objects Reddit Bitcoin Censorship, Decides to Censor Moderators," Cointelegraph, August 01, 2016, **https://cointelegraph.com/news/coinbase-ceo-objects-reddit-bitcoin-censorship-decides-to-censor-moderators**.
8. u/nullc, "An Initiative to Bring Advanced Privacy Features to Bitcoin Has Been Opened in the Bitcoin Core Issue Tracker," r/bitcoin, reddit, August 18, 2015, **https://www.reddit.com/r/Bitcoin/comments/3hfgpo/comment/cu7mhw8/?context=9**.
9. u/Theymos, "It's Time for a Break: About the Recent Mess & Temporary New Rules," r/bitcoin, Reddit, August 16, 2015, 5:50 p.m. PDT, **https://www.reddit.com/r/Bitcoin/comments/3h9cq4/its_time_for_a_break_about_the_recent_mess/?st=ja45nlq1&sh=ab0c785c**.
10. u/zowki, "Vitalik Buterin on /r/Bitcoin censorship," r/btc, reddit, August 13, 2017, **https://www.reddit.com/r/btc/comments/6te1uu/vitalik_buterin_on_rbitcoin_censorship/**; Jamie Redman, "Andreas Antonopoulos: AMA With the 8BTC Community," **Bitcoin.com** News, July 31, 2016, **https://news.bitcoin.com/antonopoulos-ama-8btc-community/**.

11. Alexander Bowring, "'Bitcoin Jesus' Roger Ver Faces Further BCH Backlash," FullyCrypto, February 21, 2018, **https://fullycrypto.com/bitcoin-jesus-roger-ver-faces-bch-backlash.**

12. Justin O'Connell, "Coinbase Tests Bitcoin XT, Gets Removed from **Bitcoin.org,**" Bitcoinist, [2015], accessed September 6, 2022, **https://bitcoinist.com/coinbase-tests-bitcoin-xt-removed-bitcoin-org/.**

13. Mark Hunter, "Bitcoin XT: The Forgotten First Bitcoin Hard Fork," FullyCrypto, April 20, 2022, **https://fullycrypto.com/bitcoin-xt-the-forgotten-first-bitcoin-hard-fork.**

14. Gavin Andresen website, **https://gavinandresen.ninja**; Stan Schroeder, "Craig Wright to Offer 'Extraordinary Proof' He Is the Creator of Bitcoin," Mashable, May 4, 2016, **https://mashable.com/article/craig-wright-proof-nakamoto**; HAL 90210, "Bitcoin Project Blocks Out Gavin Andresen over Satoshi Nakamoto claims," *The Guardian*, May 6, 2016, 11:21 EDT, **https://www.theguardian.com/technology/2016/may/06/bitcoin-project-blocks-out-gavin-andresen-over-satoshi-nakamoto-claims.**

15. Gregory Maxwell via bitcoin-dev, "BIP Proposal: Inhibiting a Covert Attack on the Bitcoin POW Function," April 5, 2017, 14:39:39, The Mail Archive, **https://www.mail-archive.com/bitcoin-dev@lists.linuxfoundation.org/msg05055.html.**

16. Gregory Maxwell via bitcoin-dev, "BIP Proposal: Inhibiting a Covert Attack on the Bitcoin POW Function," April 5, 2017, 14:39:39, The Mail Archive, **https://www.mail-archive.com/bitcoin-dev@lists.linuxfoundation.org/msg05055.html**; Kyle Torpey, "Is a Mining Manufacturer Blocking SegWit to Benefit from ASICBOOST?," *Bitcoin Magazine*, April 10, 2017, **www.bitcoinmagazine.com/business/mining-manufacturer-blocking-segwit-benefit-asicboost**; Admin, "Regarding Recent Allegations and Smear Campaigns," **Blog.Bitmain.com**, April 7, 2017, **https://blog.bitmain.com/en/regarding-recent-allegations-smear-campaigns/.**

17. Andrey Shevchenko, "AsicBoost Dominates Bitcoin Mining, Solving Bitmain's 2017 Controversy," Cointelegraph, March 12, 2020, **https://cointelegraph.com/news/asicboost-dominates-bitcoin-mining-solving-bitmains-2017-controversy**; Laura Shin, "Will This Battle for the Soul of Bitcoin Destroy It?," *Forbes*, October 23, 2017, 1:35 p.m., **www.forbes.com/sites/laurashin/2017/10/23/will-this-battle-for-the-soul-of-bitcoin-destroy-it/?sh=5119dcb13d3c.**

18. Kyle Torpey, "Is a Mining Manufacturer Blocking SegWit to Benefit from ASIC-BOOST?," *Bitcoin Magazine*, April 10, 2017, **www.bitcoinmagazine.com/business/mining-manufacturer-blocking-segwit-benefit-asicboost.**

19. Carlo C, "Barry Silbert Leaves Second Market to Promote and Improve Bitcoin," Cointelegraph, July 27, 2014, **https://cointelegraph.com/news/-barry-silbert-leaves-second-market-to-promote-and-improve-bitcoin**; Dan Primack, "SecondMarket founder launches bitcoin conglomerate," *Fortune*, October 27, 2015, 3:14 p.m., **https://fortune.com/2015/10/27/secondmarket-bitcoin-dcg/.**

20. Sterlin Lujan, "Fork Watch: 'Bitcoin Cash' Support Grows as August 1 Draws Near," **Bitcoin.com** News, July 28, 2017, **https://news.bitcoin.com/fork-watch-bitcoin-cash-support-grows-as-aug-1-draws-near/**; Benjamin Pirus, "Opinion: Upcoming BCH fork is bad luck for big blockers," Crypto Insider,

November 14, 2018, **https://cryptoinsider.media/opinion-upcoming-bch-fork-probably-bad-luck-big-blockers/**.

21. Diwaker Gupta, "The Bitcoin Maximalist Movement Has Gotten Toxic. Bitcoin Optimalism Is a Better Way," Built In, August 31, 2022, **www.builtin.com/blockchain/bitcoin-maximalist**.

22. "Bitcoin Cash," CoinMarketCap, accessed September 6, 2022, **https://coinmar-ketcap.com/currencies/bitcoin-cash/**.

23. Adriana Hamacher, "Is Blockstream a Peril to Bitcoin's Decentralization?," Decrypt, October 16, 2020, **https://decrypt.co/45020/is-blockstream-a-peril-to-bitcoins-decentralization**.

Chapter 9

1. "About Bitcoin Magazine," accessed September 6, 2022, **https://bitcoinmagazine.com/about**.

2. Jake Frankenfield, "Cryptocurrency Airdrop," Investopedia, updated June 14, 2022, **https://www.investopedia.com/terms/a/airdrop-cryptocurrency.asp**.

3. Drew Cordell, "Colored Coins, What They Are and How They Work on the Bitcoin Blockchain," Bitcoinist, 2015, accessed September 6, 2022, **https://bitcoinist.com/colored-coins-work-bitcoin-blockchain/**.

4. Nick Szabo, "Smart Contracts: Building Blocks for Digital Markets," 1996, accessed August 20, 2022, **https://www.fon.hum.uva.nl/rob/Courses/Information-InSpeech/CDROM/Literature/LOTwinterschool2006/szabo.best.vwh.net/smart_contracts_2.html**.

5. Yoni Assia, Vitalik Buterin, Lior Hakim, Meni Rosenfeld, and Rotem Lev, "Colored Coins Whitepaper," [2013], accessed August 20, 2022, **https://www.etoro.com/wp-content/uploads/2022/03/Colored-Coins-white-paper-Digital-Assets.pdf**; "Ethereum (with Packy McCormick)," Season 8, Episode 8, Acquired, July 6, 2021, **https://www.acquired.fm/episodes/Ethereum**; David Gilson, "Master-Coin to Create New Altcoins in Bitcoin's Block Chain," CoinDesk, August 25, 2013, 2:45 a.m. PDT, updated Sep 10, 2021 at 4:30 a.m. PDT, **https://www.coindesk.com/markets/2013/08/25/mastercoin-to-create-new-altcoins-in-bitcoins-block-chain/**; Vitalik Buterin, "Ethereum White Paper: A Next Generation Smart Contract & Decentralized Application Platform," 2013, accessed August 21, 2022, **https://blockchainlab.com/pdf/Ethereum_white_paper-a_next_genera-tion_smart_contract_and_decentralized_application_platform-vitalik-buterin.pdf**; Laura Shin, *The Cryptopians: Idealism, Greed, Lies, and the Making of the First Big Cryptocurrency Craze* (New York: PublicAffairs, 2022); Camila Russo, *The Infinite Machine: How an Army of Crypto-hackers Is Building the Next Internet with Ethereum* (New York: Harper Business, 2020).

6. Nick Paumgarten, "The Prophets of Cryptocurrency Survey the Boom and Bust," *The New Yorker*, October 22, 2018, **https://www.newyorker.com/magazine/2018/10/22/the-prophets-of-cryptocurrency-survey-the-boom-and-bust**; CoinYuppie, "*Time Magazine* Feature: Vitalik is Worrying About the Future of the Crypto Industry," CoinYuppie, March 19, 2022, 10:22, **https://coinyuppie.com/**

time-magazine-feature-vitalik-is-worrying-about-the-future-of-the-crypto-industry/; Laura Shin, *The Cryptopians: Idealism, Greed, Lies, and the Making of the First Big Cryptocurrency Craze* (New York: PublicAffairs, 2022).

7. Camila Russo, *The Infinite Machine: How an Army of Crypto-hackers Is Building the Next Internet with Ethereum* (New York: Harper Business, 2020); see also note 6.

8. Laura Shin, *The Cryptopians: Idealism, Greed, Lies, and the Making of the First Big Cryptocurrency Craze* (New York: PublicAffairs, 2022).

9. "Investor Bulletin: Initial Coin Offerings," US Securities and Exchange Commission, July 25, 2017, **https://www.sec.gov/oiea/investor-alerts-and-bulletins/ ib_coinofferings**; Laura Shin, *The Cryptopians: Idealism, Greed, Lies, and the Making of the First Big Cryptocurrency Craze* (New York: PublicAffairs, 2022); "SEC Director Hinman's Remarks Confirm that Ether and Bitcoin Are Not Securities," Ropes & Gray, June 18, 2018, **www.ropesgray.com/en/newsroom/ alerts/2018/06/SEC-Director-Hinmans-Remarks-Confirm-that-Ether-and-Bitcoin-Are-Not-Securities**.

10. Protos Staff, "Former SEC director Hinman made millions from a pro-Ethereum firm during tenure," Protos, May 13, 2022, 3:16 p.m., **www.protos.com/former-sec-director-hinman-made-millions-from-a-pro-ethereum-firm-during-tenure**; Thomas Yeung, "ETHGate 2022: The Ethereum Scandal XRP Investors Are Calling 'Bigger Than Enron,'" Nasdaq, January 6, 2022 03:26PM EST, **https:// www.nasdaq.com/articles/ethgate-2022%3A-the-ethereum-scandal-xrp-investors-are-calling-bigger-than-enron**.

11. Nick Paumgarten, "The Prophets of Cryptocurrency Survey the Boom and Bust," *The New Yorker*, October 22, 2018, **https://www.newyorker.com/ magazine/2018/10/22/the-prophets-of-cryptocurrency-survey-the-boom-and-bust**; see also Russo, *Infinite Machine* (note 7) and Shin, *Cryptopians* (note 8).

12. Adriana Hamacher, "Who are Ethereum's co-founders and where are they now?," Decrypt, July 28, 2020, **https://decrypt.co/36641/who-are-ethereums-co-founders-and-where-are-they-now**.

13. Russo, *Infinite Machine* (note 7) and Shin, *Cryptopians* (note 8).

14. "Ethereum Token Sale Statistics," CoinCodex, accessed September 7, 2022, **https://coincodex.com/ico/ethereum/**.

15. Adriana Hamacher, "The 10 Biggest ICOs: Here's Where the Money Went," Decrypt, January 14, 2021, **https://decrypt.co/53950/the-10-biggest-icos-heres-where-the-money-went**.

16. Sergio D. Lerner, "Lessons from the DAO incident," RSK, accessed September 7, 2022, **https://blog.rsk.co/noticia/lessons-from-the-dao-incident/**.

17. Nathaniel Popper, "Paper Points Up Flaws in Venture Fund Based on Virtual Money," *New York Times*, May 27, 2016, **https://www.nytimes.com/2016/05/28/ business/dealbook/paper-points-up-flaws-in-venture-fund-based-on-virtual-money.html**; Ernesto Frontera, "A History of 'The DAO' Hack," CoinMarketCap Alexandria, last updated [November 2021], **https://coinmarketcap .com/alexandria/article/a-history-of-the-dao-hack**.

18. Joon Ian Wong and Ian Kar, "Everything you need to know about the Ethereum 'hard fork,'" Quartz, July 18, 2016, last updated July 20, 2022, **https://qz.com/730004/ everything-you-need-to-know-about-the-ethereum-hard-fork/**.

19. "Code is Law," Ethereum Classic, February 21, 2022, **https://ethereumclassic .org/why-classic/code-is-law**.

20. Barry Silbert, "Bought my first non-bitcoin digital currency...Ethereum Classic (ETC). At $0.50, risk/return felt right. And I'm philosophically on board," Twitter, July 25, 2016, 10:29 a.m., **https://twitter.com/BarrySilbert/status/757628841 938472961?s=20&t=qzFv8ZR2dVvFkx4kk-RHjA.**

21. Laura Shin, "Exclusive: Austrian Programmer and Ex Crypto CEO Likely Stole $11 Billion of Ether," *Forbes*, February 22, 2022, 6:30 a.m. EST, **https://www .forbes.com/sites/laurashin/2022/02/22/exclusive-austrian-programmer- and-ex-crypto-ceo-likely-stole-11-billion-of-ether/?sh=759fabde7f58;** Davit Babayan, "Controversial TenX Responds to Outrage, Crypto Community Not Happy," NewsBTC, [2018], accessed September 7, 2022, **https://www.newsbtc .com/news/controversial-tenx-responds-to-outrage-crypto-community- not-happy/.**

22. Mat Di Salvo, "Former Crypto CEO Denies Responsibility for $11 Billion Ethereum DAO Hack," Decrypt, February 22, 2022, **https://decrypt.co/93547/crypto-ceo- denies-11-billion-ethereum-dao-hack.**

23. Bilal Jafar, "Grayscale's Ethereum Trust Holds $12 Billion Worth of ETH," Finance Magnates, June 9, 2021, 8:15 GMT, **https://www.financemagnates. com/cryptocurrency/news/grayscales-ethereum-trust-holds-12-billion- worth-of-eth/.**

Chapter 10

1. Office of Investor Education and Advocacy, "Ponzi Schemes Using Virtual Currencies," US Securities and Exchange Commission Pub. No. 153, July 2013, **https:// www.sec.gov/files/ia_virtualcurrencies.pdf.**

2. Sam Klemens, "How Long Does a Bitcoin Transaction Take? Bitcoin Unconfirmed Transactions," Crypto News, July 03, 2020, **https://www.exodus.com/news/ how-long-does-a-bitcoin-transaction-take/;** Alyssa Hertig, "A Guide to Saving on Bitcoin's High Transaction Fees," CoinDesk, February 26, 2021 at 12:31 p.m., updated September 14, 2021 at 5:18 a.m., **https://www.coindesk.com/ tech/2021/02/26/a-guide-to-saving-on-bitcoins-high-transaction-fees/.**

3. Eric Markowitz, "How Instagram Grew from Foursquare Knock-Off to $1 Billion Photo Empire," *Inc.*, accessed September 11, 2022, **https://www.inc.com/ eric-markowitz/life-and-times-of-instagram-the-complete-original-story. html;** "Was YouTube a Dating Site?" BrandMentions, accessed September 11, 2022, **https://brandmentions.com/wiki/Was_YouTube_a_Dating_Site;** Katharine A. Kaplan, "Facemash Creator Survives Ad Board," *Harvard Crimson*, November 19, 2003, **https://www.thecrimson.com/article/2003/11/19/ facemash-creator-survives-ad-board-the/;** Eliana Dockterman, "How 'Hot or Not' Created the Internet We Know Today," *TIME*, June 18, 2014, 1:18 p.m., **https://time.com/2894727/hot-or-not-internet/;** Malcom A. Glenn, "For Now, Facebook Foes Continue Fight Against Site," *Harvard Crimson*, July 27, 2007, **https://www.thecrimson.com/article/2007/7/27/for-now-facebook-foes- continue-fight/.**

4. Till Musshoff, "The Bitcoin Block Size Wars Explained," bitrawr, June 23, 2021, **www.bitrawr.com/bitcoin-block-size-debate-explained.**
5. Murtuza Merchant, "Utility Tokens vs. Equity Tokens: Key Differences Explained," Cointelegraph, May 16, 2022, **https://cointelegraph.com/explained/ utility-tokens-vs-equity-tokens-key-differences-explained#:~:text= Usually%20associated%20with%20initial%20coin,to%20develop%20a%20 cryptocurrency%20project.**
6. Team Blockdata, "Top Banks Investing in Crypto and Blockchain," Blockdata, June 14, 2022, last updated: September 4th, 2022, **https://www.blockdata .tech/blog/general/top-banks-investing-in-crypto-and-blockchain-may-2022-update.**
7. Ekin Genç, "How Are Institutions and Companies Investing in Crypto?," Coin-Desk, June 24, 2022, 2:27 p.m. PDT, **https://www.coindesk.com/learn/how-are-institutions-and-companies-investing-in-crypto/.**
8. Justin Harper, "How Much Gold Is There Left to Mine in the World?," BBC, September 23, 2020, **https://www.bbc.com/news/business-54230737.**
9. Jake Frankenfield, "HODL," Investopedia, updated July 18, 2022, **https:// www.investopedia.com/terms/h/hodl.asp#:~:text=HODL%20is%20a%20 term%20derived,forum%20where%20the%20typo%20appeared.**
10. Luke Conway, "Bitcoin Halving: What You Need to Know," Investopedia, updated November 29, 2021, **https://www.investopedia.com/bitcoin-halving-4843769.**
11. Altcoin Daily. (2022, July 7). "Michael Saylor speaks on Bitcoin, Ethereum, Cardano, & Altcoin Market!" YouTube. Retrieved October 3, 2022, from **https:// www.youtube.com/watch?v=JGvdMWvyRAA.**
12. Michael Bellusci and Christine Lee, "Michael Saylor Lost Big in the Dot-Com Bubble and Bitcoin's Crash. Now He Aims to Rebound Again." CoinDesk Latest Headlines RSS. CoinDesk, August 4, 2022, **https://www.coindesk.com/ business/2022/08/04/michael-saylor-lost-big-in-the-dot-com-bubble-and-bitcoins-crash-now-he-aims-to-rebound-again/.**
13. Jordan Tuwiner, "Microstrategy Bitcoin Holdings Chart & Purchase History." Buy Bitcoin Online: 9+ Best Trusted Sites (2022). Accessed October 3, 2022, **https:// buybitcoinworldwide.com/microstrategy-statistics/.**
14. Ryan Smith, "Michael Saylor Announces 'Bitcoin for Corporations' Educational Event." BeInCrypto, January 12, 2021, **https://beincrypto.com/michael-saylor-announces-bitcoin-for-corporations-educational-event/.**

Chapter 11

1. James Royal, "Bitcoin's Price History: 2009 to 2022," Bankrate, June 14, 2022, **https://www.bankrate.com/investing/bitcoin-price-history/.**
2. "Altcoin Exchange 101: A Comprehensive Guide on How to Buy and Sell Altcoins," Cointelegraph, accessed September 8, 2022, **www.cointelegraph.com/ altcoins-for-beginners/altcoin-exchange-101-a-comprehensive-guide-on-how-to-buy-and-sell-altcoins.**

3. Justina Lee, Yuji Nakamura, and Benjamin Robertson, "How a Billionaire Crypto King Built the No. 1 Exchange in Just 8 Months," Bloomberg, March 28, 2018, 9:00 a.m. PDT, **https://www.bloomberg.com/news/articles/2018-03-28/cryptos-billionaire-trading-king-has-suddenly-run-into-problems#xj4y7vzkg**; Pamela Ambler, "From Zero to Crypto Billionaire in Under A Year: Meet the Founder of Binance," *Forbes*, February 7, 2018, 4:45am EST, **https://www.forbes.com/sites/pamelaambler/2018/02/07/changpeng-zhao-binance-exchange-crypto-cryptocurrency/**; see also Ash Jurberg, "The Former McDonalds Cook Who Made $1 Billion in Less Than 7 Months," Entrepreneur's Handbook, January 12, 2018, **https://entrepreneurshandbook.co/the-former-mcdonalds-cook-who-made-1-billion-in-less-than-7-months-6f82f811c04a**.

4. Nellie Bowles, "Everyone Is Getting Hilariously Rich and You're Not," *New York Times*, January 13, 2018, **www.nytimes.com/2018/01/13/style/bitcoin-millionaires.html**; Cryptopedia Staff, "Ethereum and the ICO Boom," Gemini, updated March 10, 2022, **https://www.gemini.com/cryptopedia/initial-coin-offering-explained-ethereum-ico**.

5. Gareth Jenkinson, "Culture Shock: Bitcoin a Part of All Walks of Life in 2017," Cointelegraph, December 31, 2017, **www.cointelegraph.com/news/culture-shock-bitcoin-a-part-of-all-walks-of-life-in-2017**; James Royal, "Bitcoin's Price History: 2009 to 2022," Bankrate, June 14, 2022, **https://www.bankrate.com/investing/bitcoin-price-history/**.

6. Tae Kim, "Warren Buffett Says Bitcoin Is 'Probably Rat Poison Squared,'" CNBC, May 5, 2018, 2:55 p.m. EDT, updated May 6, 2018, 10:48 a.m. EDT, **cnbc.com/2018/05/05/warren-buffett-says-bitcoin-is-probably-rat-poison-squared.html**; Paul Vigna, "Jamie Dimon: I 'Regret' Calling Bitcoin a Fraud," *Wall Street Journal*, updated January 9, 2018, 10:38 a.m. ET, **https://www.wsj.com/articles/jamie-dimon-i-regret-calling-bitcoin-a-fraud-1515510361?tesla=y**; Hugh Son, "JP Morgan Is Rolling Out the First US bank-backed Cryptocurrency to Transform Payments Business," CNBC, updated Thu, Feb 14 20197:13 p.m. EST, **https://www.cnbc.com/2019/02/13/jp-morgan-is-rolling-out-the-first-us-bank-backed-cryptocurrency-to-transform-payments--.html**; Kate Birch, "JP Morgan Is First Leading Bank to Launch in the Metaverse," *FinTech Magazine*, February 17, 2022, **https://fintechmagazine.com/banking/jp-morgan-becomes-the-first-bank-to-launch-in-the-metaverse**; Taylor Locke, "JPMorgan CEO Jamie Dimon Says He's Still a Crypto Skeptic: 'I'm Not a Bitcoin Supporter. I Have No Interest in It,'" CNBC, May 4, 2021, 1:40 p.m. EDT, **https://www.cnbc.com/2021/05/04/jpmorgan-ceo-jamie-dimon-im-not-a-bitcoin-supporter.html**.

7. Turner Wright, "Cato Institute CEO Says His Daughter Married the 'Bitcoin Sign Guy' from 2017 Hearing," Cointelegraph, **https://cointelegraph.com/news/cato-institute-ceo-says-his-daughter-married-the-bitcoin-sign-guy-from-2017-hearing**.

8. Shivdeep Dhaliwal, "Japan Officially Recognizes Bitcoin and Digital Currencies as Money," Cointelegraph, May 2, 2016, **https://cointelegraph.com/news/japan-officially-recognizes-bitcoin-and-digital-currencies-as-money**; Selva Ozelli, "Why Singapore Is One of the Most Crypto-friendly Countries," Cointelegraph, February 12, 2022, **www.cointelegraph.com/news/why-singapore-is-one-of-the-most-crypto-friendly-countries**; Adriana Hamacher, "'Blockchain

Island' Strategy Led to $70 Billion Passing Through Malta," Decrypt, June 22, 2021, **www.decrypt.co/74204/blockchain-island-strategy-led-to-70-billion-passing-through-malta-report;** Cryptopedia Staff, "Ethereum and the ICO Boom," Gemini, updated March 10, 2022, **https://www.gemini.com/cryptopedia/initial-coin-offering-explained-ethereum-ico.**

9. Evelyn Cheng, "Digital Currency Ripple Soars Nearly 56 percent, Becomes Second-Largest Cryptocurrency by Market Cap," CNBC, updated December 30, 2017, 12:47 p.m., **https://www.cnbc.com/2017/12/29/ripple-soars-becomes-second-biggest-cryptocurrency-by-market-cap.html;** "Ripple (XRP) Price Per Day from August 2013 to September 5, 2022," Statista, accessed September 8, 2022, **https://www.statista.com/statistics/807266/ripple-price-monthly/.**

10. Brent Xu, Dhruv Luthra, Zak Cole, and Nate Blakely, "EOS: An Architectural, Performance, and Economic Analysis," **https://cdn0.tnwcdn.com/wp-content/blogs.dir/1/files/2018/11/EOS_Report.pdf;** "Report: Censorship-Prone EOS 'Needs to Re-Architect Its Infrastructure,'" *Bitcoin News*, November 19, 2018, **https://thebitcoinnews.com/report-censorship-prone-eos-needs-to-re-architect-its-infrastructure/;** Mark Hunter, "BitMEX Reopens EOS Debate by Re-posting Damning Report," Fully Crypto, November 25, 2018, **https://fullycrypto.com/bitmex-reopens-eos-debate-by-re-posting-damning-report;** Thomas B. Cox, "Yes, EOS Is a Blockchain," Medium, November 6, 2018, **https://thomasbcox.medium.com/yes-eos-is-a-blockchain-a5921e5497d5.**

11. Philipp Traugott, "Dan 'The Butterfly' Larimer Is Flitting from One Token to Another. After BitShares, Steemit and EOS, Is He Going to Start Another Project?" **CaptainAltcoin.com**, October 25, 2019, **https://captainaltcoin.com/dan-the-butterfly-larimer-is-flitting-from-one-token-to-another-after-bitshares-steemit-and-eos-is-he-going-to-start-another-project/.**

12. Christopher Harland-Dunaway, "The Many Escapes of Justin Sun," The Verge, March 9, 2022, 11:00 a.m. EST, **https://www.theverge.com/c/22947663/justin-sun-tron-cryptocurrency-poloniex;** "Tron's Whitepaper Is Copied, Plagiarized," Trustnodes, August 1, 2018, 11:54 a.m., **https://www.trustnodes.com/2018/01/08/trons-whitepaper-copied-plagiarized.**

13. Shareen Pathak, "When Lambo? How Lamborghini Became the Status Brand of the Crypto Boom," Digiday, May 24, 2018, **https://digiday.com/?p=288731;** Dominik Stroukal, "Bitcoin Bull Markets: Four Different Stories of Bitcoin Highs," SatoshiLabs, Trezor Blog, December 10, 2020, **https://blog.trezor.io/what-happens-in-a-bullrun-four-different-histories-of-bitcoin-highs-3371e8073264.**

14. "$24 Million Iced Tea Company Says It's Pivoting to the Blockchain, and Its Stock Jumps 200%," CNBC, updated December 26, 2017, 11:03 a.m. EST, **https://www.cnbc.com/2017/12/21/long-island-iced-tea-micro-cap-adds-blockchain-to-name-and-stock-soars.html;** Nathaniel Popper, "Floyd Mayweather and DJ Khaled Are Fined in I.C.O. Crackdown," *New York Times*, November 29, 2018, **https://www.nytimes.com/2018/11/29/technology/floyd-mayweather-dj-khaled-sec-fine-initial-coin-offering.html.**

15. "The Inside Story of the CryptoKitties Congestion Crisis," ConsenSys, February 20, 2018, **https://consensys.net/blog/news/the-inside-story-of-the-cryptokitties-congestion-crisis/;** Stan Higgins, "From $900 to $20,000: Bitcoin's Historic 2017 Price Run Revisited," CoinDesk, December 29, 2017 at 5:30 a.m.

PST, https://www.coindesk.com/markets/2017/12/29/from-900-to-20000-bitcoins-historic-2017-price-run-revisited/.

16. John P. Njuion, "It Might Be Time to Forgive Charlie Lee For Selling his Litecoin Bag," Ethereum World News, February 14, 2021, https://en.ethereum worldnews.com/it-might-be-time-to-forgive-charlie-lee-for-selling-his-litecoin-bag/.

17. Ali Raza, "Vitalik Buterin: Ethereum Foundation Made $100 Million by Selling ETH at ATH," Bitcoinist, 2019, accessed September 8, 2022, https://bitcoinist .com/ethereum-foundation-made-100-million-by-selling-eth/; Vitalik Buterin, "*All* crypto communities, Ethereum included, should heed these words of warning. Need to differentiate between getting hundreds of billions of dollars of digital paper wealth sloshing around and actually achieving something meaningful for society," Twitter, December 27, 2017, 3:59 a.m., https://twitter.com/VitalikButerin/status/945987507941978112?ref_src=twcamp%5Eshare%7Ctwsrc%5Em5%7Ct wgr%5Eemail%7Ctwcon%5E7046%7Ctwterm%5E3.

18. Aaron Hankin, "Americans Lost $1.7 Billion Trading Bitcoin in 2018 – and More Than Half Don't Know They Can Claim a Deduction," MarketWatch, January 15, 2019 at 9:44 a.m. ET, https://www.marketwatch.com/story/americans-lost-17-billion-trading-bitcoin-in-2018-and-more-than-half-dont-know-they-can-claim-a-deduction-2019-01-15.

Chapter 12

1. Kira Belova, "What Are Layer 2 Blockchain Scaling Solutions and What Benefits Do They Offer?," PixelPlex, January 10, 2022, https://pixelplex.io/blog/what-is-layer-2/; Ekin Genç, "What Is Optimism?" CoinDesk, June 3, 2022, https:// www.coindesk.com/learn/what-is-optimism/.

2. Ekin Genç, "Cardano Hits All-Time High as Crypto Market Rally Continues," Decrypt, August 28, 2021, https://decrypt.co/79133/cardano-reaches-all-time-high-as-rally-continues.

3. "Crusher of the Month," Crush Crypto, September 28, 2018 https://crushcrypto .com/ethereum-crusher-september-18/.

4. Mason Marcobello, "What Is Defi? Don't Start in Defi until You've Read This Guide," The Defiant, May 18, 2022, https://www.thedefiant.io/what-is-defi.

5. Jon Russell, "Cryptocurrency Exchange Etherdelta Suspends Service Following Alleged Hack," TechCrunch, December 21, 2017, https://techcrunch .com/2017/12/20/etherdelta-suspends-service/; Eduard Kovacs, "U.S. Government Asks Victims of 2017 Etherdelta Hack to Come Forward," SecurityWeek, May 24, 2021, https://www.securityweek.com/us-government-asks-victims-2017-etherdelta-hack-come-forward; Securities Exchange Act of 1934: Release No. 84553, November 8, 2018, Administrative Proceeding File No. 3-18888, https:// www.sec.gov/litigation/admin/2018/34-84553.pdf.

6. "Introducing Bancor 3," November 29, 2021, https://blog.bancor.network/introducing-bancor-3-962a3c601c25; Joon Ian Wong, "Ethereum Unleashed the 'Initial Coin Offering' Craze, but It Can't Handle Its Insane Success,"

Quartz, June 15, 2017, **https://qz.com/1004892/the-bancor-ico-just-raised-153-million-on-ethereum-in-three-hours/**; Vitalik Buterin, "On Path Independence," Vitalik.ca, accessed September 7, 2022, **https://vitalik.ca/general/2017/06/22/marketmakers.html**.

7. Shardus, "Bancor vs UNISWAP Where to List Your erc20 Token," Medium, November 19, 2020, **https://shardus.medium.com/bancor-vs-uniswap-where-to-list-your-erc20-token-60052e7de28e**.

8. Alexander Behrens, "Sushiswap Set to Drain Nearly $1 Billion from Rival Uniswap," Decrypt, September 9, 2020, **https://decrypt.co/41349/sushiswap-drain-nearly-1-billion-rival-uniswap**.

9. "Sushi 2.0: A Restructure For the Road Ahead," April 25, [2022], accessed September 9, 2022, **https://forum.sushi.com/t/sushi-2-0-a-restructure-for-the-road-ahead/10111**.

10. "Synthetix Launches Crypto-Backed Synthetic Asset Platform After Rebranding from Havven," BusinessWire, December 06, 2018, 09:00 a.m., **https://www.businesswire.com/news/home/20181206005225/en/Synthetix-Launches-Crypto-Backed-Synthetic-Asset-Platform-After-Rebranding-From-Havven;** Nikolai Kuznetsov, "Compound's Comp Token Takes Defi by Storm, Now Has to Hold Top Spot," Cointelegraph, June 29, 2020, **https://cointelegraph.com/news/compounds-comp-token-takes-defi-by-storm-now-has-to-hold-top-spot**.

11. "ChainLink," ICO Drops, September 18, 2017, **https://icodrops.com/chainlink/**; Ariane Ville, "Notes on the Ethlend ICO," Medium, October 5, 2017, **https://medium.com/@ArianeZambiras/notes-on-the-ethlend-ico-85e4e1c74251**.

12. Robert Stevens, "The 2020 Year in Review: DEFI," Decrypt, December 26, 2020, **https://decrypt.co/52298/the-2020-year-in-review-defi**.

13. "What Is EIP-1559? How Will It Change Ethereum?" ConsenSys, June 22, 2021, **https://consensys.net/blog/quorum/what-is-eip-1559-how-will-it-change-ethereum/**; "Polkadot," accessed September 9, 2022, **https://coinmarketcap.com/currencies/polkadot-new/**.

14. Prashant Jha, "Binance Smart Chain and Binance Chain Become BNB Chain," Cointelegraph, February 15, 2022, **https://cointelegraph.com/news/binance-smart-chain-becomes-bnb-chain;** Eduardo Próspero, "Is the Binance Smart Chain Going off the Rails? BSC Validators Rise Up," **Bitcoinist.com**, November 20, 2021, **https://bitcoinist.com/is-the-binance-smart-chain-going-off-the-rails-bsc-validators-rise-up/**.

15. "Solana USD (SOL-USD)," Yahoo! Finance, accessed September 9, 2022, **https://finance.yahoo.com/quote/SOL-USD/history?period1=1609459200andperiod2=1612051200andinterval=1dandfilter=historyandfrequency=1dandincludeAdjustedClose=true;** Camille Lemmens, "4 Questions Everyone Must Know How to Answer About Solana," Altcoin Buzz, August 22, 2022, **https://www.altcoinbuzz.io/cryptocurrency-news/product-release/4-questions-everyone-must-know-how-to-answer-about-solana/**; "History," Solana Foundation, accessed September 9, 2022, **https://docs.solana.com/history;** Steven Ehrlich, "Meet the World's Richest 29-Year-Old: How Sam Bankman-Fried Made a Record Fortune in the Crypto Frenzy," *Forbes*, April 21, 2022, **https://www.forbes.com/sites/stevenehrlich/2021/10/06/the-richest-under-30-in-the-world-all-thanks-to-crypto/?sh=4f3e890a3f4d**.

16. Dominic Basulto, "Is Solana Trying to Become the Apple of the Crypto World?" The Motley Fool, August 4, 2022. **https://www.fool.com/investing/2022/08/04/is-solana-trying-to-become-the-apple-of-the-crypto/**.

17. Iliana Mavrou and Raphael Sanis, "Polkadot Price Prediction: Connecting All Blockchains," **Capital.com,** updated September 1, 2022, 10:34, **https://capital.com/polkadot-forecast-will-dot-price-rise**.

18. "Top Smart Contracts Tokens by Market Capitalization," CoinMarketCap, accessed September 9, 2022, **https://coinmarketcap.com/view/smart-contracts/**.

Chapter 13

1. "Cryptocurrency Prices, Charts and Market Capitalizations," CoinMarketCap, accessed September 8, 2022, **https://coinmarketcap.com/**.

2. Pete Schroeder, "Stablecoins to Face Bank-like U.S. Regulation Under Draft House Bill – Source," Reuters, Thomson Reuters, July 20, 2022. **https://www.reuters.com/markets/us/stablecoins-face-bank-like-us-regulation-under-draft-house-bill-source-2022-07-20/**.

3. Top USD Stablecoin Tokens by Market Capitalization," CoinMarketCap, accessed September 8, 2022, **https://coinmarketcap.com/view/usd-stablecoin/**; "ISO 20022 Message Definitions," ISO20022, accessed September 8, 2022, **https://www.iso20022.org/iso-20022-message-definitions?business-domain=1**.

4. Turner Wright, "US Treasury Sanctions USDC and ETH Addresses Connected to Tornado Cash," Cointelegraph, August 8, 2022, **https://cointelegraph.com/news/us-treasury-sanctions-usdc-and-eth-addresses-connected-to-tornado-cash;** Gary Gensler, "President's Working Group Report on Stablecoins," SEC, November 1, 2021. **https://www.sec.gov/news/statement/gensler-statement-presidents-working-group-report-stablecoins-110121**.

5. "What Is a Blockchain Oracle?," Chainlink, last updated September 14, 2021, **https://chain.link/education/blockchain-oracles**.

6. Elon Musk (@elonmusk), "Who Controls the Memes, Controls the Universe," Twitter, June 26, 2020, 12:35 a.m., **https://twitter.com/elonmusk/status/1276418907968925696?lang=en**.

7. "YOLO" is an acronym for the term "You Only Live Once" made popular by the music group Lonely Island; "Yolo (featuring Adam Levine & Kendrick Lamar) – Single by The Lonely Island," Apple Music, January 1, 2013, **https://music.apple.com/us/album/yolo-feat-adam-levine-kendrick/1444328910**.

Chapter 14

1. "Fundamental vs. Technical Analysis." AMG Funds, July 13, 2022. **https://www.amgfunds.com/research-and-insights/investment-essentials/fundamental-vs-technical-analysis/**.

2. Robert McMillan, "Take a Tour of Robocoin, the World's First Bitcoin ATM," *Wired*, October 29, 2013, **https://www.wired.com/2013/10/bitcoin-atm-gallery/**.

3. Maria Gracia Santillana Linares, "Crypto ATMS Lose Traction in Tarnished Market," *Forbes*, August 9, 2022, **https://www.forbes.com/sites/ mariagraciasantillanalinares/2022/08/08/crypto-atms-lose-traction-in-tarnished-market/?sh=574315501731**.

4. "Safest and Best Crypto Exchanges USA," Koinly, last updated: August 1, 2022, **https://koinly.io/blog/best-crypto-exchange-usa/**; Jackson Wood, "Custodial Wallets vs. Non-Custodial Crypto Wallets," CoinDesk, March 9, 2022, **https://www.coindesk.com/learn/custodial-wallets-vs-non-custodial-crypto-wallets/**; Jack Kubinec, "The Nine Largest Crypto Hacks in 2022," Blockworks, July 26, 2022, **https://blockworks.co/the-nine-largest-crypto-hacks-in-2022/**.

5. Joshua Stoner, "Luna/UST Fallout Update: 3AC, Celsius, Voyager, and Vauld," Securities.io, August 25, 2022, **https://www.securities.io/luna-ust-fallout-update-3ac-celsius-voyager-and-vauld/**.

6. "Everything You Need to Know about Decentralized Finance (DEFI)," Cryptopedia, Gemini, accessed September 8, 2022, **https://www.gemini.com/ cryptopedia/story/a-deep-dive-into-defi**.

7. For more, check out this article: Valerio Puggioni, "Crypto Rug Pulls: What Is a Rug Pull in Crypto and 6 Ways to Spot it," Cointelegraph, February 06, 2022, **https://cointelegraph.com/explained/crypto-rug-pulls-what-is-a-rug-pull-in-crypto-and-6-ways-to-spot-it**.

8. Maurie Backman, "Warren Buffett Has This Advice for Investing in a Volatile Market: Dollar-Cost Averaging," *USA Today*, October 28, 2020, **https://www .usatoday.com/story/money/investing/2020/10/28/warren-buffett-has-this-advice-for-investing-in-a-volatile-market/114480910/**.

Chapter 15

1. "Paper Trading," AVA Trade, accessed September 11, 2022, **https://www .avatrade.com/education/correct-trading-rules/paper-trading**.

2. Coffee Tea Investment, "USD Tether: The Largest Ticking Time Bomb in Modern Financial History," Predict, December 26, 2021, **https://medium.com/ predict/usd-tether-the-largest-ticking-time-bomb-in-modern-financial-history-8ac839c9aea**; Amy Castor, "The Curious Case of Tether: A Complete Timeline of Events," Amy Castor Blog, January 17, 2019, **https://amycastor. com/2019/01/17/the-curious-case-of-tether-a-complete-timeline-of-events/**; Elizabeth Lopatto, "The Tether Controversy, Explained," The Verge, August 16, 2021, 8:00am EDT **https://www.theverge.com/22620464/tether-backing-cryptocurrency-stablecoin**; Jake Frankenfield, "Tether (USDT): Meaning and Uses for Tethering Crypto Explained," Investopedia, updated May 12, 2022, **https://www.investopedia.com/terms/t/tether-usdt.asp**.

3. Stuart Langridge, "What Is Tokenomics?," CoinMarketCap Alexandria, last updated July 2022, accessed September 11, 2022, **https://coinmarketcap.com/ alexandria/article/what-is-tokenomics.**

4. Krisztian Sandor and Ekin Genç, "The Fall of Terra: A Timeline of the Meteoric Rise and Crash of UST and LUNA," CoinDesk, updated August 19, 2022, 10:20 a.m. PDT, **https://www.coindesk.com/learn/the-fall-of-terra-a-timeline- of-the-meteoric-rise-and-crash-of-ust-and-luna/.**

5. Frankie Candles, YouTube channel, accessed September 11, 2022, **https://www .youtube.com/c/FrankieCandles.**

Chapter 16

1. Kate Irwin, "What Is Virtual Land? How NFTs Are Shaping the Metaverse," Decrypt, August 31, 2022, **https://decrypt.co/resources/what-is-virtual- land-how-nfts-are-shaping-the-metaverse.**

2. "The History of NFTS & How They Got Started," Portion Blog, August 11, 2022, **https://blog.portion.io/the-history-of-nfts-how-they-got-started/;** Andrew Steinwold, "The History of Non-Fungible Tokens (NFTs)," Medium, October 7, 2019, **https://medium.com/@Andrew.Steinwold/the-history-of-non- fungible-tokens-nfts-f362ca57ae10.**

3. "The History of NFTs on Ethereum," NonFungible.com, accessed September 7, 2022, **https://nonfungible.com/news/utility/the-history-of-nfts-on- ethereum;** Bradley Keoun, "'Rare Pepe' Steeped in Bitcoin History Fetches $500k on NFT Market OpenSea," CoinDesk, August 31, 2021, **https://www.coindesk.com/ markets/2021/08/31/rare-pepe-steeped-in-bitcoin-history-fetches-500k- on-nft-market-opensea/;** Chris Williams, "Ethereum NFT Collectors Are Digging up Digital Skulls," Crypto Briefing, January 11, 2022, **https://cryptobriefing .com/ethereum-nft-collectors-rush-dig-up-digital-skulls/.**

4. Andrew Hayward, "What Are Cryptopunks? The Ethereum NFT Sensation," Decrypt, February 7, 2022, **https://decrypt.co/resources/what-are- cryptopunks-ethereum-nft-avatars;** Natasha Dailey, "The Massively Popular Cryptopunks NFT Collection Was Buggy and Unnoticed at Launch – Until All 10,000 Suddenly Sold in 24 Hours," Business Insider, Nov 14, 2021, **https:// markets.businessinsider.com/news/currencies/cryptopunks-nft- collection-buggy-unnoticed-launch-wired-ethereum-blockchain-2021-11.**

5. Fitz Tepper, "People Have Spent over $1m Buying Virtual Cats on the Ethereum Blockchain," TechCrunch, December 3, 2017, **https://techcrunch .com/2017/12/03/people-have-spent-over-1m-buying-virtual-cats-on-the- ethereum-blockchain/;** Dean Takahashi, "Cryptokitties Explained: Why Players Have Bred over a Million Blockchain Felines," VentureBeat, October 6, 2018, **https://venturebeat.com/business/cryptokitties-explained-why-players- have-bred-over-a-million-blockchain-felines/;** "Herding One-Million Cats," Medium, CryptoKitties, September 19, 2018, **https://medium.com/ cryptokitties/herding-one-million-cats-7dbec6c77476.**

6. Bryan Mears, "The 10 Biggest NBA Top Shot Sales to Date," The Action Network, December 9, 2021, **https://www.actionnetwork.com/nba/the-10-biggest-nba-top-shot-sales-to-date;** Randy Ginsburg, "The Impressive Rise and Untimely Fall of NBA Top Shot," NFT Now, May 31, 2022, **https://nftnow.com/features/what-happened-to-nba-top-shot/.**

7. Aaron Chow, "Fidenza Art Blocks NFT Bought for $1,400 USD Sells for $3.3 Million USD," Hypebeast, March 2, 2022, **https://hypebeast.com/2021/8/art-blocks-fidenza-nft-1400-to-3-million-ethereum.**

8. Kyle Chayka, "How Beeple Crashed the Art World," *The New Yorker*, March 22, 2021, **https://www.newyorker.com/tech/annals-of-technology/how-beeple-crashed-the-art-world;** "Mike Winkelmann Has Created a New Artwork Every Day for 3,416 Consecutive Days (Nearly 10 Years)," BOOOOOOOM!, January 1, 1970, **https://www.boooooooom.com/2016/09/07/mike-winkelmann-has-created-a-new-artwork-every-day-for-3416-consecutive-days-nearly-10-years/.**

9. Cameron Knight, "Cincinnati Photographer Got Great Views of Cities, Not-so-Great Views of Justice System," *Cincinnati Enquirer*, August 14, 2022, **https://www.cincinnati.com/story/news/2022/08/11/isaac-wright-climbing-photographer/10170207002/.**

10. "Welcome to the Bored Ape Yacht Club," accessed September 9, 2022, **https://boredapeyachtclub.com/;** Shalini Nagarajan, "Yuga Labs Faces Potential Class Action Lawsuit Over 'Inflated' BAYC NFTs," Blockworks, July 25, 2022, 6:42 a.m. EDT, **https://blockworks.co/yuga-labs-faces-potential-class-action-lawsuit-over-inflated-bayc-nfts/;** Sam Dunn, "The All-Star Owners of the Bored Ape Yacht Club," Boardroom, May 13, 2022, **https://boardroom.tv/bored-ape-nft-celebrity-owners;** Lucas Matney, "Bored Apes maker Yuga Labs acquires CryptoPunks NFT collection," TechCrunch, March 11, 2022, 3:32 p.m. PST, **https://techcrunch.com/2022/03/11/bored-apes-maker-yuga-labs-acquires-cryptopunks-nft-collection/.**

11. Nansen Team, "How to Find and Track NFT Whales," Nansen, September 1, 2022, **https://www.nansen.ai/guides/how-to-find-and-track-nft-whales.**

12. Anton Telitsyn, "Cryptocurrency and Online Multiplayer Games," InfoQ, November 30, 2017, **https://www.infoq.com/articles/cryptocurrency-online-games/;** Jex Exmundo and Rupendra Brahambhatt, "What Are Play-to-Earn Games? A Guide to Your Future Side-Hustle," NFT Now, August 15, 2022, **https://nftnow.com/guides/the-best-play-to-earn-games-for-nft-and-crypto-lovers/.**

13. Langston Thomas, "Here's Why Many Gamers (Rightfully) Aren't so Game on NFTs," NFT Now, July 19, 2022, **https://nftnow.com/features/heres-why-many-gamers-rightfully-arent-so-game-on-nfts/;** J. Clement, "Percentage of Adults in the United States Who Ever Play Video Games in the United States in 2020 and 2021," Statista, May 13, 2022, **https://www.statista.com/statistics/499703/share-consumers-ever-play-video-games-by-age-usa/;** Abram Brown, "The War Between Gamers and Cryptominers – and the Scarce Global Resource That Sparked It," *Forbes*, June 23, 2021, **https://www.forbes.com/sites/abrambrown/2021/05/24/gamers-cryptocurrency-cryptominers-gpu-microchip/?sh=7753c017dbf8.**

14. Mia Sato, "Coachella Will Sell Lifetime Festival Passes as NFTs," The Verge, February 1, 2022, **https://www.theverge.com/2022/2/1/22912255/coachella-lifetime-passes-nfts**; Leeor Shimron, "How Musicians Are Using NFTs to Revolutionize Fan Engagement," *Forbes*, February 28, 2022, 9:30 a.m. EST, **https://www.forbes.com/sites/leeorshimron/2022/02/28/how-musicians-are-using-nfts-to-revolutionize-fan-engagement/?sh=45bb99551fed**.

Chapter 17

1. Madhurkant Sharma, "Comparison Between Web 1.0, Web 2.0 and Web 3.0," GeeksforGeeks, last updated August 2, 2022, **https://www.geeksforgeeks.org/web-1-0-web-2-0-and-web-3-0-with-their-difference**; Tim O'Reilly, "Web 2.0 and the Emergent Internet Operating System," O'Reilly Media, accessed September 9, 2022, **https://www.oreilly.com/tim/p2p/**.
2. Darcy DiNucci, "Fragmented Future," originally published in *Print: America's Graphic Design Magazine*, April 1999, available at **http://darcyd.com/fragmented_future.pdf** (accessed September 9, 2022); Peter Suciu, "Social Media Is Making The Political Divide Even Worse," *Forbes*, August 20, 2020, **https://www.forbes.com/sites/petersuciu/2020/08/20/social-media-is-making-the-political-divide-even-worse/?sh=f366643102cf**; Emma Fletcher, "Social Media a Gold Mine for Scammers in 2021," Federal Trade Commission, January 25, 2022, **https://www.ftc.gov/news-events/data-visualizations/data-spotlight/2022/01/social-media-gold-mine-scammers-2021**; Emma Shapiro, "Censorship on Social Media Not Only Limits Artists' Online Reach – It Can Prevent Future Opportunities, Too," *The Art Newspaper: International Art News and Events*, April 18, 2022, **https://www.theartnewspaper.com/2022/04/18/censorship-on-social-media-not-only-limits-artists-online-reachit-can-prevent-future-opportunities-too**.
3. "Emerge Web3: Lovisa Björna in Conversation with Gavin Wood," Emerge, **https://www.whatisemerging.com/videos/gavin-wood-on-web3#:~:text=Gavin%20Wood%2C%20coined%20the%20term,Parity%20and%20the%20Web3%20Foundation**; Crystal Stranger, "How Blockchain Became a Dirty Word," *Cryptoweek*, Medium, January 22, 2019, **https://medium.com/@cryptoweek/how-blockchain-became-a-dirty-word-50f43c01d16**.
4. Ben Sisario, "Musicians Say Streaming Doesn't Pay. Can the Industry Change?" *New York Times*, 7 May 2021, **https://www.nytimes.com/2021/05/07/arts/music/streaming-music-payments.html**; Cameron DeFaria, "Audius Deemed a 'Spotify Rival' after Revealing High-Profile Investors," *Dancing Astronaut*, September 22, 2021, **https://dancingastronaut.com/2021/09/audius-deemed-a-spotify-rival-after-revealing-high-profile-investors/**.
5. Peter Kafka, "Web3 Is the Future, or a Scam, or Both," *Vox*, February 1, 2022, **https://www.vox.com/recode/22907072/web3-crypto-nft-bitcoin-metaverse**; Ephrat Livni, "Jack Dorsey and Venture Capitalists Clash over the Future of Cryptocurrency," *New York Times*, December 22, 2021, **https://www.nytimes.com/2021/12/22/business/jack-dorsey-bitcoin-web3-vc.html**;

Jack Dorsey, "You don't own 'web3.' The VCs and their LPs do ...," Twitter, December 21, 2021, **https://twitter.com/jack/status/1473139010197508098.**

6. Title 17, Chapter II, Part 230, Regulation D: Rules Governing the Limited Offer and Sale of Securities Without Registration Under the Securities Act of 1933, § 230.501, last amended June 8, 2022, **https://www.ecfr.gov/current/title-17/ chapter-II/part-230/subject-group-ECFR6e651a4c86c0174/section-230.501;** Adam Hayes, "Accredited Investor Defined: Understand the Requirements," Investopedia, August 29, 2022, **https://www.investopedia.com/terms/a/ accreditedinvestor.asp;** Electronic Code of Federal Regulations, "§230.501 Definitions and Terms Used in Regulation D," **https://www.ecfr.gov/current/ title-17/chapter-II/part-230/subject-group-ECFR6e651a4c86c0174/sec-tion-230.501;** Lydia Beyoud, "SEC 'Accredited Investor' Definition Tweak Faces Equity Concerns," Bloomberg Law, February 23, 2022, 3:00 a.m., **https://news. bloomberglaw.com/securities-law/sec-accredited-investor-definition-tweak-faces-equity-concerns.**

7. Nick Marinoff. "SEC Chairman: Cryptocurrencies Like Bitcoin Are Not Securities, but Most ICOS Are," *Bitcoin Magazine*, June 7, 2018, **https://bitcoinmagazine .com/business/sec-chairman-cryptocurrencies-bitcoin-are-not-securities-most-icos-are;** Daniel Roberts, "Secret SEC Investigation into ICOs Puts Startups at Risk," Decrypt, February 25, 2021, **https://decrypt.co/3622/sec-tightens-the-noose-on-ico-funded-startups.**

8. SJR 16: Financial services: investor certification examination process, California Senate Joint Resolution, 2021–2022 Regular Session, Open States, last updated June 22, 2022, **https://openstates.org/ca/bills/20212022/SJR16/;** H.R. 4753: Accredited Investor Self-Certification Act, 117th Congress (2021–2022), **Congress.gov**, accessed September 10, 2022, **https://www.congress.gov/ bill/117th-congress/house-bill/4753?s=1&r=80.**

9. Vitalik Buterin, "Moving Beyond Coin Voting Governance," Vitalik.ca, August 16, 2021, **https://vitalik.ca/general/2021/08/16/voting3.html;** "Governance Overview," Optimism Docs, updated July 6, 2022, **https://community. optimism.io/docs/governance/;** Team Gitcoin, "Quadratic Funding = Wisdom of the Crowds," Gitcoin, July 20, 2022, **https://gitcoin.co/blog/quadratic-funding#:~:text=Quadratic%20Funding%20optimizes%20for%20the,as%20 %241%20to%20a%20project.**

10. "What Is Habbo?," page archived between December 29, 2016, and Jan 11, 2022, **https://web.archive.org/web/20190809204005/https://help.habbo.com/hc/ en-us/articles/221643428;** Ingrid Lunden, "After Losing over Half Its 9m Users in a Pedophile Scandal, Habbo Hotel Hopes for New Life as a Gaming Platform," *TechCrunch,* November 27, 2012, **https://techcrunch.com/2012/11/27/after-losing-over-half-its-9m-users-in-a-pedophile-scandal-habbo-hotel-hopes-for-new-life-as-a-gaming-platform/;** Kayleigh Partleton, "Sulake's Networking Title Habbo Celebrates Its 20th Anniversary," **PocketGamer.biz**, October 15, 2020, 03:13 p.m., **https://www.pocketgamer.biz/news/74772/suklakes-networking-title-habbo-celebrates-its-20th-anniversary/.**

11. Viktor Hendelmann, "The World's First Metaverse: What Happened to Second Life?," Productmint, accessed September 10, 2022, **https://productmint.com/ what-happened-to-second-life/.**

12. Trent Murray, "Valve's Skin Gambling Ban and How It Affects the Esports Industry," Esports Observer, July 15, 2016, **https://archive.esportsobserver.com/ valves-skin-gambling-ban-and-how-it-affects-the-esports-industry/**; Owen Good, "NFT Mastermind Says He Created Ethereum Because Warcraft Nerfed His Character," Polygon, October 4, 2021, **https://www.polygon.com/22709126/ ethereum-creator-world-of-warcraft-nerf-nft-vitalik-buterin**.

13. Jacob Kastrenakes and Alex Heath, "Facebook Is Spending at Least $10 Billion This Year on Its Metaverse Division," The Verge, October 25, 2021, **https:// www.theverge.com/2021/10/25/22745381/facebook-reality-labs-10-billion-metaverse**; Justin Bariso, "Facebook Changing Its Name to Meta Is a Brilliant Business Move. But It's Also Bad News for the Future," Inc., November 29, 2021, **https://www.inc.com/justin-bariso/facebook-meta-mark-zuckerberg-innovators-dilemma-why-did-facebook-change-its-name.html**.

14. Dean Takahashi, "Animoca Brands Acquires Sandbox Game Developer Pixowl for $4.875 Million." VentureBeat, 27 Aug. 2018, **https://venturebeat.com/ games/animoca-brands-acquires-sandbox-game-developer-pixowl-for-4-875-million/**; "Animoca Brands Raises US$358,888,888 at over US$5B Valuation to Grow the Open Metaverse." *Animocabrands*, **https://www.animocabrands. com/animoca-brands-raises-usd358888888-at-usd5b-valuation-to-grow-the-open-metaverse**.

15. "Our Portfolio," Digital Currency Group, accessed September 10, 2022, **https:// dcg.co/portfolio/**.

16. Lucas Matney. "Bored Apes Founders on Their Plans for Otherside Metaverse." *TechCrunch*, TechCrunch, 26 Aug. 2022, **https://techcrunch.com/2022/07/19/ bored-apes-founders-on-their-plans-for-otherside-metaverse/**.

17. "Motion Sickness in Virtual Reality: Causes and Solutions," WalkOVR, accessed September 10, 2022, **https://walkovr.com/motion-sickness-in-vr/ #:~:text=In%20brief%2C%20it%20occurs%20when,drowsiness%2C%20 disorientation%2C%20and%20apathy**; Tomislav Bezmalinovic, "Meta Quest 2: These Bugs Are Incredibly Annoying." Mixed, March 6, 2022, **https://mixed-news .com/en/meta-quest-2-these-bugs-are-incredibly-annoying/**; Kaylee Fagan, "Here's What Happens to Your Body When You've Been in Virtual Reality for Too Long," Business Insider, March 4, 2018, **https://www.businessinsider .com/virtual-reality-vr-side-effects-2018-3**.

18. Paige Leskin, "American Kids Want to Be Famous on YouTube, and Kids in China Want to Go to Space: Survey." Business Insider, 17 July 2019, **https://www .businessinsider.com/american-kids-youtube-star-astronauts-survey-2019-7**; Vittoria Elliott, "Workers in the Global South Are Making a Living Playing the Blockchain Game Axie Infinity," Rest of The World, 19 Aug. 2021, **https:// restofworld.org/2021/axie-infinity/**; "Axie Infinity Live Player Count and Statistics," Axie Infinity, accessed September 10, 2022, **https://activeplayer.io/ axie-infinity/**.

19. Rohan Seth, "What Zoom's Rise Tells Us About Future of Work Culture," *Deccan Herald*, 2 Apr. 2020, **https://www.deccanherald.com/opinion/what-zoom-s-rise-tells-us-about-future-of-work-culture-820438.html**.

20. Denis Campbell. "Depression in Girls Linked to Higher Use of Social Media." *The Guardian*, 4 Jan. 2019, **https://www.theguardian.com/society/2019/jan/04/**

depression-in-girls-linked-to-higher-use-of-social-media;PeterSuciu. "Social
Media Is Making the Political Divide Even Worse." *Forbes*, 20 Aug. 2020, **https://
www.forbes.com/sites/petersuciu/2020/08/20/social-media-is-making-
the-political-divide-even-worse/**.

Chapter 18

1. Eric Brazil, "Parents Fear Girl Was Lured Via Cyberspace," SFGATE, June 6, 1995,
   **https://www.sfgate.com/news/article/Parents-fear-girl-was-lured-via-
   cyberspace-3145247.php**; Greenbiz Editors, "Critics Wary of e-Commerce Effects
   on Environment," Greenbiz, August 28, 2001, **https://www.greenbiz.com/
   article/critics-wary-e-commerce-effects-environment**; Amelia Tait, "25 Years
   on, Here Are the Worst Ever Predictions about the Internet," New Statesman, April
   4, 2022, **https://www.newstatesman.com/science-tech/2016/08/25-years-
   here-are-worst-ever-predictions-about-internet**.
2. Chainalysis Team, "Crypto Crime Trends for 2022: Illicit Transaction Activity Reaches All-Time High in Value, All-Time Low in Share of All Cryptocurrency Activity," Chainalysis, January 6, 2022, **https://blog.chainalysis.com/
   reports/2022-crypto-crime-report-introduction/**.
3. Rudolph J. Rummel, *Statistics of Democide: Genocide and Mass Murder Since 1900*
   (London: Transaction Books, 1999).
4. Joen Coronel, "'Bitcoin Ban' in US May Happen Soon, Predicts American Billionaire Ray Dalio: Will This Change Its Value?" Tech Times, March 29, 2021, **https://
   www.techtimes.com/articles/258518/20210329/bitcoin-ban-predicts-
   american-billionaire-ray-dalio.htm**; Kevin Helms, "Robert Kiyosaki Says
   'We Are in Biggest Bubble in World History' – Warns Government Will Seize All
   Cryptocurrencies," Bitcoin News, March 10, 2022, **https://news.bitcoin.com/
   robert-kiyosaki-biggest-bubble-in-world-history-warns-government-will-
   seize-all-cryptocurrencies/**; Robert T. Kiyosaki, *Rich Dad Poor Dad: What
   the Rich Teach Their Kids About Money That the Poor and Middle Class Do Not!*
   (Twenty-fifth anniversary ed. Scottsdale: Plata Publishing, 2022).
5. Samuel Sherwood, "A Brief History of China Fud: Exodus." *Exodus Crypto News
   & Insights*, July 19, 2021, **https://www.exodus.com/news/a-brief-history-of-
   china-fud/**; Kim Lyons, "China's Central Bank Bans Cryptocurrency Transactions to Avoid 'Risks,'" The Verge, September 24, 2021, **https://www.theverge
   .com/2021/9/24/22691472/china-central-bank-cryptocurrency-illegal-
   bitcoin**; MacKenzie Sigalos, "Bitcoin Mining Has Totally Recovered from Chinese Ban." CNBC, December 11, 2021, **https://www.cnbc.com/2021/12/10/
   bitcoin-network-hashrate-hits-all-time-high-after-china-crypto-
   ban.html**; MacKenzie Sigalos, "China Is Kicking out More than Half the
   World's Bitcoin Miners – and a Whole Lot of Them Could Be Headed to Texas,"
   CNBC, July 20, 2021, **https://www.cnbc.com/2021/06/15/chinas-bitcoin-
   miner-exodus-.html**.
6. Brody Ford, "Crypto Lobbying Spree Includes Facebook, Coinbase, Ripple,
   IBM, Fidelity." Bloomberg, March 8, 2022, **https://www.bloomberg.com/**

news/articles/2022-03-08/crypto-lobbying-skyrocketed-last-year-and-quadrupled-since-2018.

7. Liz Wolfe, "Legislators Hid a Sneaky Crypto Reporting Provision in the Infrastructure Bill," *Reason*, December 16. 2021, **https://reason.com/2021/12/16/legislators-hid-a-sneaky-crypto-reporting-provision-in-the-infrastructure-bill/**;Victoria Guida, "Washington Wakes up to Crypto Influence amid Infrastructure Fight," POLITICO, **https://www.politico.com/news/2021/08/09/cryptocurrency-influence-washington-infrastructure-fight-502792.**

8. James Taylor, "Lacking Regulatory Clarity: The Single Biggest Obstacle to Institutional Crypto Adoption in U.S.," Nasdaq, April 26, 2022 11:38AM, **https://www.nasdaq.com/articles/lacking-regulatory-clarity%3A-the-single-biggest-obstacle-to-institutional-crypto-adoption.**

9. Cristina Criddle, "Bitcoin Consumes 'More Electricity than Argentina,'" BBC, February 10, 2021, **https://www.bbc.com/news/technology-56012952**; Greenbiz Editors, "Critics Wary of e-Commerce Effects on Environment," **Greenbiz.com**, August 28, 2001, **https://www.greenbiz.com/article/critics-wary-e-commerce-effects-environment**; Rachel Rybarczyk, Drew Armstrong, and Amanda Fabiano, "On Bitcoin's Energy Consumption: A Quantitative Approach to a Subjective Question," Galaxy Digital, May 2021, **https://www.lopp.net/pdf/On_Bitcoin_Energy_Consumption.pdf**; Morgan Erickson-Davis, "Slash-and-Burn Clearing Nears Indigenous Park as Brazil's Fire Season Ignites," *Mongabay Environmental News*, June 11, 2021, **https://news.mongabay.com/2021/06/slash-and-burn-clearing-nears-indigenous-park-as-brazils-fire-season-ignites/.**

10. Michael Grullon, "Crypto Will Be as Volatile as Gold in the Future: Vitalik Buterin Says." Watcher Guru, September 2, 2022, **https://watcher.guru/news/crypto-will-be-as-volatile-as-gold-in-the-future-vitalik-buterin-says**.

11. Khristopher Brooks, "Bitcoin Has Its Own 1% Who Control Outsized Share of Wealth," CBS Interactive, December 21, 2021 **https://www.cbsnews.com/news/bitcoin-cryptocurrency-wealth-one-percent/**; Georgi Georgiev, "Top 5 Richest Bitcoin Addresses Belong to Exchanges." **Bitcoinist.com**, November 20, 2018, **https://bitcoinist.com/richest-bitcoin-addresses-exchanges/#:~:text=Binance%20is%20the%20world's%20largest,holds%20141%2C096%20BTC%20worth%20%24749%2C654%2C668.**

12. Valeria Bednarik, "Coinbase, Binance or Coincheck down for Maintenance. Top 4 Scenarios and How to Deal with Crypto Exchange Problems." FXStreet, n.d., **https://www.fxstreet.com/cryptocurrencies/resources/brokers-down-maintenance**; Jeff Benson, "Coinbase, Binance Go down amid Crypto Crash, Highlighting Appeal of Decentralized Exchanges." Decrypt, May 19, 2021, **https://decrypt.co/71431/coinbase-binance-go-down-amid-crypto-crash-highlighting-appeal-decentralized-exchanges.**

13. Karen Martin, "Waiting for Quantum Computing: Why Encryption Has Nothing to Worry About," TechBeacon, January 22. 2019. **https://techbeacon.com/security/waiting-quantum-computing-why-encryption-has-nothing-worry-about.**

Chapter 19

1. Cryptopedia Staff, "Crypto Wallets: Hot vs. Cold Wallets," Gemini, updated March 10, 2022, **https://www.gemini.com/cryptopedia/crypto-wallets-hot-cold.**
2. Marcus Chan, "Are Blockchain Bridges Safe? Why Bridges Are Targets of Hacks." CoinDesk, 17 Aug. 2022, **https://www.coindesk.com/learn/are-blockchain-bridges-safe-why-bridges-are-targets-of-hacks/.**
3. Ryan Browne, "Nearly All of the $600 Million Stolen in a Huge Crypto Heist Has Been Returned – but There's a Catch." CNBC, 17 Aug. 2021, **https://www.cnbc .com/2021/08/13/poly-network-hack-nearly-all-of-600-million-in-crypto-returned.html;** Lawrence Abrams, "$620 Million in Crypto Stolen from Axie Infinity's Ronin Bridge." BleepingComputer, 29 Mar. 2022, **https://www.bleeping-ingcomputer.com/news/cryptocurrency/620-million-in-crypto-stolen-from-axie-infinitys-ronin-bridge/;** Eliza Gkritsi, "North Korean Hackers Stole $400M in 2021, Mostly in Ether," CoinDesk, updated Feb 7, 2022 at 10:32 a.m., **https://www.coindesk.com/tech/2022/01/14/north-korean-hackers-stole-400m-in-2021-mostly-in-ether/.**
4. Jordan Tuwiner, "Bitfinex Hack 2016: 119,756 Bitcoin Stolen," Buy Bitcoin Worldwide, updated August 4, 2022, **https://buybitcoinworldwide.com/bitfinex-hack/;** "Two Arrested for Alleged Conspiracy to Launder $4.5 Billion in Stolen Cryptocurrency," US Department of Justice, February 8, 2022, **https://www .justice.gov/opa/pr/two-arrested-alleged-conspiracy-launder-45-billion-stolen-cryptocurrency;** Zeke Faux, "Bitfinex Hack: How This NYC Couple Allegedly Stole $8b in Bitcoin (BTC)." Bloomberg, 30 June 2022, **https://www .bloomberg.com/news/features/2022-06-30/how-the-world-s-biggest-bitcoin-btc-hack-at-bitfinex-got-botched;** Lawrence Lewitinn, "'Like Genghis Khan, but with More Pizzazz': What We Know about the Accused Bitfinex Money Launderers." CoinDesk, 8 Feb. 2022, **https://www.coindesk.com/ business/2022/02/08/like-genghis-khan-but-with-more-pizzazz-what-we-know-about-the-accused-bitfinex-money-launderers/.**
5. Zhiyuan Sun, "Aurora Pays $6M Bug Bounty to Ethical Security Hacker Through Immunefi," Cointelegraph, Jun 07, 2022, **https://cointelegraph.com/ news/aurora-pays-6m-bug-bounty-to-ethical-security-hacker-through-immunefi.**
6. Martin Young, "Elon Musk Impersonators Make Bank as Crypto Scammers' Profits Surge," Cointelegraph, 18 May 2021, **https://cointelegraph.com/news/ elon-musk-impersonators-make-bank-as-crypto-scammers-profits-surge;** Eli Tan, "Another Twitter Hack Hits the NFT Community." CoinDesk, 19 July 2022, **https://www.coindesk.com/business/2022/07/19/another-twitter-hack-hits-the-nft-community/.**
7. Tanzeel Akhtar, "Bored Apes NFT: Collection Warns Not to Mint NFTs After Chat Platform Hack." Bloomberg, 1 Apr. 2022, **https://www.bloomberg.com/ news/articles/2022-04-01/crypto-bored-apes-warn-not-to-mint-nfts-after-chat-platform-hack;** Jeremy Merrill, "Read That Link Carefully: Scammers Scoop up Misspelled Cryptocurrency Urls to Rob Your Wallet." *Washington Post*, 8 Oct. 2021, **https://www.washingtonpost.com/technology/2021/10/08/ cryptocurrency-scam-websites/.**

8. See also Chris Burniske (@cburniske), "'Scam' is so overused in crypto that it's lost all meaning & confuses the broader public, to the detriment of *all* cryptoassets," Twitter, December 27, 2018, 6:24 a.m.

9. Daily Hodl Staff, "Top Crypto Analyst Warns 'Vaporware' Ethereum Rivals Will Go to Zero, Says Traders Underestimating ETH's Price Trajectory," *The Daily Hodl*, 9 Apr. 2022, **https://dailyhodl.com/2022/04/09/top-crypto-analyst-warns-vaporware-ethereum-rivals-will-go-to-zero-says-traders-underestimating-eths-price-trajectory/**.

10. Tim Copeland, "The Complete Story of the QuadrigaCX $190 Million Scandal," Decrypt, March 13, 2019, **https://decrypt.co/5853/complete-story-quadrigacx-190-million;** "Statement from Jennifer Robertson, Wife and Partner of Gerald Cotten, on Behalf of QuadrigaCX," archive.today webpage capture from **https://www.quadrigacx.com/gerald-cotton**, January 15, 2019, **https://archive.ph/GAheG;** Molli Mitchell, "'The Crypto King': Who Is Gerald Cotten and Where Is Gerry Now?," *Newsweek*, March 30, 2022, **https://www.newsweek.com/who-gerald-cotten-gerry-cotten-dead-alive-crypto-king-netflix-1693417;** see also Luke Sewell, director, *Trust No One: The Hunt for the Crypto King* documentary film (1:30:00), Netflix, March 30, 2022, **https://www.netflix.com/title/81349029**.

11. Yogita Khatri, "Defi Protocol Wonderland Is Allegedly Run by Quadrigacx Co-Founder," The Block, 1 Jan. 1970, **https://www.theblock.co/post/131931/avalanche-defi-wonderland-time-0xsifu-quadrigacx-patryn;** Wonderland (TIME), CoinMarketCap, accessed September 10, 2022, **www.coinmarketcap.com/currencies/wonderland/**.

12. US Attorney's Office, Southern District of California, "Director and Promoter of BitConnect Pleads Guilty in Global $2 Billion Cryptocurrency Scheme," US Department of Justice, September 1, 2021, **https://www.justice.gov/usao-sdca/pr/director-and-promoter-bitconnect-pleads-guilty-global-2-billion-cryptocurrency-scheme;** Jake Swearingen, "The Rise and Fall of BitConnect, the Sketchiest Crypto Exchange," *Intelligencer*, January 17, 2018, **https://nymag.com/intelligencer/2018/01/ponzi-scheme-bitcoin-site-bitconnect-shuts-down.html;** David Voreacos. "BitConnect's Kumbhani Charged by U.S. in $2.4 Billion Ponzi Scam." Bloomberg, 26 Feb. 2022, **https://www.bloomberg.com/news/articles/2022-02-26/bitconnect-s-kumbhani-charged-by-u-s-in-2-4-billion-ponzi-scam;** Jeff Yeung, "BitConnect Founder Disappears Following Justice Department Indictment," Hypebeast, March 2, 2022, **https://hypebeast.com/2022/3/bitconnect-founder-satish-kumbhani-justice-department-indictment-disappearance;** Jaroslaw Adamowski, "Crypto Scam BitConnect Founder Reportedly Booked in India on Fresh Charges," *Crypto News*, August 18, 2022 08:00 a.m., **https://cryptonews.com/news/crypto-scam-bitconnect-founder-reportedly-booked-in-india-on-fresh-charges.htm**.

13. Shalini Nagarajan, "Celsius Faces Heat for at Least $1.2B Balance Sheet Hole, Customers Owed $4.7B," *Blockworks*, 15 July 2022, **https://blockworks.co/celsius-faces-heat-for-1-2b-balance-sheet-hole-customers-owed-4-7b/;** Sebastian Sinclair, "Celsius Accused of Market Manipulation by Ex-Employee." *Blockworks*, 8 Aug. 2022, **https://blockworks.co/celsius-accused-of-market-manipulation-by-ex-employee/**.

14. MacKenzie Sigalos, "From $10 Billion to Zero: How a Crypto Hedge Fund Collapsed and Dragged Many Investors down with It." CNBC, 12 July 2022, **https://www.cnbc.com/2022/07/11/how-the-fall-of-three-arrows-or-3ac-dragged-down-crypto-investors.html**; Jen Wieczner, "The Crypto Geniuses Who Vaporized a Trillion Dollars." *Intelligencer*, 15 Aug. 2022, **https://nymag.com/intelligencer/article/three-arrows-capital-kyle-davies-su-zhu-crash.html**; Wahid Pessarlay, "Where in the World Are the 3AC Founders? Speculation Abounds," Cointelegraph, August 29, 2022, **https://cointelegraph.com/news/where-in-the-world-are-the-3ac-founders-speculations-abound**; MacKenzie Sigalos and Arjun Kharpal, "One of the Most Prominent Crypto Hedge Funds Just Defaulted on a $670 Million Loan," CNBC, June 29, 2022, **https://www.cnbc.com/2022/06/27/three-arrows-capital-crypto-hedge-fund-defaults-on-voyager-loan.html**.

15. Andrew Throuvalas, "Nansen Analysis Examines How Terra Collapse Affected Celsius and Three Arrows Capital," Decrypt, 29 June 2022, **https://decrypt.co/104102/nansen-analysis-examines-how-terra-collapse-affected-celsius-and-three-arrows-capital**.

16. "Lawyer for 11,000 XRP Holders Pushing to Fight SEC in Ripple Lawsuit," *Forkast.News*, April 8, 2021, 2:14 p.m., **https://forkast.news/video-audio/xrp-fight-sec-ripple-lawsuit/**.

Chapter 20

1. Emmaline Soken-Huberty, "10 Reasons Why Privacy Rights Are Important," *Human Rights Careers*, 17 May 2020, **https://www.humanrightscareers.com/issues/reasons-why-privacy-rights-are-important/**.

2. Gargi Sarkar, "Crypto Industry Worried About Growth Amid Recent Uncertainty, Lack of Regulatory Clarity," Inc42, 19 Apr. 2022, **https://inc42.com/buzz/crypto-industry-worried-about-growth-amid-recent-uncertainty-lack-of-regulatory-clarity/**.

3. Ryan Sean Adams, "The Defi Mullet: Market Monday Lite (12/07)," Bankless, December 7, 2020, **https://newsletter.banklesshq.com/p/the-defi-mullet-market-monday-lite**.

4. "CBDC: Challenge Stablecoins' First-Mover Advantage." *CBDC: Challenge Stablecoins'First-MoverAdvantage*|PYMNTS.com, PYMNTS.com, 15 Mar. 2022, **https://www.pymnts.com/cbdc/2022/cbdc-plans-proliferate-as-governments-race-to-challenge-stablecoins-first-mover-advantage/**; Barclay Bram, "China's Digital Yuan Is a Warning to the World," *Wired UK*, 23 Aug. 2021, **https://www.wired.co.uk/article/digital-yuan-china-bitcoin-libra**; Benjamin Pimentel, "Sen. Lummis: The crypto industry can be its own worst enemy," Protocol, June 23, 2022, **https://www.protocol.com/fintech/lummis-crypto-interview**; Coinbase, "Fact Check: USD Coin Is the Largest Regulated Stablecoin in the World," Aug 6, 2021, **https://blog.coinbase.com/fact-check-usd-coin-is-the-largest-regulated-stablecoin-in-the-world-6e7f3c06cbf0**; Nikhilesh De, "Circle Confirms Freezing $100k in USDC at Law Enforcement's Request."

CoinDesk, 8 July 2020, **https://www.coindesk.com/markets/2020/07/08/ circle-confirms-freezing-100k-in-usdc-at-law-enforcements-request/**.

5. Sarah Cabral and Amy LaCombe, "Robinhood, Reddit, and Gamestop: What Happened and What Should Happen next?," Markkula Center for Applied Ethics at Santa Clara University, December 1, 2021, **https://www.scu.edu/ethics/ focus-areas/business-ethics/resources/robinhood-reddit-and-gamestop-what-happened-and-what-should-happen-next/**.

6. Rory Jones, "NFL Teams See National Revenue Increase 12% to US$347.3m for 2021 Season," SportsPro, July 25, 2022, **https://www.sportspromedia.com/ news/nfl-revenue-2021-season-green-bay-packers-finances-accounts/**; National Chicken Council, "Americans Projected to Eat 1.42 Billion Chicken Wings for Super Bowl LVI," February 2, 2022, **https://www.prnewswire.com/ news-releases/americans-projected-to-eat-1-42-billion-chicken-wings-for-super-bowl-lvi-301473903.html**.

7. "Gold's Market Cap," **CompaniesMarketCap.com**, accessed September 10, 2022, **https://companiesmarketcap.com/gold/marketcap/**; "Capital Markets Fact Book, 2022," SIFMA, July 12, 2022, **https://www.sifma.org/resources/ research/reports/fact-book/**; Bailey Reutzel, "Silly Maxis, Calm Down . . .You Can Love Bitcoin and Other Coins at the Same Time," The Defiant, September 21, 2021, **https://thedefiant.io/bitcoin-maxis**.

8. Raphael Haupt, "Regenerative Finance (ReFi)," CoinMarketCap Alexandria, accessed September 10, 2022, **https://coinmarketcap.com/alexandria/glossary/regenerative-finance-refi**.

9. Sam Kessler, "Crypto Carbon: Can Blockchain Networks Fix Carbon Offsets?," CoinDesk, March 27, 2022, **https://www.coindesk.com/layer2/mining-week/2022/03/27/crypto-carbon-can-blockchain-networks-fix-carbon-offsets/**; Petya Trendafilova, "Vlinder & Solid World DAO Partner to Restore Mangrove Forests," Carbon Herald, August 18, 2022, **https://carbonherald. com/vlinder-and-solid-world-dao-partner-to-restore-mangrove-forests/**.

10. Cryptopedia Staff, "What Is Gitcoin? The GTC Crypto Protocol Explained," Gemini, updated March 8, 2022, **https://www.gemini.com/cryptopedia/gtc-crypto-gitcoin-bounties-web3-gtc-token**.

11. Stuart James, "Proof of Humanity: An Explainer," Kleros, March 12, 2021, **https://blog.kleros.io/proof-of-humanity-an-explainer/**; Charles Schwab, "Modern Wealth Survey," May 2019, **https://content.schwab.com/web/retail/ public/about-schwab/Charles-Schwab-2019-Modern-Wealth-Survey-findings-0519-9JBP.pdf**; Stockton Economic Empowerment Demonstration (SEED), "Guaranteed Income Increases Employment, Improves Financial and Physical Health," March 3, 2021, **https://www.stocktondemonstration.org/ press-landing/guaranteed-income-increases-employment-improves-financial-and-physical-health**; McKinsey & Company, "An Experiment to Inform Universal Basic Income," September 15, 2020, **https://www.mckinsey .com/industries/public-and-social-sector/our-insights/an-experiment-to-inform-universal-basic-income**.

12. Matt Stevens and Isabella Grullón Paz, "Andrew Yang's $1,000-a-Month Idea May Have Seemed Absurd before. Not Now," *New York Times*, March 18, 2020, **https:// www.nytimes.com/2020/03/18/us/politics/universal-basic-income-andrew-**

yang.html; Andrew Yang (@AndrewYang), "Cryptocurrency is one path to universal basic income," Twitter, August 10, 2021, 1:31 p.m., **https://twitter.com/ andrewyang/status/1425193106950041600?lang=en;** Andrew Yang (@Andrew-Yang), "My goal is simple – eradicate poverty. Web3 technologies represent the biggest anti-poverty opportunity of our time. Millions of lives are being transformed and creators empowered by new ways to exchange and generate value on the blockchain. It's bottom-up not top-down," Twitter, February 17, 2022, 5:32 a.m., **https:// twitter.com/AndrewYang/status/1494303712407437318.**

13. Andrew Thurman and Sam Kessler, "Money Continues to Pour into Gamefi, but Will Developers Follow?," CoinDesk, March 28, 2022, **https://www.coindesk .com/business/2022/03/28/money-continues-to-pour-into-gamefi-but-will-developers-follow/.**

Chapter 21

1. "BNB –What Is BNB and What Is It Used For?" Binance, accessed September 26, 2022, **https://www.binance.com/en/bnb.**

2. "Brand Intimacy Study 2022," Lab, September 20, 2022, **https://mblm.com/lab/ brandintimacy-study/.**

3. Vishal Chawla, "Polygon Unveils Zk-Rollup Solution Miden to Scale Ethereum," Crypto Briefing, November 17, 2021, **https://cryptobriefing.com/polygon-unveils-zk-rollup-solution-miden-scale-ethereum/.**

4. "Zero-Knowledge Proofs," **ethereum.org,** accessed September 26, 2022, **https:// ethereum.org/en/zero-knowledge-proofs/.**

5. Naveed Iqbal, "Ripple Launches Crypto-Enabled Enterprise Payments in Brazil with Travelex Bank," *Business Wire*, August 18, 2022, **https://www .businesswire.com/news/home/20220818005147/en/Ripple-Launches-Crypto-enabled-Enterprise-Payments-in-Brazil-With-Travelex-Bank;** "Tranglo Enables Ripple's on-Demand Liquidity Service across Its 25 Payment Corridors," PRNewsWire, March 1, 2022, **https://www.prnewswire.com/ ae/news-releases/tranglo-enables-ripple-s-on-demand-liquidity-service-across-its-25-payment-corridors-898578358.html.**

6. Brenden Rearick, "ISO 20022 Cryptos: 5 Compliant Cryptos to Keep an Eye on in 2022," Yahoo!, December 22, 2021, **https://www.yahoo.com/video/iso-20022-cryptos-5-compliant-194204661.html.**

7. Brenden Rearick, "ISO 20022 Cryptos: 5 Compliant Cryptos to Keep an Eye on in 2022," Yahoo!, December 22, 2021, **https://www.yahoo.com/video/iso-20022-cryptos-5-compliant-194204661.html;** "Why Do Restaurants Fail? Restaurant Failure Rate Statistics and Facts," Complete Bar Inventory Software System, accessed September 12, 2022, **https://home.binwise.com/blog/restaurant-failure-rate.**

8. Damon Brown, "This Perfect Bill Gates Quote Will Frame Your Next Decade of Success," *Inc.*, December 4, 2019, **https://www.inc.com/damon-brown/this-perfect-bill-gates-quote-will-frame-your-next-decade-of-success.html.**

9. William Craig, "The History of the Internet in a Nutshell," WebFX, August 12, 2022, **https://www.webfx.com/blog/web-design/the-history-of-the-internet-in-a-nutshell/**; Matt O'Brien, "Report: California's Middle Class Shrinks to Below 50 Percent." *The Mercury News*, August 13, 2016. **https://www.mercurynews.com/2011/12/07/report-californias-middle-class-shrinks-to-below-50-percent/**; Mises Institute, "In October, Money Supply Growth Remained Near All-Time Highs," SeekingAlpha, December 3, 2020, **https://seekingalpha.com/article/4392716-in-october-money-supply-growth-remained-near-all-time-highs**.

10. Kimberly Amadeo, "Did Tarp Help You or the Banks?," The Balance, December 31, 2021, **https://www.thebalancemoney.com/tarp-bailout-program-3305895**; Laura Noonan, Cale Tilford, Richard Milne, Ian Mount, and Peter Wise, "Who Went to Jail for Their Role in the Financial Crisis?," *The Financial Times Limited*, September 20, 2018, **https://ig.ft.com/jailed-bankers/**.

Index